Cooking with Vegetables

Cooking with Vegetables

Original recipes by

Marika Hanbury Tenison

Illustrations by John Miller

JONATHAN CAPE
THIRTY BEDFORD SQUARE LONDON

First published 1980
Text copyright © 1980 by Marika Hanbury Tenison
Illustrations copyright © 1980 by John Miller

Jonathan Cape Ltd, 30 Bedford Square, London WC1

British Library Cataloguing in Publication Data

Hanbury Tenison, Marika
Cooking with vegetables.
1. Cookery (Vegetables)
I. Title
641.6'5   TX801

ISBN 0–224–01597–4

Acknowledgments
The illustrations are of vegetables grown at Maidenwell
by Geoffrey Marston and at Glebe Farm, Sancreed by
Norman J. Hosking

Printed in Great Britain by The Anchor Press Ltd
and bound by Wm Brendon & Son Ltd
both of Tiptree, Essex

For Robin and Michael

Contents

viii CONTENTS

Preface

Taking a New Look at Cookery for the Age We Live in

'Surely', people are always saying to me, 'there isn't anything to write about cookery that hasn't been written before or recipes to invent that haven't been tried out by someone, somewhere, in the world?' In this book I hope to prove these people wrong for I believe I have worked out a plan for a new way of cooking that will bring variety and economic good sense into our present-day way of life with recipes that are not only original but also suited to a healthy and exciting diet.

Patterns in eating have changed gradually from decade to decade throughout the world. Basic principles, certainly, remain the same; although we no longer sit down to meals of numerous courses and have at least six covered dishes for breakfast, the modern slow-cook pots are merely an extension of the heavy pottery crock which once sat overnight on a low-burning fire and we still use the same herbs and spices for flavouring that have been enjoyed for centuries. Now I feel it is time for our pattern of eating in the Western world to change yet again to meet and adapt to the restrictions which are being imposed by widespread inflation, the desire for a more varied diet which has evolved from so many people holidaying and travelling abroad and the wide general interest in cooking and cookery books.

In this new approach to cooking for today I have, to put it simply, reversed the roles of vegetables in relation to meat, poultry and fish and drawn on the cooking principles practised in the East, as well as those of the classic cuisine of the West, to produce food that is attractive to look at, relatively quick to cook and delicious to eat. Meat, poultry and fish are becoming more expensive every day and in some cases there is even a shortage of protein foods; vegetables on the other hand are improving in quality all the time. Often people are able to grow their own produce in gardens or even in patio tubs and pots, and imported vegetables of a wide variety are becoming more and more commonplace.

The last thing that most of us want is to have to resign ourselves to a restricted diet of vegetarianism and so I devised a diet which, combining certain vegetables with meat, fish and poultry, could produce the flavour of the protein ingredients without having to use the large quantities normally called for. As there is little starch and only small quantities of fat used in most of the recipes, they are also designed to promote a healthy and well-balanced pattern of eating.

The outline of *Cooking with Vegetables* was evolved while on holiday in Italy. I was finishing a cookery book on traditional British food; Robin, my explorer husband, was beginning a travel book; and our great friend John Miller, a Cornish artist, was painting the Italian landscape. It was autumn, the countryside was misty and magical and the food we ate was local, fresh and breathtakingly simple; we were relaxed, fulfilled and happy. I told John my ideas for a new cookery book about the kind of food I had begun to evolve in my own home but which I had not yet written about, food based on fresh ingredients, with the emphasis on the magical versatility of good vegetables and the combined cuisines of countries I have visited all over the world. We decided to work on the book together; I grew the vegetables in my garden, John painted them while the dew was still fresh on their leaves and they came back to the kitchen to be used for the two hundred original recipes that follow. Four seasons after our Italian holiday both the drawings and the recipes were completed.

M.H.T.

Maidenwell
Cornwall
January 1980

A Note on Measurements

You will find both Imperial and metric measurements next to the ingredients in the recipes. The American tablespoon, pint and half pint (cup) measurements are slightly smaller than those used in Britain but this difference is really too slight to make any discernible variation in the recipe. While you cook a recipe and taste it as you go along, you will realize yourself that it may need a little more liquid or perhaps a little less than the recipe may specify. One variety of carrots, for instance, will absorb slightly more liquid than another, a higher heat will tend to evaporate some cooking liquid, and some vegetables are just naturally more juicy than others. No recipe will ever come out identical in every way to the same dish cooked before; too much depends on the exact strength of heat applied, on the quality of the ingredients, on their thickness and length and on the cooking time. In any case how boring life would be if every recipe *was* the same. In the end it is the personality of the cook that should make each dish individual and I would hate to think that anyone using my recipes should not feel free to add or subtract ingredients to suit their own particular taste and preference.

AMERICAN MEASURES

16 fluid ounces = 1 American pint
8 fluid ounces = 1 American standard cup
0·5 fluid ounces = 1 American tablespoon

For use in this book it is, however, quite acceptable to work on the premise that 1 American cup is equal to ½ pint liquid and

1 oz butter, margarine or lard = 2 tablespoons
1 oz flour = 2 rounded tablespoons.

IMPERIAL AND METRIC MEASURES

Ounces	Grammes*
½ oz	15 g
1 oz	25 g
2 oz	50 g
3 oz	75 g
4 oz	100 g

5 oz	150 g
6 oz	175 g
7 oz	200 g
8 oz	225 g
9 oz	250 g
10 oz	275 g
11 oz	300 g
12 oz	350 g
13 oz	375 g
14 oz	400 g
15 oz	425 g
16 oz (1 lb)	450 g

*(Approximate figures, rounded down to nearest unit of 25)

Pints	Millilitres
$\frac{1}{4}$ pint	150 ml
$\frac{1}{2}$ pint	300 ml
$\frac{3}{4}$ pint	450 ml
1 pint	600 ml
1$\frac{1}{2}$ pints	900 ml
1$\frac{3}{4}$ pints	1000 ml (a litre)

Introduction

Notes on Some of the Ingredients Used in the Recipes

TINNED ANCHOVIES

Tinned anchovies are an old-fashioned but highly usable flavouring ingredient which go surprisingly well with meat and poultry as well as fish. Anchovies also have their uses as a garnish for both hot and cold dishes and go well in salads. If you find their flavour too strong, it can be toned down by soaking the fillets in milk for a short time and then squeezing off the excess liquid.

CHEESES FOR COOKING WITH

Use mature Cheddar for a fairly mild flavouring, Parmesan (freshly grated and not bought loose or in drums) for a stronger taste and Gruyère for a smooth, rich texture. In some recipes I combine more than one variety of cheese to get the taste I want and I almost always add cayenne pepper to dishes cooked with cheese in order to encourage the flavour. Grated cheeses, packed in small quantities, can be stored in the deep freeze and, if you are ever in Italy, great savings can be made by buying a large hunk of good-quality Parmesan and grating it as soon as you get home.

GINGER

An important ingredient in many of my recipes is *fresh* green ginger root; dried ground ginger is not at all the same thing. Fortunately it is quite easy to buy the pungent, succulent ginger roots these days (better-class greengrocer's and shops which specialize in West Indian or Eastern food should sell them) and a couple of the knobbly roots, which resemble Jerusalem artichokes, will last you some time and keep fresh for up to a month if stored in the salad compartment of a refrigerator. The root should be peeled before being used (an inch of ginger root is ample for any dish) and then the flesh is grated or very finely chopped. The flavour is quite strong and one should have just a subtle hint of the spice rather than a mouthful.

MARINADES

Marinating is one of the best forms of flavouring and tenderizing there is, since combining ingredients with a combination of oil and an acidulous ingredient such as lemon juice or vinegar helps to break down tough fibres. A recent trick I discovered is to marinate ingredients and then freeze them in the marinade; this has an excellent effect on second-quality cuts of meat or poultry which might turn out to be dull in flavour.

Marinating is also of great value when you are having to deal with fish that might prove to be rather uninteresting; even simply soaking it in oil, lemon juice and seasonings will make a lot of difference to the taste.

MUSTARD

There are so many varieties of mustard available these days that it is sometimes confusing to try to make a choice amongst them. For cooking I use a smooth mustard and my favourites are the hot English mustard or the delicious, aromatic, French Dijon mustard flavoured with allspice.

COOKING OIL

The oil you use for cooking is a matter of personal preference. I favour a lightly flavoured oil and one that is pure in colour and light in tone. I used to use a high-quality olive oil but since this has become prohibitively expensive I have now settled for 'Olivette', a light mixture of olive and other oils, or sunflower oil which I find excellent for most cooking purposes.

The larger the quantity the cheaper your oil will be, so try and find gallon tins. The oil will keep indefinitely providing it is stored in a cool, dry and dark place.

PASTA

As I love Italian food I am extremely fond of pasta in almost any form and, like rice, it has the advantage over potatoes of not needing to be peeled. Buy the best quality of pasta (in some Italian shops in London's Soho you can even buy the fresh, home-made, product) and take care not to overcook it. The varieties (there are literally hundreds) I use most are spaghetti, thin spaghetti, pasta shells and both the white and green tagliatelle.

To cook pasta, plunge it in a large pan of fast-boiling salted water. As soon as the pasta is tender but still *al dente*, it should be drained well and returned to the pan with some butter or good olive oil and mixed well, before the sauce is added. Serve as soon as possible.

PASTRY

There are not very many pastry-based dishes in this book since I have tried to keep the dishes light and in many of them vegetables take the place of a more starchy pastry topping or casing. You will, however, find some delicious recipes for quiches made with unusual fillings, some recipes for savoury choux pastry puffs with fillings and several that incorporate puff pastry. In the case of puff pastry, which takes a considerable amount of time and patience to make at home, I would always recommend buying it frozen – most of the commercial brands are excellent and they do not need a lengthy defrosting period.

The pastry I use for all quiches and pastry cases is a short one made with an egg. Since it is quite difficult to handle when fresh it is worth giving the pastry a resting period in the refrigerator before rolling it out. To prevent pastry cases shrinking when they are being cooked I also recommend freezing the lined cases before baking them. Quiche cases should be partially baked blind before the filling is added to prevent them going soggy.

Pâte Brisée for Pastry Cases and Quiche Cases

This amount of pastry can be thinly rolled to make three quiche cases. Extra pastry can be kept in the refrigerator, wrapped in a polythene bag, or it can be frozen.

1 *lb (450 g) plain white flour*   1 *large egg made up to 6 fl. oz*
8 *oz (225 g) butter, chilled*   *(175 ml) with cold water*
1 *teaspoon salt*

Sieve the flour into a bowl with the salt. Add the butter, cut into small pieces, and rub the butter into the flour using your fingertips. When the mixture resembles fine breadcrumbs make a well in the centre and add the egg, beaten with enough water to make 6 fl. oz (175 ml); work the liquid into the flour and butter until the dough is smooth and pliable – do not overwork or the pastry will become tough. Dust the pastry with flour, place it in a plastic bag and chill it in the refrigerator for at least 30 minutes before attempting to roll it out.

Roll out the pastry on a well-floured board, rolling away from you all the time, and not back and forth, getting the pastry as thin as you can. Line your cases with the pastry and prick them lightly all over with a fork. Line the cases with foil and fill them with dried beans. Freeze the cases until solid and then bake the frozen cases in a hot oven (400°F. 200°C. Reg. 6) for 10 minutes. Remove the beans and foil, press out any air bubbles with your fingers, return the cases to the oven and continue to bake for a further 5–10 minutes until crisp and lightly coloured but not brown.

Savoury Choux Pastry

Savoury choux puffs, made in the same way as éclairs, are delicious with a savoury stuffing and you can use many of the recipes in this book to stuff the cases. The puffs can be made in advance and reheated and although the cases look very professional, choux pastry is surprisingly easy to make.

5 oz (150 g) plain white flour   *3 oz (75 g) butter*
8 fl. oz (230 ml) cold water   *4 large eggs*
½ teaspoon salt

Place the water and butter in a saucepan over a medium heat. When the butter has melted, bring to the boil and add all the flour and salt, stirring vigorously with a wooden spoon, over the heat, until the mixture is smooth, comes away from the sides of the pan and the moisture in the mixture has evaporated. Remove from the heat and beat in the eggs, one by one, beating with a wire whisk after each addition until the egg is completely absorbed and the mixture is dry and glossy. Leave the mixture to stand for 10 minutes after the last egg has been added and the dough is shining and elastic.

Oil and flour a baking sheet and drop the dough from a tablespoon on to the sheet, leaving plenty of space between the mounds. Bake the pastry in a hot oven (425°F. 220°C. Reg. 7) for about 20 minutes until well risen, golden brown and firm (the puffs should sound hollow when they are tapped on the bottom). Turn off the heat and leave the puffs in the oven with the door slightly open for a further 5 minutes to prevent them collapsing.

PEPPER

Freshly ground black peppercorns are used as a seasoning in nearly all my recipes.

Dishes that are white or pale in colouring should be seasoned with ground, or freshly ground, white pepper as black flecks might look unattractive. For rich and highly spiced dishes try the red and green peppercorns which can now be found in tins and jars. These are the fresh seeds of the pepper vine picked when they have coloured but which are not left in the sun to dry. The peppercorns should be drained and crushed before being used and they have an excellent flavour, but do use them sparingly until you are able to measure their strength.

POPPADUMS

Poppadums make an excellent accompaniment to a number of hors d'oeuvres and soup recipes as well as being an essential part of a curry meal. They are quickly cooked (fry them in a little hot oil pressing the poppadums flat with a spatula and turning them half-way through the cooking time, until they have doubled in size and are really crisp). They should be drained on kitchen paper and can be cooked well in advance. Poppadums can also be re-heated if necessary although they taste just as good cold as they do hot.

RICE

I use a lot of rice in my cooking because not only is it quick and easy to cook, but it has the advantage over potatoes of not needing to be prepared in any way. Always use long-grain or Patna rice and try to avoid the commercial 'quickly cooked' or partly cooked varieties. One of the nicest rice forms is Basmati, which can be bought in Indian shops or from good delicatessens; it is a bit more expensive but worth the extra cost.

For a foolproof way to cook rice, wash it in cold water and place the rice in a pan with exactly double the quantity of cold water and some salt. Bring the rice slowly to the boil, stir it once only, cover very tightly and cook over a low heat for 20 minutes. Stir the rice with a fork to let the air in and to separate the grains, cover and leave on the side of the stove for 10 minutes or until required – it will keep hot for a surprisingly long time.

BOTTLED SAUCES

I had always been most violently against the use of tomato ketchup until I recently read that the French are beginning to use quite a lot in their cooking. I tried it out and found that, providing the sauce is used with discretion, it can be a valuable addition to the flavouring of a good many dishes. Other sauces in my cupboard include the invaluable Worcestershire sauce, Tabasco sauce (both of which should be used by the drop only), old-fashioned Harvey's sauce, anchovy sauce, soy sauce and mushroom ketchup; all of these make very valuable flavourings, although they must never be allowed to dominate the dish.

SPICES

Spices are an essential part of good cooking and especially of an imaginative cuisine but they lose a lot of their flavour if they are not used when they are as fresh as possible. Ideally, you should grind your own spices in a pestle and mortar but if time is at a premium use a good brand of ground spices, make sure you replace the lids firmly and store them in a cool, dry and dark place. As well as the more usual spices I also use mace, cumin, coriander (which grows well in the garden and produces aromatic leaves, which go well with cold food, and seeds which can be used fresh or dried), juniper berries, turmeric (also known as Greek hay and once widely used as a veterinary medicine), saffron and more of those useful spices, nutmeg (which should always be freshly ground) and cayenne, than is usual. The Eastern spices, cumin, coriander, turmeric and a blending called 'garam masala', sold ready mixed, go extremely well with meat or fish and vegetable combinations and are worth experimenting with— use them sparingly until you have discovered their potential.

STOCKS

In many of my recipes, especially in chicken dishes, the meat is cut raw from the bones leaving you with excellent material from which to make a rich and nourishing home-made stock, for use in sauces, gravies and soups. Stock cubes are a useful innovation but there is no doubt that their flavour is not nearly as good as that of real stock (Elizabeth David describes them as tasting of nothing but salt) nor their substance as smooth and rich. I find commercial stock cubes can be used in emergencies and added to home-made stock to give extra flavour, although used continuously they have the disadvantage of giving all your dishes the same taste. Good home-made stocks are like bridge hands or games of backgammon; each one is different and has its own personality.

Vegetables, vegetable peelings and trimmings add extra flavouring to a stock and are vital if a really good result is to be obtained. Vegetable peelings also help to give stock colour and therefore make it more attractive. Use onion skins, carrot peelings and tomato skins for both flavour and colour, and save celery tops, cucumber skins, the tops of tender young carrots, leek trimmings and the core and seeds of peppers and tomatoes to enhance the taste of meat- and poultry-based soups. Beware of turnip, swede, parsnip and kohlrabi skins as their flavour can be overpowering. Brassicas—the cabbage family—should be avoided in stock-making as it is when they are cooked for a long time that their smell and taste becomes offensive.

For a brown stock the bones or carcass should be browned in a little dripping or oil (the fat should then be drained off) before any vegetables are added. Peppercorns add a sharper seasoning than ground pepper and a bouquet of herbs is essential. Stocks can also be made entirely from vegetables although they will need a longer period of boiling to reduce the liquid and produce a good flavour. For white stocks onion and tomato skins should be omitted.

Put all your stock ingredients into a large saucepan and cover them with cold water. Bring to the boil, skim off any scum that rises to the surface, cover tightly and simmer for 2–3 hours (this process can be carried out in a low oven or the stock can be cooked in a pressure cooker or slow-cook pot). Strain the stock into a bowl, leave it to cool and then refrigerate until any fat has formed a skin across the surface. Remove the fat, return the stock to a clean pan, bring to the boil and boil rapidly until the stock has reduced and the flavour is enriched. Taste every now and then and, if absolutely necessary, add a stock cube or some tomato purée to increase the flavour.

If stocks are not to be used within 24 hours they should be re-boiled or frozen.

TINNED TOMATOES

When tinned tomatoes are used in place of fresh tomatoes their flavour can be improved by boiling and reducing the liquid.

TOMATO PURÉE AND PASTE

Both tomato purée and paste play a role in many of my recipes but care must always be taken not to allow the flavour of the tomato to dominate other ingredients; both purée and paste can also help to thicken soups, casseroles and sauces. If you grow your own tomatoes you can make your own tomato paste and either bottle or freeze it. Home-made tomato paste has an even better flavour than the commercial products and can be made by stewing really ripe tomatoes with herbs (oregano, basil and bay leaves), spices (cumin, nutmeg and ginger) and a little wine

vinegar, sugar and white wine until the ingredients are
thoroughly reduced. Purée the ingredients through a food mill
to remove the seeds.

VINEGAR

Cider or wine vinegars are used throughout the recipes. Malt
vinegar is best forgotten as its flavour is far too harsh for normal
cooking purposes.

Herbs

One of the great delights of growing your own food is the herb
garden: aromatic, attractive to look at and, in the summer, a
haven for multicoloured butterflies. Here, at Maidenwell, I
planted my herb garden before I embarked on the large areas of
vegetables and fruit we now grow. As a result that particular
corner is now twenty years old—with the air of having been
there for ever—and while some of the more old-fashioned herbs
like 'old lady', 'old man' and 'salad burnet' are not much used,
many of the others are picked almost daily. Most herbs are easy
to grow and since many of them are closely related to weeds
the problem is often one of keeping them in check rather than
having to give them encouragement.

Although some herbs do dry satisfactorily, especially now the
new process of freeze-drying has been brought in, their flavour
is not exactly that of the fresh herb and they do tend to have a
rather dusty overtone. Fresh herbs can be preserved very satisfactorily in the deep freeze; remove stalks, chop if necessary
and package in small quantities. (I also freeze small bunches of
herbs on the stalk to use as bouquets garnis during the winter
months.)

THE USE OF HERBS WHEN COOKING

Many cookery books put an emphasis on the careful and discreet
use of herbs in cooking and although I agree with this maxim
where some of the stronger herbs like sage, thyme and tarragon

are concerned, I do believe that the more mild herbs like parsley, marjoram and oregano can be used in quite large quantities with the greatest of success. I tend to double all the quantities of parsley that are usually suggested (in some dishes I will actually use as much as half a pound at a time to give a marvellous fresh and country flavour to a casserole or a chicken pie) and I am also extremely lavish in the use of bay leaves, adding three or four rather than one or two to a casserole or stew.

Recipes specifying that herbs are to be *finely* chopped do mean exactly that, as it should be the flavour of the herbs rather than the texture which is used to enhance a dish. One of the easiest ways of chopping herbs (unless you have an electric food processor which does the job admirably) is to strip off the leaves into a mug and snip them finely with kitchen scissors.

So, whenever possible, use fresh herbs as their flavour is far and away superior to those that are dried. If you can grow your own, also try to preserve some by freezing them for the winter months. Mint (do grow more than one variety – the apple and pineapple mint are both particularly good), parsley, chives, chervil, coriander, dill, lovage, oregano, marjoram, bay, sorrel and savory all grow well out of doors and basil can be grown in pots. If you are restricted for space, most herbs can be grown in pots or window boxes and the only ones that need a lot of room are parsley, chervil, sorrel and horseradish.

If you do have to use dried herbs, make sure you buy a good brand, always put the lid firmly back on the jar after use and store them in a cool, dry, dark place. Dried herbs will have a better flavour if they are soaked for a short time in a little lemon juice and warm water before being used.

PARSLEY AND CHERVIL

Both these herbs have a considerable amount to offer in the way of flavouring, as well as adding colour and as a garnish, and the mistake people often make is to use them too sparingly. If they are for flavouring, use them with a fairly lavish hand and reserve the stalks to flavour stocks. Deep-fry large sprigs of parsley to use as a delicious garnish for fried foods (drop the sprigs into very hot, deep oil and cook for a few seconds until they have shrivelled and are crisp – drain well on kitchen paper).

CHIVES

If you have to use dried herbs choose a brand that is 'freeze-dried' as these have by far the best flavour; or, better still, substitute very finely chopped spring onion tops for the required chives. Chives have a fairly mild flavouring and can be used quite generously.

CORIANDER

Fresh coriander leaves have a definite, pungent flavour which goes well with tomato and fish dishes. They are also good sprinkled over salads and almost any dish which has a curry flavouring. Chop the leaves finely before using them. The green seeds can be crushed and added to casseroles and stews.

ROSEMARY

Easily grown, an attractive addition to any garden (if it flowers well, legend says, you can be sure that the lady of the house 'wears the pants' in the establishment) and an essential part in the cooking of lamb and many good roast chicken dishes. This is a strong herb and should normally be used sparingly. If you barbecue, some branches thrown on the coals just before cooking give lamb chops or chicken a marvellous flavour.

DILL

This is traditionally a herb to use with fish but I find it also goes well with chicken. Dill is a strong herb and, unless you want its flavour to be dominant in a dish, I suggest using it with caution. Dill grows well in the garden and both leaves and flowers can be frozen for winter use. In the time of the famous herbalist Culpeper, it was widely used as a medicine for expelling wind.

LOVAGE

One of the old-fashioned herbs that is frequently overlooked these days. It grows to a height of about 7 or 8 feet and was used to screen greenhouses in the summer months. It looks attractive in the garden, is no trouble at all to grow and has a flavour that is similar to celery with a touch of anise about it. The stalks can be used as a vegetable in the same way as celery, and the leaves for flavouring or garnishing.

OREGANO AND MARJORAM

These come from the same family and are both pleasant-tasting herbs that go well with vegetables, meat, fish and poultry. Oregano is particularly good in dishes which have a tomato base and marjoram goes very well indeed with beef dishes. Both grow in poor soil although they do need a certain amount of sunshine.

BAY

This is another herb which I feel is often used too sparingly. In a recipe that calls for one bay leaf I inevitably treble the quantity, and I always add three or four leaves to a stock. This is one of the few herbs which does dry well and although the flavour changes slightly it also tends to intensify on drying.

SAVORY

The classic herb to use with broad beans and especially the young beans. It also goes well with other vegetables and I make a point of always adding a sprig to the water in which I cook French or runner beans.

SORREL

You really do have to grow sorrel yourself because, sadly, this delicious summer herb is seldom seen in the greengrocer's. It grows very easily, needs only a poor soil, and the more you cut the plant down the more strongly it will flourish. Domestic sorrel is a near relation of the long, bright, bitter-sweet leaves you find growing wild in country fields (once a very popular salad ingredient) but the cultivated leaves have a less bitter and sharp taste and are much larger and more succulent. It is a perennial plant and to produce enough for a vegetable you will require a minimum of eight plants. The leaves are washed, dried and cooked exactly like spinach; a small number add a fillip to salads and are a delicious part of a good many sauces that go well with fish and poultry.

Growing Your Own Vegetables

Every seed-merchant's new catalogue is filled with more and more exciting ideas for vegetables you can grow and harvest in your back garden. Horticultural research is going on all the time and new strains of vegetables are always available for anyone who has a plot to dig. Providing you are prepared to lavish a certain amount of care on your garden you can produce the most amazing results and a wide variety of well-known and exotic vegetables. Our home is 800 feet high on Bodmin Moor, beset by violent winds and cold rain for much of the year. Yet we grow aubergines in cloches, have no fewer than twenty-four varieties of herbs and, in a good summer, can produce a healthy crop of those sweet but ugly giant Mediterranean tomatoes out of doors.

Freezing has almost become a mania and one of the mistakes most people seem to make is to plant too much of one crop. It is better to stagger your planting of peas and beans, your carrots and lettuces, and to rotate crops. Spend some time working out a plan to harvest fresh vegetables all the year round instead of becoming a slave to your freezer during the good days of summer.

One of the delights of growing your own vegetables pinpoints the greatest advantage you have over those who have to buy them. Do experiment by picking your crops in all their stages. Every stage has its own merits and young or immature vegetables can also prove to be a revolution in taste and texture; the tops of broad beans, nipped off to make better growth, are a highly sophisticated delicacy; immature beans only a few inches long, cooked whole, have a marvellously individual flavour and the larger beans are a boon to summer salads. Baby, finger-sized, carrots have just as much to offer as the firm and crisp large ones and only need to be wiped over with a scouring cloth rather than being peeled.

Work your menus around your garden, picking your vegetables when they are *au point* and then deciding what to do with them, rather than setting your sights on a certain dish and using produce that is not quite right for the job.

Buying Fresh Vegetables

In most city areas or larger towns you will find at least *one* greengrocer who is prepared to go beyond the run-of-the-mill range of vegetables and offer some exotic produce. You will usually be able to find a local market, too, which provides a source of cheaper and fresher vegetables; patronize markets if you can, and beware of those cleaned and rather anaemic-looking packaged vegetables that are often sold in supermarkets – heat has to be used in some of the sealing processes of packaging and the vegetables inside can turn out to be a disappointment. Find out when shops get deliveries (most of them work on a three-day rota) and buy on the morning when new stock arrives. Be thoroughly critical about buying anything but the best, finger the goods if necessary, whatever the signs say, and pick vegetables that are heavy for their size and which feel springy and full of sap.

Preparing Your Vegetables

No one could be more of an advocate of British cooking than I am but I do have to argue with our attitude to the preparation of fresh vegetables. We miss a lot by serving them virtually as they come out of the ground and not experiencing the excitemeat of the texture of vegetables that are sliced, chopped and shredded to produce an ever-changing contrast. Small, young, crisp vegetables such as baby carrots, immature miniature broad beans, needle-slim French beans, snowball cauliflowers and home-grown new potatoes of marble size should be left whole, but for many of the recipes in the book the cutting of large vegetables plays an important role in the success of the dishes.

Watching top-class chefs, particularly Chinese and Japanese cooks, chopping by hand is a constant delight; they do it so swiftly that the eye can hardly follow their movements and they make the process seem ridiculously easy. With practice this kind of preparation is not as difficult as it looks providing you have some really sharp knives in your kitchen. You cannot sharpen your kitchen knives too often and I try to make a habit of sharpening each one every time I use it. Once you have developed the art of slightly more sophisticated chopping and slicing you will find it infinitely rewarding and remarkably therapeutic and soothing.

Find out the size of knife that suits you most comfortably; my own favourite is one with a rather thick blade and a curved end for slicing and shredding larger vegetables; for more intricate work I prefer a smaller, pointed, instrument. A good handle is important so that you get a firm grip on your knife.

For cutting and slicing, hold the knife firmly but not rigidly with your thumb and index finger gripping the top of the blade. Make your movements smooth and as quick as possible, keeping slices to an even thickness. When slicing round objects (potatoes, whole carrots etc.) it helps to cut a thin sliver off the bottom of the vegetable so that it will not rotate while you are working on it. Slice at right angles to the chopping board with sharp, quick, movements.

To cut larger vegetables into long diagonal slices, trim a thin slice from one side so that the vegetable will lie flat on the board. Starting from the thicker end, cut a diagonal slice from one side and continue to make diagonal, wafer-thin slices.

To produce matchstick or julienne strips, cut the vegetables first into long, wafer-thin slices and then into thin, matchstick strips. The slices can be placed one on top of the other so that it is easy to julienne a number of slices at once.

To chop onions or shallots evenly, peel the onion or shallot and cut it into half lengthwise. Lay one half, cut side down, on the board and make thin vertical slices towards the centre without cutting right through, thus keeping the onion from falling apart. Holding the onion or shallot firmly by the root end, cut through with thin horizontal slices, producing uniform, small, dice.

Keeping Cut Vegetables

There are times when you will want to prepare your vegetables in advance and keep them for some time before cooking them. In order to prevent prepared vegetables going soft or losing colour, cover them with cold salted water and keep them in a cool place (preferably a refrigerator) away from the light. When required, the vegetables should be well drained and patted as dry as possible on kitchen paper.

Some vegetables, such as celeriac and salsify, discolour once they are peeled. Prevent this by dropping the prepared vegetables into cold water to which a couple of teaspoonfuls of lemon juice have been added.

Storing Fresh Vegetables

If you grow your own vegetables pick them, if possible, just before they are to be used. Avoid picking them in full sunlight as this detracts from their flavour. When you buy vegetables do not buy too large a quantity at one time. Store them, without cleaning, in the bottom of a refrigerator or in a really cool place such as a garage or cellar, keeping them away from the light.

Slicing and Cutting: Meat and Poultry

Many of my recipes require meat and poultry to be cut into wafer-thin slices or strips. Meat should always be cut against the grain and, if you want really thin slices, put the meat into the freezer for about half an hour or so before cutting and this will compact the fibres.

Use razor-sharp knives for cutting meat and try to keep the slices as uniform as possible. Steel, rather than stainless-steel, knives obtain the best results although they are a chore to clean.

When a recipe calls for minced meat use a food processor, if you own one, for chopping or 'grinding' meat rather than a mincing machine which tends to squeeze out some of the essential juices from the flesh. Unless the meat is inclined to be on the tough side, do not mince or grind it too finely as this destroys the texture. Allow a fair percentage of fat to meat as the fat helps to tenderize the ingredients.

By carefully jointing and cutting an uncooked chicken or duck carcass you can get a surprisingly large amount of meat and still be left with the bones from which to make a rich and nourishing stock. Remove the wings and legs first (leg joints can be cut in two) and slice the meat from each side of the breast bone in one piece using a really sharp, pointed knife. If the skin is to be removed add this to your stock pot.

When cutting up a cooked bird make sure it is absolutely cold before you start work. Be careful to baste birds extremely well during cooking time if they are to be used cold and continue to baste a few times after they have been removed from the oven to keep the flesh moist.

Asparagus

Surely the King (or the Queen) of all vegetables and, from a grower's point of view, more time-consuming, space-taking and yet more rewarding than any other crop in the garden. However, providing your soil is right, asparagus is not a difficult vegetable to produce—it takes time and patience but once a bed is established it will serve you well for a long time, providing you are never too greedy and always leave some stalks to grow into the ferns that will enrich the following year's crop.

One slight drawback to asparagus (seldom mentioned for obvious reasons) is the effect of a very volatile asperagine which results in its giving a strange and somewhat disagreeable smell to the urine for some hours after it has been eaten. Culpeper, the great father of all dieticians, felt strongly that, because of this unpleasant smell, the results of eating the plant must be beneficial to the insides; it helps, he suggests, to wear down stones in the kidneys and 'to provoke urine' and being taken 'several mornings together, stirreth up bodily lust in man or woman'.

It is from the Greeks that the myth associating asparagus with cuckoldry derived—their story was that the plant originated from a ram's horn stuck in the ground. Nevertheless they found it an extremely pleasing vegetable, as indeed did the Romans who carried its fame with them as they conquered their enemies.

The history of asparagus is a long one since it grows wild in many parts of the world and has been used since time immemorial as a vegetable ingredient. In England asparagus beds, raised and dressed with sea sand or seaweed, formed a feature of the red-brick walled kitchen gardens of the eighteenth century. In

America, although wild asparagus was to be found there too, the first cultivation of the vegetable is said to have been by a consul for the Dutch royal family in Massachusetts in the mid-eighteenth century. Since then asparagus has become very much a feature of American eating with some of the best 'jumbo' spears, thick, long and succulent, being produced in California and exported to Europe and the British Isles. These larger and fatter stems should be peeled, using a sharp knife and taking off only a thin sliver from the outer layer of the stalk, before being cooked and the peelings, if they are plentiful, contain enough flavour to make it worthwhile cooking them in some stock to make the basis of an asparagus-flavoured soup.

Chicken and Asparagus Soup

Serves 6

6 oz (175 g) raw or cooked
  breast of chicken
8 oz (225 g) asparagus
1 potato
1 small onion
1 oz (25 g) butter
1 tablespoon plain flour
1½ pints (900 ml) good
  chicken stock

2 egg yolks, beaten
¼ pint (150 ml) single cream
2 teaspoons very finely chopped
  fresh tarragon or savory
salt and white pepper
pinch ground nutmeg

Wash and trim the asparagus removing all coarse fibres. Remove the tips and set them aside and chop the stalks. Peel and dice the potato and peel and chop the onion. Place the asparagus stalks in a saucepan with the potato and onion, season with salt and pepper, add just enough cold water to cover, bring to the boil and simmer for about 15 minutes or until the vegetables are absolutely tender. Purée the vegetables through a food mill or in an electric blender or food processor.

Steam the asparagus tips until they are just tender. Cut the chicken into very small dice or thin strips. Melt the butter in a clean saucepan. Add the flour and mix well. Gradually add the chicken stock, stirring continually until the soup comes to the boil and is thick and smooth. Add the vegetable purée to the soup base and mix well until thoroughly blended. Add the chicken and simmer for 2 minutes if the chicken is already cooked or for about 5 minutes if it is raw.

Beat the egg yolks with the cream. Add the cream mixture to the soup and stir, without boiling, until the soup is hot through. Add the asparagus tips, season with salt, pepper and nutmeg and mix in the tarragon or savory. Thin the soup, if necessary, with a little extra chicken stock, milk or cream.

Note: In the winter I serve this soup with a garnish of minute, crisply fried bread *croûtons*; in the summer I sometimes have it ice cold with a garnish of some flaked and roasted almonds.

Asparagus and Macaroni Cheese

A pleasing dish that can be served as a starter or as a light main course.
Serves 4

8 oz (225 g) asparagus
8 oz (225 g) macaroni
8 oz (225 g) ham
½ pint (300 ml) single cream
2 eggs, beaten
2 oz (50 g) freshly grated
  Parmesan cheese

salt and freshly ground black
  pepper
pinch ground nutmeg
4 tablespoons dried breadcrumbs
1½ oz (40 g) melted butter

Cook the asparagus in boiling salted water until it is just tender (about 8 minutes). Drain off the cooking water into a large saucepan (add more water if necessary), bring back to the boil and add the macaroni. Cook the macaroni until it is just tender (about 15 minutes) and drain well.

Trim off any coarse ends from the asparagus. Chop the ham. Arrange the macaroni, ham and asparagus in layers in a well-buttered baking dish.

Mix the cream with the eggs and half the Parmesan cheese and season with salt and pepper and nutmeg. Pour the custard mixture over the macaroni, scatter over the breadcrumbs mixed with the remaining cheese and dribble over the melted butter.

Bake in a hot oven (400°F. 200°C. Reg. 6) for 20 minutes until the custard is set and the topping is crisp and golden brown.

Serve with a tomato salad and a green vegetable.

Asparagus with Chicken and Tarragon Sauce

A good luncheon or supper dish for those first hot days of summer when asparagus is in season.
Serves 4

2 *chicken breasts*
1 *lb (450 g) asparagus*
salt and white pepper
1 *onion*
1 *carrot*
1 *stick celery*
1 *bay leaf*
1 *oz (25 g) butter*
1 *tablespoon flour*

½ *pint (300 ml) strong chicken stock*
2 *teaspoons lemon juice*
¼ *pint (150 ml) double cream*
2 *egg yolks*
1 *tablespoon very finely chopped fresh tarragon*
2 *hard-boiled eggs*

Trim the asparagus so that all the rough fibres are removed. Cook the asparagus in boiling salted water until it is *just* tender and drain well. Peel and roughly chop the carrot and onion and chop the celery.

Place the chicken breasts (with the skin removed) in the chicken stock, season with salt and pepper and add the onion, carrot, celery and bay leaf. Bring gently to the boil and poach the chicken breasts over a low heat for about 15 minutes or until just cooked. Drain off the stock, discard the vegetables and bay leaf and leave the breasts to cool.

Melt the butter in a small saucepan. Add the flour and mix well. Gradually blend in the stock, stirring continually until the sauce is thick and smooth and comes to the boil. Season with salt and pepper, mix in the tarragon and lemon juice and simmer for 3 minutes.

Cut the chicken breasts into thin matchstick strips and mix them into the sauce. Beat the egg yolks with the cream, add it to the sauce and stir gently over a low heat until the sauce becomes satiny (do not boil).

Arrange the asparagus on a heated dish and pour the chicken and tarragon sauce over it. Garnish with a 'mimosa' of hard-boiled egg yolks rubbed through a coarse sieve.

Accompany the dish with new potatoes and a young green vegetable or a salad. You can also serve the chicken and asparagus in a ring of freshly boiled and fluffy long-grain rice.

B

Fillets of Fish with Asparagus, Cheese and Mustard Sauce

Asparagus is so tender and delicate in both texture and flavour that it goes particularly well with rather bland ingredients such as white fish and chicken. This is an elegant and very delicious dish; it can be served as a fairly substantial starter or as a light main course for a summer's day. Try to rescue the bones of the fish from your fishmonger.

Serves 4

4 large or 8 small fillets of white
    fish such as whiting, sole,
    plaice, sea bass, grey mullet etc.
12 oz (350 g) asparagus
¼ pint (150 ml) dry white wine
water
1 carrot
1 onion
1 stick celery
bouquet garni
2 bay leaves
1 oz (25 g) butter

1 tablespoon flour
2 oz (50 g) Cheddar cheese
½ oz (15 g) freshly grated
    Parmesan cheese
salt and freshly ground black
    pepper
pinch ground nutmeg
2 teaspoons French Dijon
    mustard
2 egg yolks
¼ pint (150 ml) single cream
pinch cayenne pepper

Trim off any tough fibres from the asparagus stalks and cook the asparagus in boiling salted water until it is just tender. Drain well reserving the cooking water.

Wash and roughly chop the carrot. Peel and halve the onion. Roughly chop the celery.

Combine the asparagus water, vegetables, white wine, bouquet garni and bay leaves with any fish trimmings, bring to the boil and cook over a high heat for 20 minutes. Strain the stock and leave to cool.

Place the fish fillets in a shallow pan, pour over the stock and bring gently to the boil. Simmer the fillets for about 8 minutes until they are just cooked and lift them gently out of the stock. Arrange the fillets in a lightly buttered fireproof serving dish and top each one with asparagus. Strain the stock and measure off ½ pint (300 ml) liquid.

Melt the butter in a small saucepan, add the flour and mix well. Gradually blend in the fish stock, stirring continually until the sauce comes to the boil and is thick and smooth. Add the

Cheddar cheese and the mustard and continue to stir until the cheese has melted. Season the sauce with salt and pepper and a pinch of ground nutmeg.

Beat the egg yolks with the cream, add the mixture to the sauce and stir over a low heat (do not boil) until the sauce is satiny.

Pour the sauce over the fish and asparagus, top with the Parmesan cheese and a very little pinch of cayenne pepper and put under a hot grill until the top is golden brown and the dish is hot through.

Serve at once with new potatoes, mashed potatoes or rice and a green salad or green vegetable.

Beef Olives with Asparagus

Last summer, trying to earn some money to pay for urgently needed renovations to my Cornish farmhouse, I joined the tourist bonanza and had a party of American ladies to stay for ten days of 'gourmet cooking'. This was a recipe I made up for them and it has always remained a great satisfaction for me to discover it really is possible to produce an excellent dinner party based on an extremely conservative quantity of that delectable but outrageously expensive ingredient, fillet steak. The asparagus, by the way, came from the garden.
Serves 6

1 lb (450 g) fillet steak in one piece
12 oz (350 g) asparagus
12 very thin slices Parma ham or streaky bacon
3 onions
salt and freshly ground black pepper
pinch allspice
French Dijon mustard
½ oz (15 g) butter
3 tablespoons oil
2 tablespoons brandy
1 tin consommé
1 tablespoon tomato purée
1 carton (5 fl. oz, 150 ml) sour cream
pinch of paprika
1½ tablespoons finely chopped parsley

Chill the fillet steak in the deep freeze for about 30 minutes to make it easier to slice. Cut the steak into 12 very thin slices, place the slices between two sheets of greaseproof paper and beat them gently with a meat mallet until they are almost paper thin. Stretch the bacon rashers with the back of a knife and trim off the rinds.

Trim the asparagus stalks and cook them in boiling salted water until they are only just tender. Drain well. Peel the onions, slice them thinly and divide them into rings.

Season one side of each steak with a little salt, pepper and allspice and spread them with a very little Dijon mustard. Place a rasher of bacon (or the Parma ham) on each steak and top with asparagus stems. Roll up the steaks very neatly and secure them with toothpicks.

Heat the butter and oil together in a large heavy frying pan. Add the onions and cook over a low heat until the onions are soft and transparent. Remove the onions with a slotted spoon, raise the heat under the pan, add the beef olives and cook them quickly until they are browned on all sides. Add the brandy, shake the pan, set light to the brandy and continue to shake the pan until the flames die.

Arrange the onions in the bottom of a fireproof baking dish, place the beef olives on top of the onions and pour over the consommé. Cover the dish tightly with foil and braise the olives in a moderately hot oven (375°F. 190°C. Reg. 5) for about 30 minutes or until the meat is absolutely tender.

Transfer the olives to a clean, heated serving dish and arrange the onions on top of them. Strain the juices from the dish into a small saucepan and mix in the tomato purée and sour cream. Season with salt, pepper and a small pinch of paprika, heat through without boiling and pour the sauce over the olives. Sprinkle with chopped parsley.

Serve the olives with new potatoes, mashed or jacket potatoes and with a crisp green vegetable.

Aubergines (Eggplants)

From the growing point of view aubergines (relations of the potato) must surely be one of the most attractive and exotic fruits/vegetables that can be grown in the greenhouse. They need plenty of heat but if given that will thrive and I have had as many as eight aubergines from each of my plants. In a good summer you can grow them out of doors in a sheltered corner of the garden or in a cold frame but in less fine years they need the protection of a greenhouse to get good results.

I grow the plants in pots and find each stage a delight. The leaves are attractively shaped, the flowers, large and pale purple, are a delight to look at and the glossy purple fruit must surely be amongst the most luscious of all harvests. Aubergines are certainly a plant well worth growing in your house, for decoration as well as food value, if you haven't a greenhouse or cold frame. In addition if, like me, you enjoy cooking with them you will find that a considerable saving is derived from growing your own aubergines.

Aubergines are native to southern Asia and although they have always been a popular form of food in the East, when they were first imported into Europe in the thirteenth century they were totally disregarded as gastronomic material and grown merely for their decorative value. Gradually, influenced by the Turks and the Arabs, Europeans overcame their fear that the aubergine (sometimes known as the 'raging apple') was highly poisonous and liable to cause insanity and now it is one of the most widely and successfully used vegetables in the world.

Aubergines come in many forms, from the white, perfectly

egg-shaped variety to the long, thinner, purple version which is the most hardy and which succeeds best for home growing. The slightly bitter flavour that comes from the juice of the raw fruit nearly always disappears by the time the vegetable has been cooked and it is not necessary to follow the practice recommended in many cookery books of soaking the prepared aubergines in salted water or even sprinkling them with salt and leaving them to 'sweat' for a time before cooking, unless the dish you are making requires the removal of some of the excess liquid in the vegetable. The salting process, followed by careful drying with kitchen paper, is advisable if aubergine slices are to be fried. Much of the flavour of the aubergine lies in the skin, so avoid removing the skin unless this is absolutely necessary.

Aubergine is a natural accompaniment to lamb in combined meat and vegetable dishes and it has that very valuable quality of absorbing the flavour of the ingredients it is cooked with. The vegetable is also extremely rich and filling as well as having a fine, almost oily, texture and it is therefore a tremendous asset in stretching meat and other more expensive ingredients to almost amazing lengths with excellent results.

If you grow your own aubergines use them as soon as possible after they have been picked. If you buy your aubergines make sure their skin is still glossy and shining and has not become dull and that the flesh is not bruised and is firm to the touch.

Aubergines should be stored in the salad compartment of the refrigerator.

Ox Tongue Cooked with Aubergines

A rather sharp sauce made from vegetables in this dish helps to counteract the slightly rich sweetness of tongue.
Serves 6–8

1½ lb (675 g) ox tongue,
  cooked
2 medium aubergines
¼ pint (150 ml) dry white wine
½ pint (300 ml) chicken stock

1 teaspoon French Dijon
  mustard
2 bay leaves
1 teaspoon finely chopped basil
  and chervil

1 *pinch finely chopped marjoram*
salt and freshly ground black
  pepper
2 *tablespoons olive oil*
2 *onions*
1½ *oz (40 g) butter*

1 *oz (25 g) flour*
a little milk
3 *tablespoons finely chopped*
  parsley
2 *tablespoons finely chopped*
  chives or spring onion tops

Cut the tongue into very thin slices.

Trim the ends of the aubergines and cut the flesh (without peeling) into ½ inch (1½ cm) thick matchstick strips. Sprinkle the strips with salt and leave to 'sweat' in a colander for at least 30 minutes.

Combine the wine, stock, mustard and herbs in a saucepan. Season with salt and pepper, bring to the boil and simmer gently for 30 minutes. Cool the liquid, strain it through a fine sieve and add enough milk to make ¾ pint (450 ml).

Dry the aubergines on kitchen paper and fry them in the oil for 20 minutes over a medium heat, stirring every now and then to prevent sticking and adding a little more oil if they get too dry. Peel and finely chop the onions.

Melt the butter in a fairly large saucepan, add the onions and cook over a low heat until the onions are soft and transparent. Add the flour and mix well. Gradually add the liquid, stirring continually over a medium high heat until the sauce comes to the boil and is thick and smooth. Fold in half the parsley and chives and the aubergines. Check the seasoning and if the sauce is not quite sharp enough for your taste, add a little more Dijon mustard.

Arrange the slices of tongue in a lightly buttered fireproof dish, pour over the sauce and heat through in a medium hot oven (400°F. 200°C. Reg. 6) for 25 minutes and sprinkle over the remaining parsley and chives before serving.

Serve with potatoes cooked with fennel (see page 129).

Maidenwell Steak Tartar

Steak tartar is one of my passions in life, along with some of the other more expensive forms of food in the world. While economy was a necessary evil I was nevertheless loath to give up my pleasures entirely, so I worked out a compromise which seemed to present the best of all possible worlds – a first-class dish with all the flavour of a steak tartar while using a reduced quantity of shaved or minced raw meat. The steak is combined with cooked, puréed aubergine and the usual ingredients that go towards making this exciting dish. The result is *almost* better than the traditional classic recipe.

The meat for steak tartar has to be lean and tender. I prefer to use rump steak rather than the slightly smooth fillet steak but it is necessary to remove all the fat and any tough fibres or sinews from the meat before you prepare it. Ideally, the meat should be shaved into minute slivers with a very sharp knife but you can get almost the same result by chopping the meat, very finely, in an electric food processor. Failing either of these methods you could also mince the meat through the coarse blades of a mincing machine.

The great joy of steak tartar, apart from its delicious flavour, is the fact that it needs no extra vegetables on the side. You can serve it with a green or mixed salad but there is no need for anything else at all. What is more, it is the ideal food for the slimmer or the figure conscious since its calories are very low indeed.

Serves 2 (double the quantity for four servings)

8 *oz (225 g) lean rump steak with the fat and gristle trimmed off*
8 *oz (225 g) aubergine*
1 *tablespoon olive or vegetable oil*
1 *clove garlic*
1 *green pepper*
2 *firm ripe tomatoes*
1 *tablespoon very finely chopped onion*

1 *teaspoon finely chopped capers*
salt and freshly ground black pepper
Worcestershire and Tabasco sauce
½ *teaspoon French Dijon mustard*
2 *eggs*
1 *tablespoon finely chopped parsley*

Cut the meat into very, very thin slivers with a really sharp knife or mince it through the coarse blades of a mincing machine or very finely chop the meat in an electric food processor.

Peel and very finely chop the aubergine, sprinkle it with salt and place in a colander. Cover with a weight and leave the aubergine to 'sweat' for 30 minutes. Drain off excess liquid from the aubergine and pat the vegetable dry with kitchen paper. Cook the aubergine in the oil, over a moderately low heat until it is completely soft. Purée the aubergine by mashing it with a fork until it is smooth or put it through a food mill, an electric liquidizer or a food processor. Leave to cool.

Peel and crush the garlic. Remove the seeds and core from the green pepper and very finely chop the flesh. Cover the tomatoes with boiling water and leave for 2 minutes. Drain them and slide off the skins. Remove the core and seeds and chop the flesh very, very finely.

Combine the meat, aubergine purée, pepper, tomatoes, onion, garlic and capers, and season with salt and pepper. Add the mustard and mix in a few drops of Worcestershire sauce and Tabasco sauce. Shape the mixture into two circles on cold plates, break a raw egg into the centre of each circle and dust with the parsley. Chill before serving.

Parmigiana with Fish

Parmigiana is basically a vegetable dish with layers of aubergines, cheese and tomato sauce topped by a generous sprinkling of Parmesan cheese. It is very well flavoured and has a rich texture and aroma and I found that by adding some steamed and flaked fish one could produce a really first-class main course.
Serves 8

1 lb (450 g) firm-fleshed white fish (coley, cod, whiting etc.)
3 lb (1350 g) aubergines
1 large onion
8 oz (225 g) carrots
2 stalks celery
4½ tablespoons olive or vegetable oil
1 medium tin (14 oz, 392 g) tomatoes
2 teaspoons tomato purée

6 fl. oz (175 ml) dry white wine
salt and freshly ground black pepper
pinch oregano
2 tablespoons flour
8 oz (225 g) mozzarella or Bel Paese cheese
3 oz (75 g) grated Parmesan cheese

Thinly peel and slice the aubergines. Sprinkle the slices with 1 tablespoon salt, pack them in a colander, weight them down with a plate and leave them to 'sweat' for 1 hour.

Peel and finely chop the onion. Peel and grate the carrots. Very finely chop the celery stalks. Heat 1½ tablespoons oil, add the onion, carrot and celery and cook over a low heat until the onion is soft and transparent. Add the tomatoes, tomato purée and wine. Season with salt and pepper, add the oregano, bring to the boil, cover tightly and simmer gently for 30 minutes.

Dry the aubergine slices with kitchen paper and dredge one side of the slices with the flour. Heat the remaining oil in a frying pan. Add the aubergine slices (do not try to fry too many at one time) floured side down and fry them for a few minutes until lightly browned. Drain off excess oil on kitchen paper.

Steam the fish until *just* cooked. Remove any skin and bones and lightly flake the flesh. Lightly mix the fish into the tomato sauce. Thinly slice the mozzarella or Bel Paese cheese.

Layer the aubergine slices, the tomato and fish sauce and the cheese slices in a lightly greased casserole dish sprinkling each layer with just a little grated Parmesan and finishing with tomato sauce.

Sprinkle over the remaining Parmesan and bake in a moderately hot oven (375°F. 190°C. Reg. 5) for 30 minutes until the casserole is hot through and the top is bubbling and golden brown.

Fillets of White Fish with an Aromatic Topping

I have also made this dish with small, whole, dabs which have had their dark skin removed. The quality of the fish you use will depend on the price you want to pay but the sauce which tops the fillets is so good that the dish may well be made with inexpensive fillets of fish such as whiting. The method is also good for mackerel.

Serves 4

4 *fillets of fish*
3 *large ripe tomatoes*
1 *medium aubergine*
1 *onion*

1 *clove garlic*
2½ *tablespoons olive or vegetable oil*
salt and freshly ground black
  pepper

2 oz (50 g) butter
1 teaspoon lemon juice
pinch oregano

2 oz (50 g) Gruyère cheese,
grated

Cover the tomatoes with boiling water for 2 minutes, slide off the skin, remove the core and seeds and chop the tomato flesh. Cut the aubergine into very small dice. Peel and chop the onion. Peel and very finely chop the garlic. Heat 2 tablespoons oil in a heavy pan. Add the onion, garlic and two-thirds of the aubergine and cook over a low heat, stirring to prevent sticking, until the onion is soft and transparent. Add the tomatoes, season with salt and pepper, mix in the oregano, bring to the boil, cover tightly and simmer for 30 minutes until the vegetables are really soft and have an almost puréed texture.

Season the fillets and cook them gently in the butter and ½ tablespoon of oil until they are just tender and have lost their opaque look. Arrange the fillets in a shallow baking dish and pour over the lemon juice and juices from the pan.

Spread the sauce over the fillets, sprinkle over the cheese and put under a medium hot grill until the cheese has melted and the dish is hot through.

Beetroot

Today the beetroot is a much-underrated vegetable, although centuries ago it was considered not only a delicacy but also a curer of many ills. How many people in Britain these days, for instance, actually eat the leaves of the beetroot? Yet it was for those attractive red-veined leaves that the Greeks and Romans grew the plant, not only eating them but also adding them to wine which had gone sour in order to make it drinkable. The leaves can be used like spinach and they are also an excellent addition to a vegetable soup or a rich and nourishing *bortsch*.

There seems to be no very good reason why the beetroot hasn't gained the status in Britain and America that it has in the Eastern European countries where it appears daily in winter menus. Since its arrival in Europe and, later, its importation by the Dutch into the United States in the days of the early settlers, it seems to have made little impact. In the southern states of America it is the leaves alone that are served as a vegetable and it is only in New England cuisine that the root has achieved some fame, being an essential ingredient of two traditional dishes, Red Flannel Hash and Harvard Beets.

The beetroot is a hardy plant and being a native of both Europe and Asia it is easy to grow. For a time the juice which colours the water as you cook the root was thought to have great medicinal properties, provided, for some reason, it was sniffed up the nose. You have to be careful about this bleeding when you cook the root and although you should scrub it well to remove any dirt before the beetroot is boiled, a good inch of the stalks should be left on. As it takes a long cooking time to become tender, cooking beetroot in a pressure cooker rather than an ordinary saucepan is to be recommended. The roots can also be baked in an oven and once tender they are left to cool and then the skin is rubbed off before they are used.

It is a mistake to relegate cooked beetroot to the role of a salad vegetable (so often it discolours the other ingredients and, frequently over-soused with vinegar, swamps the flavour of other ingredients). As a cooked vegetable, served with a sweet and sour sauce or in a rich cheese sauce, it can be delicious and it makes a valuable winter vegetable.

Two years ago I began growing the golden as well as the red beetroot and these have been highly successful providing they are lifted when they are reasonably small. The golden beet have several advantages: they do not bleed much when cooking; they do not stain any other ingredients which are to be served with them; and although their flavour is similar to that of the red variety they are not so sweet.

Tongue, Beetroot and Spring Onion Salad

Serves 4

8 oz (225 g) cooked tongue
1 medium beetroot, cooked
4 spring onions
3 tablespoons olive or vegetable oil
1 tablespoon white wine vinegar
½ teaspoon French Dijon
   mustard

salt and freshly ground black
   pepper
1 teaspoon freshly grated
   horseradish root
1 tablespoon finely chopped
   parsley

Cut the tongue into thin matchstick strips. Peel the beetroot, cut it into slices and then into thin matchstick strips. Trim the spring onions and cut them into thin slices. Combine the oil, vinegar and mustard, season with salt and pepper and mix well. Add the horseradish and parsley to the vinaigrette and beat the sauce with a fork. Add the tongue, beetroot and spring onions and toss lightly. Turn on to a serving dish and chill before serving.

A Salad of Tongue, Beetroot and Cucumber

If you grow it or can buy it the golden beetroot is infinitely preferable for all salad dishes, as the red variety does tend to dye any other ingredients it comes into contact with and the finished dish, made with the red beetroot, appears a rather strong colour. The taste of this dish, nevertheless, is delicious and the slight sweetness of the beetroot is well counteracted by the fairly sharp dressing.

Serves 4

8 oz (225 g) tongue
12 oz (350 g) beetroot, cooked
½ small cucumber
1 crisp eating apple
1 carton (5 fl. oz, 150 ml) yoghurt
2 tablespoons mayonnaise
1 teaspoon grated horseradish root (or 2 teaspoons horseradish sauce)

1 teaspoon French Dijon mustard
salt and freshly ground black pepper
1 bunch watercress
1 tablespoon finely chopped chives or spring onion tops

Cut the tongue into thin strips. Thinly slice the beetroot and cut into thin strips. Peel and thickly slice the cucumber and cut the slices into thin strips. Peel and core the apple, cut it into thin slices and cut the slices into thin strips.

Combine the yoghurt with the mayonnaise, horseradish and mustard, season with a little salt and pepper and mix well. Add all the ingredients for the salad, except the watercress and chives, to the yoghurt sauce and mix lightly together.

Remove the stalks from the watercress and spread the leaves on a shallow serving dish. Pile the salad on to the leaves and garnish with the finely chopped chives or spring onion tops.

Marinated Mackerel and Beetroot Salad

A delicious summer salad dish, richly coloured and marvellously piquant and cool. Despite using the relatively humble mackerel

this is a dish I consider to be of dinner party material; if you have
it as a first course, serve it with small glasses of oily, really well-
chilled vodka (put the bottle of vodka in the freezer for at least
six hours before serving it) and if the salad is to make the main
course of your meal accompany it with a really well-chilled rosé
wine.

This is a dish I often produce for a summer luncheon or
dinner buffet party. It looks very pretty and it certainly tastes as
good as it looks.

Serves 4

4 *small mackerel*
10 *peppercorns*
1 *large onion*
pinch mace
4 *cloves*
4 *bay leaves*
pinch allspice
1 *sprig thyme*
2 *sage leaves*
salt and white wine vinegar
1 *large beetroot, cooked*

1 *crisp eating apple*
2 *cooked potatoes*
½ *teaspoon made English*
   mustard
1 *tablespoon mixed finely*
   chopped parsley and chives
2 *tablespoons olive oil*
2 *tablespoons sour cream or*
   yoghurt
1 *crisp lettuce*

Clean the mackerel and remove their heads and tails. Cut out
the backbones (or fillet the fish) and arrange the mackerel in a
lightly oiled baking dish. Cover with the peppercorns, the onion,
peeled and cut into rings, the herbs and spices. Season with salt
and pour over enough vinegar to cover the fish. Bake in a
moderate oven (350°F. 180°C. Reg. 4) for 40 minutes.

Carefully lift out the fish, removing any of the flavouring
ingredients, place in a clean dish and strain over the vinegar
mixture. Cool and then chill for at least 4 hours.

Peel the beetroot and cut it into small dice. Peel, core and dice
the apple. Dice the potatoes. Drain off the vinegar from the
mackerel and mix 3 tablespoons of the liquid with the mustard,
olive oil, sour cream or yoghurt and the herbs. Cut the mackerel
into ½ inch (1½ cm) wide slices with a pair of kitchen scissors.
Lightly mix the beetroot, apple and potato together and arrange
them on a bed of crisp lettuce leaves, top with the slices of
mackerel and pour over the dressing. Serve chilled.

Pan-fried Fillets of Mackerel with Sweet and Sour Beetroot

The sharpness of the sauce used in this dish helps to counteract the sweetness of the beetroot and the richness of the mackerel.
Serves 4

4 *large or* 8 *small fillets of*
  mackerel
flour
salt and freshly ground black
  pepper
2 *medium beetroots, cooked*
2½ *oz (65 g) butter*

1 *tablespoon vegetable oil*
3 *tablespoons white wine or cider*
  vinegar
2 *tablespoons sugar*
1 *tablespoon finely chopped*
  parsley

Lightly coat the mackerel fillets with seasoned flour. Peel the beetroots and cut them into small dice.

Melt 1½ oz (40 g) butter with the oil, add the mackerel fillets and cook over a medium heat, turning once, until the fillets are golden brown and cooked through. Transfer the fish to a heated serving dish, pour over any juices from the pan and keep warm while making the sauce.

Melt 1 oz (25 g) butter in a saucepan. Add 1 teaspoon salt, the vinegar and the sugar and stir over a low heat until the sugar has melted. Add the beetroot and toss over a medium high heat until the sauce is very hot. Spoon the sauce over the mackerel and dust with finely chopped parsley before serving.

Fish with Beetroot and Peppers in a Sweet and Sour Sauce

A sweet and sour sauce helps to counteract the slight sweetness of beetroot and the luscious dark-red colour of this dish looks good against a background of fluffy boiled rice.
Serves 4

12 *oz (350 g) firm white fish*
  fillet
3 *medium beetroots, cooked*

1 *green pepper*
1 *onion*
1 *inch (2½ cm) fresh ginger root*

2 *cloves garlic*

1 *small dried red chilli pepper or*
   1 *fresh green chilli pepper*

3 *carrots*

½ *pint (300 ml) chicken stock*

1 *tablespoon cornflour*

1 *tablespoon soy sauce*

3 *tablespoons white wine vinegar*

3 *tablespoons sugar*

4 *tablespoons vegetable oil*

salt

Peel and chop the onion. Remove the seeds and core from the green pepper and cut the flesh into thin strips. Peel the ginger and cut the flesh into very, very fine strips. Peel and finely chop the garlic. Finely chop the chilli (remove the seeds if you don't like your food too hot). Peel the carrots and cut them into ¼ inch (¾ cm) thick matchstick strips. Peel the beetroots and cut the flesh into fairly thick matchstick lengths about ¼ inch (¾ cm) thick. Remove the skin from the fish and cut it into ¼ inch (¾ cm) thick strips.

Combine the chicken stock, cornflour, soy sauce, vinegar and sugar and mix well.

Heat the oil in a Chinese *wok* or deep frying pan. Add the onion, garlic, ginger and chilli pepper and cook over a high heat stirring all the time, for 1 minute. Add the carrots and continue to stir for 8 minutes. Add the pepper and cook for a further 2 minutes.

Pour in the stock mixture and stir until the sauce is thick and glossy. Mix in the fish and beetroot, season with a little salt and cook for about 3 minutes until the fish is no longer opaque. Serve as quickly as possible.

Sweet and Sour Beetroot and Cucumber with Strips of Fried Fish and Sprigs of Deep-fried Parsley

You can use any inexpensive white fish fillets for this dish. The beetroot and cucumber in a sharp sauce provide an interesting contrast to the fish and the dish looks attractive.

Serves 6

2 *medium beetroots, cooked*
1 *small cucumber or ½ large cucumber*
1 *lb (450 g) fillets of white fish (use plaice, lemon sole, dabs, whiting etc.)*
1 *egg, beaten*
dried breadcrumbs
12 *sprigs parsley*

2 *oz (50 g) butter*
salt and freshly ground black pepper
2 *tablespoons white wine vinegar*
2 *tablespoons sugar*
deep oil for frying
wedges of lemon
sauce tartare

Peel the beetroots, cut them into ¼ inch (¾ cm) thick slices and then cut the slices into matchstick strips. Peel the cucumber, cut it into half lengthwise and scoop out the seeds. Cut the two halves into ¼ inch (¾ cm) thick slices, sprinkle them with salt and leave them to 'sweat' in a colander for 20 minutes. Shake off excess liquid and pat the cucumber slices dry on kitchen paper.

Cut the fish into ½ inch (1½ cm) thick diagonal strips. Dip the strips into the beaten egg and then coat them in breadcrumbs Remove most of the tough stalk of the parsley.

Melt the butter in a heavy pan. Add the beetroot, cucumber, vinegar and sugar and season with pepper and plenty of salt. Cook over a low heat, stirring gently so as not to break up the beetroot, until the sugar has melted. Transfer to a heated serving dish and keep warm while cooking the fish.

Heat some deep oil until a cube of bread added to the oil will turn golden almost as soon as it is dropped into the pan. Add the strips of fish a few at a time, and cook until the fish is golden brown. Remove the fish and drain it on kitchen paper. When all the fish has been cooked add the sprigs of parsley to the oil and cook them for a few seconds until they are crisp. Drain the parsley on kitchen paper.

At the last minute before serving, pile the fish on to the bed of beetroot and cucumber and garnish with the parsley and wedges of lemon. Serve with sauce tartare.

Beetroot Tops with Bacon and a Cheese Sauce

Beetroot tops should never be discarded as they make a first-rate vegetable as well as an excellent soup ingredient. Prepare them

just like spinach and take care that they are not overcooked. The
liquid the tops were cooked in can be used as a soup base or for
stock.

This is a recipe that very much comes under the category of
'supper' dishes. It is nourishing, flavoursome and substantial and
it is also extremely inexpensive.
Serves 4

1 *lb (450 g) beetroot tops*
8 *rashers streaky, smoked bacon*
butter
1½ *oz (40 g) flour*
¾ *pint (450 ml) milk*
2 *teaspoons French Dijon*
   mustard
2½ *oz (65 g) Cheddar cheese,*
   grated

1 *egg*
salt and freshly ground black
   pepper
pinch of ground nutmeg
2 *oz (50 g) fresh white*
   breadcrumbs
1 *tablespoon vegetable oil*

Wash the beetroot tops and trim off any tough stalks. Cook
the tops in a little boiling salted water until they are just tender.
Drain them well and chop them roughly with a pair of kitchen
scissors.

Cook the rashers of bacon, without extra fat, over a medium
high heat until they are nicely crisped. Drain off and reserve the
bacon fat from the pan, remove the rinds from the rashers and
cut the rashers into 1 inch (2½ cm) wide strips.

Arrange the beetroot tops in a lightly buttered fireproof dish
and place the chopped bacon on top of the greens.

Add enough butter to the bacon fat to make 2 tablespoons of
fat, place the fat in a saucepan and mix in the flour. Gradually
stir in the milk, beating continually over a medium high heat
until the sauce comes to the boil and is thick and smooth. Add
three-quarters of the cheese, season with salt, pepper, nutmeg
and mustard and continue to stir until the cheese has melted.
Lower the heat and beat in the egg. Pour the sauce over the
beetroot tops and bacon.

Combine the remaining cheese with the breadcrumbs and
sprinkle the mixture over the top of the dish. Dribble over the oil
and bake in a hot oven (400°F. 200°C. Reg. 6) for 15 minutes
until the topping is crisp and golden brown.

Slices of Tongue or Ham with Beetroot and Onions

This is one of those miraculously quickly cooked and prepared dishes (providing the beetroots are already cooked when you start the preparations) that are invaluable to have at your fingertips for those occasions when you want to create a dish with flair at short notice. I find it useful to keep a tin of ham or tongue in the larder for just such an occasion.
Serves 4

4 *thick slices ham or tongue*
2 *large beetroots, cooked*
2 *large onions*
3 *oz (75 g) butter*

¼ *pint (150 ml) double cream*
salt and freshly ground black
   pepper
French Dijon mustard

Cut the peeled beetroots into small dice. Peel and chop the onions. Melt the butter in a frying pan, add the onions and cook them over a low heat until they are soft and transparent. Add the beetroot, cover tightly and cook over a low heat, shaking the pan every now and then, for 10 minutes. Season the beetroot and onions with salt and pepper, mix in the cream and heat through without boiling.

Spread the ham or tongue slices with a very thin layer of mustard and arrange them in a shallow serving dish. Spread the beetroot and onion mixture over the ham or tongue and heat through for about 10 minutes in a moderate oven (350°F. 180°C. Reg. 4).

Serve with rice or with mashed potatoes and, if you like, a green salad on the side.

The Great Family Brassica

Some of my best friends have been known to turn up their noses at the common cabbage. Not for them to talk of 'cabbages and kings' in the same breath; they think of the family of *Brassica oleracea* as being a humble smelly plant that smacks of watery schoolday meals, dingy bedsitting-rooms and slovenly landladies. How much they miss, all those who don't or won't appreciate the cabbage in all its many varieties. Cabbage is still the cheapest vegetable on the market and one or other of its varieties can be grown all the year round in the vegetable garden; most are extremely easy to grow, hardy, and need the minimum of care and attention. In addition the members of the cabbage family are probably more versatile for cooking purposes than any other vegetable. Certainly the vitamin and calcium content of fresh brassicas is very high indeed and, provided these virtues are not killed by overcooking, there is no doubt that a cabbage a day can be as much good as an apple a day or any number of other things.

People tend to think of the brassica family as consisting only of spring cabbage, firm round white cabbage, crinkly-leaved, dark-toned Savoys and the richly coloured red cabbage which is so popular pickled. In fact the *Brassica oleracea* family has a hundred different varieties and is also closely related to the tight miniature Brussels sprouts, cauliflowers and the various broccolis, kale and curly greens. I think that, over the years and during a lot of

travelling, I have eaten cabbage in one form or another in every
country I have ever visited, including way-out haunts such as the
Amazonas and New Guinea.

The smell of the brassica family as it cooks can be unpleasant
and it is this that has, so often, led to cabbages, Brussels sprouts
and other brassica cousins being given a bad name. In fact this
smell should never occur—it is produced only if the vegetables
are wilted or past their prime or if they are cooked for too long.
Make sure your vegetables, whether you buy or grow them, are
crisp and a good colour, discard any leaves that have wilted or
turned yellow and eat the vegetables as soon as you can after
picking or buying them. If you have to store them, do so in a
really cool, dark place. Cook the vegetables in a minimum
amount of water for only just long enough to tenderize them
while still retaining that essential crisp quality that makes all the
difference between something really delicious and a vegetable
that is definitely mediocre.

For a foolproof way to cook cabbage, shred firm green or
white cabbage leaves and put them into 1 inch (2½ cm) of cold
water with ½ teaspoon of salt. Put on a tight-fitting lid, bring to
the boil and turn over the cabbage to ensure even cooking.
Cook for 7 minutes only over a moderately high heat, drain off
any water that has not been absorbed into the vegetables and
then toss quickly in some butter and add a seasoning of freshly
ground black pepper and a pinch of ground nutmeg.

The thick white stalks of outside cabbage leaves obviously
take longer to cook than the leaves themselves and a separate
vegetable can be made by cutting out the stalks, trimming them
and cooking them in boiling salted water in the same way as
you would asparagus. Serve the stalks with melted butter. For
stuffing the large leaves of cabbage the stalks should also be
removed and the leaves blanched in boiling salted water.

Many members of the brassica family also make good salad
material, especially in the winter when more conventional salad
stuff is difficult to get or tends to be very expensive. Young
Brussels sprouts and tender cabbage leaves can be shredded,
broccoli can be lightly cooked, well drained and left to get cold
before being dressed with a vinaigrette or a well-flavoured
mayonnaise, and cauliflowers can be lightly steamed or left raw
and divided into florettes for an attractive winter or early spring
salad dish.

If you grow your own varieties of the brassica family, don't overdo it because anyone will get bored by too much of a good thing in the end and they are a most prolific family. Twenty-five plants should produce about seventy-five pounds of vegetables, so vary your varieties providing a wide choice of succulent and healthy green produce all the year round.

Keep an eye open too for new varieties of cabbage now appearing on the market. There is, for instance, the pale and extremely crisp Chinese cabbage which looks rather like a cos lettuce and can be eaten in a salad or as a vegetable.

Above all do remember that eating cabbages can cause flatulence and, indeed, this form of food is included in the list of vegetables forbidden to astronauts before they set out for a trip into space. If you are planning to do justice to a large amount of any of the cabbage family or its relations, especially if they are to be served raw, bear this in mind when planning the rest of your day's or night's entertainment.

Many excellent dishes can be made by combining the brassica family with meat, poultry or fish. The flavours can complement each other admirably and the enzymes of the vegetables can do a lot to tenderize and enhance the texture of protein ingredients.

Red Cabbage with Chilli

A really richly flavoured and robust dish that is made by combining layers of blanched red cabbage with spiced and succulent chilli con carne. The dish is finished with a crisp topping of combined breadcrumbs and cheese.
Serves 8

1 lb (450 g) minced beef or
 lamb
2 lb (900 g) red cabbage
2 onions
3 cloves garlic
1 green pepper
1 green chilli pepper
5 tablespoons olive or vegetable oil
1 medium tin (14 oz, 392 g)
 tomatoes
2 tablespoons tomato purée

¼ pint (150 ml) red wine
2 teaspoons chilli powder
salt and freshly ground black
 pepper
3 oz (75 g) fresh white
 breadcrumbs
1½ oz (40 g) finely grated
 Cheddar cheese
1 tablespoon French Dijon
 mustard

Shred the cabbage. Peel and finely chop the onions and garlic. Remove the seeds and core of the green pepper and chilli pepper and chop the flesh. Heat 4 tablespoons of oil in a heavy saucepan. Add the onion, garlic, chilli and pepper and cook over a low heat until the onion is soft and transparent. Raise the heat, add the meat and stir lightly until the meat is browned on all sides. Add the tomatoes, tomato purée and wine, bring to the boil, mix in the chilli powder, season with salt and pepper, cover tightly and simmer for 45 minutes. Remove the cover and continue to cook, stirring every now and then, for 10 minutes until the mixture is moist but not liquid.

Blanch the cabbage in boiling salted water for 6 minutes and drain well. Arrange a third of the cabbage in a lightly buttered baking dish, cover with half the meat mixture and continue to layer the ingredients, finishing with a third layer of cabbage. Combine the breadcrumbs and cheese with the mustard and 1 tablespoon of oil and mix well. Spread the breadcrumb mixture on top of the cabbage and press down the contents of the dish firmly. Bake the dish in a moderate oven (350°F. 180°C. Reg. 4) for 45 minutes.

Lamb with Cabbage, Gin and Orange

A most successful and delicious dish. The gin gives just that hint of juniper to the meat, paprika adds a richness and the final addition of parsley and garlic butter provides a mouth-watering aroma.
Serves 4–6

1 *lb (450 g) lean lamb from leg*
  or shoulder
1 *large onion*
1 *small red cabbage*
flour
salt and freshly ground black
  pepper
3 *teaspoons paprika*
1½ *lb (675 g) potatoes*

4 *tablespoons vegetable oil*
3 *tablespoons gin*
¼ *pint (150 ml) orange juice*
stock
2 *bay leaves*
1½ *oz (40 g) butter*
1 *tablespoon finely chopped*
  parsley
2 *cloves garlic, crushed*

Peel and chop the onion. Shred the red cabbage. Cut the lamb into fairly small cubes and coat them lightly in flour seasoned with salt, pepper and paprika. Peel the potatoes and cut them into dice of the same size as the lamb.

Heat half of the oil in a frying pan. Add the onion and cook over a low heat until soft and transparent. Add the cabbage and continue to cook over a low heat, stirring every now and then, for about 5 minutes until the oil has all been absorbed.

Heat the remaining oil in a flameproof casserole or heavy pan. Add the meat and brown quickly on all sides. Add the gin, bring to the boil, set the gin alight and shake the pan until the flames die down. Add the orange juice and mix well. Add the onions, cabbage and potatoes to the meat and pour in enough stock just to cover the ingredients. Add the bay leaves, bring to the boil, cover tightly and cook over a low heat for 45 minutes or until the lamb is tender. Remove the lid and continue to cook for a further 10 minutes until most of the liquid has been absorbed into the ingredients.

Mix the butter with the crushed garlic and parsley, add the mixture to the casserole and stir well. Serve at once, with an extra vegetable on the side.

Note: This casserole can be made in advance and then re-heated, with the butter mixture being added at the last minute.

Lamb and Aubergine in Red Cabbage Leaves

You can use large green cabbage leaves instead of the red leaves but they don't have quite the same flavour. The colour of the leaves does run during the blanching time but this is compensated for by the tomato and red wine sauce. The wrapped lamb emerges with rewarding succulence.
Serves 6

12 oz (350 g) lean minced lamb
3 oz (75 g) streaky bacon
6 large red cabbage leaves
2 onions

1 medium aubergine
3 tablespoons olive or vegetable oil
2½ oz (65 g) fresh white
   breadcrumbs

2 *eggs, beaten*
½ *teaspoon each of ground*
  fenugreek, turmeric and
  coriander
1 *tablespoon tomato purée*
1 *tablespoon finely chopped*
  parsley

salt and freshly ground black
  pepper
1 *small tin (7 oz, 200 g)*
  tomatoes
¼ *pint (150 ml) red wine*

Cut the bottom off a large red cabbage and gently prize off the outside six large leaves from the head. Blanch the red cabbage leaves in fast-boiling salted water for 3 minutes. Drain well and leave to cool. Peel and very finely chop the onions. Chop the aubergine and pass it through the coarse blades of a mincing machine. Remove the rinds from the bacon and mince the rashers.

Heat the oil in a frying pan. Add the onions and aubergine and cook, stirring every now and then to prevent sticking, for 4 minutes. Raise the heat, add the lamb and bacon and continue to stir for about 3 minutes until the lamb is lightly browned.

Place the breadcrumbs in a bowl, add the beaten eggs, fenugreek, turmeric, coriander and tomato purée and mix well. Add the meat and parsley, season with salt and pepper and beat with a wooden spoon to combine all the ingredients.

Divide the meat mixture into six portions, place each portion on a cabbage leaf, roll up into a neat parcel and place them in a shallow, lightly greased baking dish.

Break up the tomatoes with a fork and mix them with the red wine. Spread the mixture over the stuffed cabbage leaves, cover tightly with foil and bake in a moderate oven (350°F. 180°C. Reg. 4) for 1¼ hours.

Serve with rice or sauté potatoes (peel and parboil the potatoes, cut them into thickish slices and fry them until really crisp and golden brown in very hot vegetable oil with a little very finely slivered garlic. Drain the potatoes on kitchen paper and sprinkle them with a little salt before serving).

Chicken Danielle

Another of those layered dishes, this time with a combination of cabbage and chicken, a good marriage of textures and flavours,

which are finished off with a rich velouté sauce lightly flavoured with nutmeg and cheese.
Serves 6

12 oz (350 g) cooked chicken
1 lb (450 g) drum head or firm cabbage
8 oz (225 g) firm button mushrooms
3 oz (75 g) butter
2 tablespoons flour
½ pint (300 ml) chicken stock

2 eggs
¼ pint (150 ml) single cream
salt, freshly ground black pepper
pinch of ground nutmeg
1 oz (25 g) grated Parmesan cheese

Very thinly shred the cabbage. Cut the chicken into very thin slices. Very thinly slice the mushrooms.

Cook the cabbage in boiling salted water for 8 minutes until just tender. Drain well.

Melt half the butter in a frying pan. Add the mushrooms and cook over a low heat, tossing the pan every now and then, for 5 minutes. Arrange the cabbage, chicken and mushrooms in a lightly buttered casserole dish, starting and finishing with layers of cabbage.

Melt the remaining butter in a saucepan. Add the flour and mix well. Gradually add the stock, stirring continually over a medium high heat until the sauce comes to the boil and is thick and smooth. Season with salt, pepper and a little nutmeg and remove from the heat.

Beat the eggs with the cream until smooth. Add the egg and cream mixture to the sauce and mix until well blended. Pour the sauce over the ingredients in the casserole, sprinkle over the cheese and bake in a moderately hot oven (375°F. 190°C. Reg. 5) for about 30 minutes or until the casserole is really hot through and the top is bubbling and golden brown.

Breast of Lamb with Cabbage

I find this an exceptionally good way to deal with the cheap but rather fatty cut that makes up a breast of lamb. The juices from the lamb go into the cabbage as the dish cooks, adding flavour to the cabbage while, at the same time, the cabbage helps to tenderize and flavour the lamb.
Serves 4

2 *breasts of lamb*
1 *lb (450 g) cabbage*
1 *small onion*
3 *oz (75 g) streaky bacon*
1 *oz (25 g) butter*
3 *oz (75 g) fresh brown*
  breadcrumbs

grated rind of 1 *lemon*
2 *tablespoons finely chopped*
  parsley
salt and freshly ground black
  pepper
2 *tablespoons double cream*
2 *tablespoons vegetable oil*

Very finely shred the cabbage. Peel and finely chop the onion. Remove the rinds from the bacon and finely chop the rashers. Blanch the cabbage in boiling salted water for 5 minutes and drain really well. Melt the butter in a small frying pan, add the onion and bacon and cook over a low heat until the onion is soft and transparent.

Combine the cabbage, breadcrumbs, onion, bacon, parsley and lemon rind. Mix in the cream and season with salt and pepper. Trim off excess fat from the lamb and cut it into fingers in between the bones.

Arrange the cabbage in a lightly buttered serving dish, place the pieces of lamb, skin side up, on top and dribble over the oil.

Roast the meat in a hot oven (425°F. 220°C. Reg. 7) for 15 minutes and then reduce the heat to moderate (350°F. 180°C. Reg. 4) and continue to cook, basting every now and then with the juices from the pan, for a further 1 hour or until the meat is tender.

Serve the dish with new potatoes or rice and a green vegetable or salad.

Ragout of Lamb with Cabbage

Serves 4

1 *lb (450 g) lean lamb*
1 *medium onion*
3 *large ripe tomatoes*
1 *medium cabbage*
2 *oz (50 g) dripping or lard*

1 *teaspoon paprika*
$\frac{1}{4}$ *pint (150 ml) water or stock*
salt
$\frac{1}{4}$ *pint (150 ml) sour cream*

Cut the meat into 1 inch (2½ cm) cubes. Peel and chop the onion. Cover the tomatoes with boiling water for 2 minutes, drain them and remove the skins. Quarter the tomatoes.

Heat the lard or dripping in a large heavy saucepan, add the onion and cook over a low heat until the onion is soft and transparent. Add the paprika and mix well. Remove from the heat, add the meat and tomatoes and pour over ¼ pint (150 ml) water or stock. Season with salt, cover tightly and cook over a low heat for 45 minutes.

Remove the tough outer leaves of the cabbage and cut it into six through the centre. Cook the cabbage in a little salted water for 5 minutes and drain really well.

Place the cabbage on top of the meat, cover and continue to cook for a further 20 minutes or until the meat is really tender. Pour over the sour cream, heat through for 3 minutes and then remove the cabbage to a serving dish with a slotted spoon, cover the cabbage with the meat and tomatoes and pour over any liquid from the pan.

Stir-fry Chinese Cabbage with Beef

A recipe with Chinese overtones that is exceptionally quick to make and, I think, very good indeed. The flavour of these dishes is always improved if you cook them in a Chinese *wok* as the heat in these pans is usually much higher and more evenly distributed than in a conventional frying pan. If you do use a frying pan, pick a large one with a heavy bottom and make sure it is really hot before you begin to add the ingredients of the dish.

One of the great secrets of this type of quick cooking is that the dish must be served as quickly as possible after it has been cooked. If you use a *wok* and combine it with a small and inexpensive butane gas camping stove which gives a very strong heat you can, if you like, cook the dish at the table after you have served and eaten the first course.

Serves 4

8 oz (225 g) beef flank or rump
1½ lb (675 g) Chinese cabbage
2½ tablespoons soy sauce
2 tablespoons sherry
2 teaspoons cornflour

¼ pint (150 ml) beef consommé
4 spring onions
2 cloves garlic
2 tablespoons sunflower oil

Chill the beef in the deep freeze for 30 minutes to make for easy slicing. Cut into wafer-thin slices against the grain and then into ¼ inch (¾ cm) thick strips. Combine 1 tablespoon soy sauce with 1 tablespoon sherry and 1 teaspoon cornflour and mix well. Add the beef and marinate for 1 hour.

Combine half the consommé with the remaining soy sauce, sherry and cornflour and mix well.

Thickly shred the cabbage into about 1 inch (2½ cm) wide slices. Cut the spring onions into thin lengthwise strips. Peel and finely chop the garlic.

Heat the oil in a hot *wok* or frying pan over a high heat. When the oil is smoking, add the beef and cook, tossing all the time, for 1 minute. Remove the meat with a slotted spoon. Add the spring onions and garlic and cook, tossing or stirring, for 30 seconds. Add the cabbage and stir over a high heat for 2 minutes. Add the meat and the consommé, soy sauce and sherry mixture and continue to stir over a high heat for 1 minute or until the meat is just tender.

Serve with fluffy boiled rice.

Cream of Brussels Sprout Soup with Bacon and Chives

Although this is a good soup and a useful way to use up Brussels sprouts which may have grown a little on the large side, it does tend to have a rather bland flavouring which is markedly improved by the addition of some crisply fried, crumbled bacon and some finely chopped chives added at the last minute.
Serves 6–8

2 lb (900 g) Brussels sprouts
  (you can use sprout tops)
8 oz (225 g) potatoes
1 onion
2 oz (50 g) butter
1½ pints (900 ml) good stock
½ pint (300 ml) milk
salt and freshly ground black
  pepper

pinch each of ground nutmeg and
  cayenne pepper
¼ pint (150 ml) single cream
2 rashers streaky bacon
2 tablespoons finely chopped
  chives or spring onion tops

Trim and wash the sprouts and drain well. Peel and finely chop the potatoes and onion. Melt the butter in a large heavy saucepan. Add the onion and potatoes and cook over a low heat until the butter has been absorbed into the vegetables. Add the Brussels sprouts and mix well. Add the stock and milk, bring to the boil, season with salt, pepper, nutmeg and cayenne, cover and simmer for about 20 minutes or until the sprouts are tender. Strain off the liquid and purée the vegetables through a fine sieve, a food mill, an electric liquidizer or food processor.

Fry the bacon until crisp without extra fat. Drain well on kitchen paper, leave to cool and then remove the rinds and crumble the rashers.

Combine the vegetable purée and cooking liquid and mix well. Bring to the boil, lower the heat and mix in the cream. Check the seasoning and sprinkle each serving with bacon and chives.

A Pâté of Brussels Sprouts, Herbs and Chicken

I became very enthusiastic about vegetable pâtés when I was working on recipes for this book. Not only are they a lovely colour but their texture is light and they provide a most unusual start to a meal. Instead of the garlic mayonnaise suggested here, you can serve the pâtés with a strongly spiced, home-made tomato sauce or with the yoghurt and cucumber sauce given as an accompaniment to the pâté of carrots and gammon on page 72.
Serves 6

6 oz (175 g) raw chicken from   2 slices white bread
   the breast   2 eggs, beaten
1 lb (450 g) Brussels sprouts   1½ oz (40 g) melted butter
a small bunch of sorrel, parsley   ½ teaspoon garam masala
   and chives   extra butter
salt and freshly ground black
   pepper

Trim the sprouts and remove the tough stalks from the sorrel and parsley. Cook the sprouts and herbs in a little boiling salted water until they are just tender and drain really well. Purée the sprouts and herbs through a fine food mill or in an electric liquidizer or food processor. Very finely mince the chicken.

Remove the crusts and soak the bread in a little warm water. Squeeze out excess water. Add the bread, chicken, melted butter and the beaten eggs to the puréed sprouts, season with salt and pepper, add the garam masala and mix really well.

Line a terrine with strips of well-buttered foil, leaving the edges of the foil to hang over the edge of the terrine. Pack the pâté mixture into the terrine, fold over the strips of foil and cover the terrine with another two thicknesses of foil. Stand the terrine in a *bain marie* of hot water and bake the pâté in a moderate oven (350°F. 180°C. Reg. 4) for 1½ hours. Leave to cool and chill until set firm. Lift out the pâté with the ends of the foil, turn it upside down on to a serving dish and carefully remove the foil.

Serve the pâté with a home-made mayonnaise flavoured with a little French Dijon mustard and some crushed garlic.

Fillet of Pork with Brussels Sprouts

Cleaned and sliced sprouts should need only a few minutes' cooking time. In this recipe they are gently cooked in butter and great care must be taken not to let them overcook.
Serves 4

1 *fillet of pork, approximately*
  1 *lb (450 g)*
1 *lb (450 g) Brussels sprouts*
1½ *tablespoons cornflour*
3 *tablespoons port*
½ *teaspoon ground turmeric*
salt

freshly ground black pepper
2 *oz (50 g) butter*
3 *tablespoons vegetable oil*
¼ *pint (150 ml) chicken stock*
¼ *pint (150 ml) single cream*
1 *tablespoon finely chopped*
  parsley

Trim the Brussels sprouts and cut them into ¼ inch (¾ cm) thick slices. Cut the pork fillet into ¼ inch (¾ cm) thick slices, place the slices between two sheets of greaseproof paper and beat them with a wooden mallet or rolling pin until the slices have about doubled in size. Combine the cornflour with the port and turmeric and season it with salt and pepper. Add the slices of pork and mix well so that the slices are coated with the mixture. Leave to stand for 30 minutes.

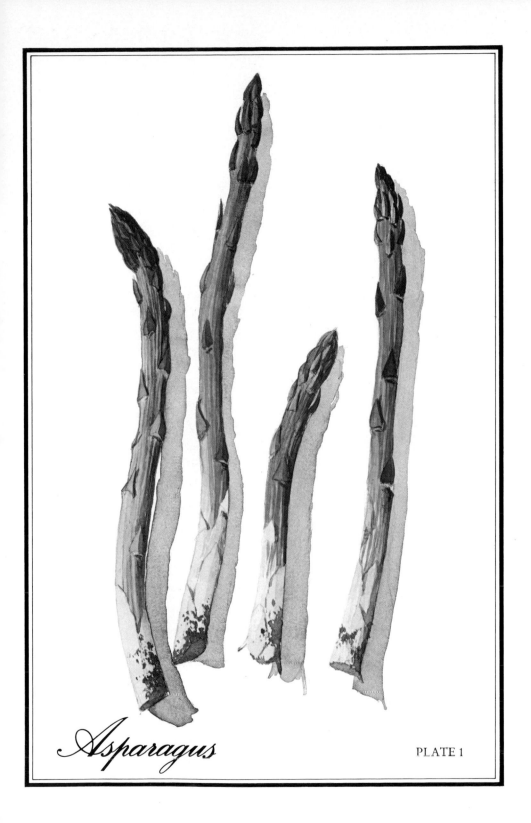

Asparagus

PLATE 1

Beetroot

PLATE 2

Heat the butter in a heavy saucepan. Add the Brussels sprouts, season with salt and plenty of pepper and cook, covered, over a low heat, shaking the pan every now and then to prevent burning, for about 6 minutes or until the sprouts are tender. Transfer the sprouts to a heated serving dish and keep warm.

Heat the oil in a frying pan. Add the slices of pork and fry over a high heat for about 6 minutes, turning once, until the meat is browned and tender. Remove the meat with a slotted spoon and arrange the slices on top of the Brussels sprouts. Add the stock to the juices in the pan and mix well. Stir in the cream, heat through without boiling, and strain the sauce over the meat. Dust with finely chopped parsley before serving.

C

Broad Beans

I once actually met someone who considered broad beans to be a 'boring and uninteresting vegetable'. French beans, this gentleman maintained, were all right, runner beans were bearable but what was there in broad beans to get so excited about? Well, I suppose we all have our peculiarities and maybe some would maintain I was more peculiar than others when I say I find broad beans in all their many guises one of the great joys of life; a natural magic that, unlike most things, seems to improve with every season and, like the Romans, I firmly believe they are 'good for you'.

The magic of broad beans is as old as their origins (they were one of the first vegetables to be cultivated and were the only 'bean' in Britain until the runner arrived a lot later). Country people will tell you how a cut raw bean rubbed daily on a wart will make it disappear and how nettle stings can be soothed by rubbing them with the white fur from the inside of the pod; the Romans, who always knew a good thing, for centuries followed the admirable practice of nibbling on young broad beans and Pecorino cheese as they sampled the first of their *vino verde* and they maintained that seven raw broad beans eaten every day of the season will help to increase the virility.

Broad beans are not only a summer vegetable. They can be sown in July as well as in the autumn and spring so that in a well-planned garden it should be possible to harvest three times a year. The plants need good manuring, deep trenching and a sheltered position. They also need to be protected against blackfly and chocolate spot.

Broad beans have four stages from the culinary point of view and each is delicious in its own right. When the plants flower, in order to make them bush out and to guard against an invasion of blackfly, the top 6 inches (15 cm) of the plants are nipped out and these make a really well-flavoured vegetable with a taste that seems to be half-way between spinach and baby broad beans. The tops should be well washed and then plunged into a small amount of fast-boiling, lightly salted water and cooked for only about 10 minutes so that they are still on the crisp side. They should then be well drained and tossed with butter or oil and some freshly ground black pepper.

The next stage is the very young broad bean, picked when they are only about 4 inches (10 cm) long. These tender pods are cooked whole, thus eliminating the boring process of podding and also retaining the full flavour of the bean and its casing. Again the beans must not be overcooked and this vegetable, like indeed the tops of the plants, makes a delicious salad if the beans are left to cool after cooking and then dressed with vinaigrette.

In the third stage the beans will have to be podded but will not have to be skinned. They should not be larger than an old sixpenny piece and are delicious hot or cold. In the final stage (unfortunately the stage one comes across most often in the greengrocer's shop) the pods are thick and long and the beans have a tough skin which should be removed after they have been cooked. Again this is a time-consuming job but it is worth while and the resulting bright-green bean has a good nutty flavour that is very pleasant.

Savory is the traditional herb to cook with broad beans and I make a practice of growing a plant or two at the end of my row of beans to remind me to cut a sprig when I am harvesting the beans.

Materlone

Delicious broad bean tops are served with an aromatic sauce made from minced lamb and onions with a tomato flavouring – the combination is really excellent and one that I can highly recommend. I like this part of the vegetable so much that I sometimes wonder if I grow the plants more for the tops than for the beans themselves.

Serves 3–4

6 oz (175 g) minced raw lamb
2 oz (50 g) fat bacon rashers,
   minced
1 lb (450 g) broad bean tops
2 sprigs savory
2 onions
1 clove garlic
4 tablespoons olive or vegetable oil

1 tablespoon finely chopped
   marjoram
4 bay leaves
1 tablespoon flour
1 tablespoon tomato purée
1 tablespoon mushroom ketchup
salt and freshly ground black
   pepper

Peel and finely chop the onions. Peel and finely chop the garlic. Heat 2 tablespoons of oil in a small saucepan, add the onions and garlic and cook over a low heat until the onion is soft and transparent. Add the meat and bacon and cook over a moderately high heat until the meat is browned. Add the flour and mix well. Mix in the tomato purée, mushroom ketchup, marjoram and bay leaves, season with salt and pepper, cover and cook over a low heat, stirring now and then to prevent sticking, for about 20 minutes or until the meat is tender.

Cook the broad bean tops with the savory in 1 inch (2½ cm) only of boiling salted water for about 10 minutes over a high heat or until the bean tops are just tender. Drain them well, remove the savory, add the remaining 2 tablespoons of oil, season them lightly with ground pepper and transfer them to a heated serving dish. Remove the bay leaves from the meat and pour the sauce over the broad beans.

Serve with potatoes or rice.

Broad Beans with Mint

A dish so good it can stand by itself as a first course in the early summer months. Use young beans picked before the skins get tough.
Serves 4–6

2 lb (900 g) broad beans
2 anchovy fillets
3 tablespoons olive oil
1 tablespoon white wine vinegar

freshly ground black pepper
1 tablespoon finely chopped mint
1 tablespoon finely chopped chives
2 ripe tomatoes

Pod the beans and cook them in boiling salted water until just tender. Drain at once and plunge them into cold water to prevent them continuing to cook. Drain well.

Finely chop the anchovies. Pound them in a mortar with a pestle until almost smooth and gradually blend in the olive oil and vinegar. Season with ground pepper and mix in the chopped mint and chives.

Plunge the tomatoes into boiling water and leave for 2 minutes. Strip off the skins, halve them, remove the tough core and seeds and finely chop the flesh.

Add the chopped tomatoes and beans to the dressing, turn into a serving dish and chill for at least 1 hour before serving as a salad, with cold meats or with buttered slices of brown bread, for a first course.

Terrine of White Fish Fillets and Broad Beans

An unusual and very delicious delicately green-coloured terrine which makes a sensational start to a dinner party. The terrine can also be served as a main course for a summer lunch and you can accompany it with a piquant home-made tomato sauce or a garlic mayonnaise. I use whiting fillets but you can substitute any other reasonably good-quality white fish.
Serves 6–8

12 oz (350 g) white fish fillets
3 oz (75 g) fresh white
  breadcrumbs
3 tablespoons fish stock or
  chicken stock
12 oz (350 g) shelled broad
  beans

2 small eggs, well beaten
salt and white pepper
pinch ground nutmeg
pinch ground coriander
pinch cayenne pepper
2 oz (50 g) melted butter
extra butter

Finely mince the white fish fillets or purée the flesh in a liquidizer or electric food processor.

Soak the breadcrumbs in the fish or chicken stock until soft. Cook the beans in boiling salted water until soft and purée them through a fine food mill (the skins of young beans will go through the mill but those of larger beans should be discarded).

Combine the fish with the beans, breadcrumbs and eggs and beat until the mixture is smooth (this can be done in an electric mixer or food processor). Season with salt, pepper (be quite generous as cold dishes require more seasoning than those that are hot), the nutmeg, coriander and cayenne. Add the melted butter and mix well.

Cut two strips of foil with which to line an earthenware, enamel or porcelain terrine, allowing enough foil to overlap the edges of the dish. Generously butter the foil and pack the fish mixture into the dish, pressing it down firmly and banging the dish once or twice to make sure the ingredients are tightly packed. Cover tightly with buttered foil and place the dish in a *bain marie* of very hot water. Bake in a moderate oven (350°F. 180°C. Reg. 4) for 45 minutes. Cover the top of the terrine with a board of the same size and weight it down with a heavy object. Leave to cool and then refrigerate for at least 8 hours.

Turn out the terrine, remove the foil and serve well chilled and cut into thick slices.

Broad Bean Salad

Serves 4

1 *lb (450 g) shelled broad beans*
4 *tablespoons olive oil*
1 *tablespoon white wine vinegar*
½ *tablespoon finely chopped parsley*
pinch *fresh or dried savory*

1 *tablespoon finely chopped chives or spring onion tops*
½ *teaspoon made English mustard*
salt and freshly ground black pepper

Cook the beans in boiling, salted water until just tender. (Peel them if necessary.)

Combine all other ingredients in a screw-topped jar and shake well to mix. Pour the sauce over the hot beans and leave to cool. Serve chilled.

A Salad of Broad Beans, Courgettes and Bacon Flavoured with Turmeric

A very successful side salad which can also be served as a main course with an accompanying rice salad if the quantity of bacon is doubled. The turmeric gives the vegetables a wonderful golden-green colouring as well as a subtle and delicious taste. Serves 6

1 *lb (450 g) young shelled broad beans*
4 *small firm courgettes*
5 *tablespoons olive or sunflower oil*
1 *teaspoon French Dijon mustard*
1 *tablespoon white wine vinegar*
1 *teaspoon ground turmeric*

salt and freshly ground black pepper
1 *tablespoon finely chopped parsley*
1 *tablespoon finely chopped chives*
4 *rashers streaky bacon*

Thinly slice the courgettes.

Cook the broad beans in boiling salted water for 6 minutes, add the courgettes and cook for a further 4 minutes until the beans and courgettes are *just* tender. Drain well.

Combine the oil, mustard and vinegar, mix in the turmeric, season with salt and pepper and pour the dressing over the vegetables while they are still warm. Mix well, leave to cool and mix in the parsley and chives.

Cook the bacon without extra fat, over a medium high heat, until it is crisp. Drain well on kitchen paper, cut off the rinds with kitchen scissors, leave the rashers to cool and then crumble into fairly small pieces.

Scatter the bacon over the salad before serving. The salad makes an excellent partner to the Terrine of White Fish Fillets and Broad Beans on page 57.

Chicken with a Green Stuffing

In this recipe a chicken is stuffed with a mixture of chopped broad beans, onion and bacon with the traditional herb that accompanies broad beans, savory. The skin of the breast of the chicken is lifted and seasoned, softened butter spread over the breast and under the skin to moisten the bird while it is cooking. I believe that the broad beans act as a tenderizer to the chicken

meat; they certainly add a delicious flavour and the stuffing is not only a meat-stretcher but also an extra vegetable as well. I chop the beans, bacon and onion in my electric food processor but you can put them through the coarse blades of a mincing machine instead.
Serves 6

1 *large roasting chicken*
chicken liver and heart
8 *oz (225 g) shelled broad beans*
2 *oz (50 g) softened butter*
3 *oz (75 g) streaky bacon with
    the rinds removed*
1 *small onion*

1 *teaspoon finely chopped savory*
*salt and freshly ground black
    pepper*
pinch ground mace
2 *tablespoons olive oil*
2 *tablespoons soy sauce*

Working carefully, slide a small sharp pointed knife under the skin of the bird at the back of the breast. Making small jabbing slashes separate the skin from the breast, working towards the legs and the front neck end of the bird. Season the softened butter with salt and pepper and push the butter under the skin. Press the skin with your fingers to get the butter evenly distributed over the breast of the bird.

Peel and finely chop the onion. Finely chop the chicken liver and heart, the bacon and broad beans. Combine the onion, bacon, liver, heart, broad beans and savory, season with a little salt, pepper and mace and mix well. Fill the cavity of the bird with this mixture and skewer the opening of the bird to keep the stuffing in place.

Brush the bird with the oil and soy sauce and roast in a hot oven (450°F. 230°C. Reg. 8) for 15 minutes. Reduce the heat to moderate (350°F. 180°C. Reg. 4) and continue to roast, basting every now and then, for about 1 hour or until the chicken is tender.

Serve with new potatoes and peas.

White Fish and Broad Bean Pie

An unusual but delicious combination. Use any firm white fish.
Serves 4

1 *lb (450 g) cod, hake, haddock
    or firm white-fleshed fish*

1 *lb (450 g) shelled broad beans*
1 *oz (25 g) butter*

1 *tablespoon flour*
½ *pint (500 ml) milk*
4 *oz (100 g) grated Cheddar*
  cheese
salt and freshly ground black
  pepper

pinch of ground nutmeg
2 *oz (50 g) fresh white*
  breadcrumbs
2 *tablespoons finely chopped*
  parsley

Steam the fish over boiling water for about 20 minutes or until the flesh is just coming away from the bones. Leave the fish to cool a little, then remove the skin and bones and flake the flesh.

Cook the beans in boiling salted water for about 20 minutes until just tender. Melt the butter in a saucepan, add the flour and mix well. Gradually blend in the milk, stirring continually over a medium high heat until the sauce comes to the boil and is thick and smooth. Add half the cheese, season with salt, pepper and a pinch of nutmeg and simmer, stirring, until the cheese has melted.

Arrange the beans in the bottom of a lightly buttered baking dish, spread the flaked fish over them and sprinkle the bread-crumbs and remaining cheese over the top. Bake in a moderately hot oven (375°F. 190°C. Reg. 5) for about 15 minutes or until the dish is hot through and the top is golden brown and crisp. Sprinkle with finely chopped parsley before serving.

Broad Beans with Bacon

Serves 4

1 *lb (450 g) shelled broad beans*
8 *oz (225 g) lean bacon rashers*
1 *onion*
½ *oz (15 g) lard*
beef stock

salt and freshly ground black
  pepper
2 *tablespoons finely chopped*
  parsley

Remove the rinds from the bacon and chop the rashers into small pieces. Peel and finely chop the onion. Heat the lard, add the bacon and onion and cook over a low heat for 3 minutes. Drain off the fat, add the beans and pour over just enough stock to cover. Season with salt and pepper and bring to the boil,

Cover and simmer for 20 minutes or until the beans are soft. Add the parsley, mix well and serve at once.

Note : If you are a garlic fancier add a clove or two of finely chopped garlic to the bacon and onion when adding the broad beans.

Thin Steaks of Lamb Cooked with a Medley of Vegetables

To be honest, I felt this dish was almost *too special* to be shared; the meat emerges tender and succulent, the combination of many flavours results in an overall taste that I consider spectacular and the crisp topping is exquisite with a delicate nutty texture. The dish is reasonably quick to prepare and needs only the accompaniment of some new or mashed potatoes or rice and a good bottle of red wine to make a sensational main course. Serves 4

8 *very thin slices cut from the top of a boned leg of lamb*
4 *medium carrots*
8 *spring onions*
flour
4 *tablespoons olive oil*
1 *teaspoon ground fenugreek*
1 *tablespoon mint jelly*
¼ *pint (150 ml) dry white wine*

1 *medium tin (14 oz, 392 g) tomatoes*
salt and freshly ground black pepper
8 *oz (225 g) large broad beans, shelled weight*
2 *oz (50 g) fresh brown breadcrumbs*
1 *oz (25 g) butter*

Peel the carrots, cut them into thin, lengthwise slices and then into matchstick strips. Trim the spring onions leaving on the green stalk. Lightly coat the meat slices with flour.

Heat 3 tablespoons of oil in a heavy frying pan. Add the carrots and spring onions and cook over a low heat, stirring to prevent sticking, for 3 minutes. Remove the carrots and spring onions with a slotted spoon. Raise the heat, add the slices of meat and cook over a high heat to brown the slices on both sides.

Arrange the slices of meat in a casserole and spread over the carrots and spring onions.

Add a tablespoon of flour to the juices in the pan and stir over a moderately high heat to brown the flour. Add the fenugreek, mint jelly, tinned tomatoes and wine and mix well. Bring to the boil and season the sauce with salt and pepper. Cover the dish tightly and cook in a moderately hot oven (375°F. 190°C. Reg. 5) for 45 minutes until the meat is tender.

Cook the beans in a little boiling, salted water until tender. Leave to cool and remove the tough outer skins of the beans. Spread the beans over the meat, top with the breadcrumbs, dot with small pieces of butter and dribble over the remaining tablespoon of oil. Return the dish to a hot oven (400°F. 200°C. Reg. 6) and continue to cook for a further 10–15 minutes until the top is crisp.

Serve the dish with new or mashed potatoes.

Broccoli

Broccoli was introduced into Britain in the eighteenth century but it has never really achieved the renown it deserves. In America, however, it is a different story. Broccoli arrived there some time later than it had in Britain and it was an immediate success, being widely used as both a hot vegetable and a salad ingredient. In Italy it is one of the most popular of vegetables, lightly cooked, *al dente*, and served with a sauce to accompany pasta dishes, and it is also eaten cold in delicious salads.

The flavour of broccoli is more delicate than cabbage and less pronounced than cauliflower. It is at the same time both subtle and pleasant. But what really appeals to me about broccoli is its texture. When cooked to perfection it is both tender and crisp. The green varieties, to which calabrese belongs, probably have the best flavour. The purple-sprouting heads, on the other hand, have the greatest endurance in cold weather, and the white-sprouting varieties are really like mini cauliflowers and can be used in their place for dishes like cauliflower cheese.

All types of broccoli are relatively easy to grow and make a valuable addition to the garden as they produce heads for a surprisingly long time. Calabrese matures in the autumn and purple-sprouting broccoli comes into its own in the late winter and spring. Spears should be picked as soon as they are about 5 inches long, keeping the plants well culled to encourage new growth.

The leaves, stems and shoots of the broccoli spears all make good eating although the leaves are usually removed if the spears are to be served in a salad. After washing and draining, the spears should be plunged into boiling salted water, cooked gently for about 8 minutes and then well drained. They can be dressed with melted butter (in Italy they are often eaten as a first course like asparagus which they closely resemble) or they can be given more special treatment with a topping of hollandaise or mornay sauce. Spears that are to be served cold should be dressed with a vinaigrette while still warm and then left to cool before being served. Thicker stalks should be halved before cooking and if they are slightly on the tough side the outside of the stalks should be scraped.

If you buy broccoli make sure the spears or heads look fresh and crisp and that they are a good colour. Check the bottom of the stalks and discard any that look dry and woody.

Calabrese or Purple-sprouting Broccoli with Savoury Meat Sauce

Part of the pleasure of eating calabrese and other members of the same family is their texture, so make sure you do not over-cook them thus ruining their flavour and producing that well-known cheap boarding-house smell of overcooked brassicas. In this recipe cooked calabrese is topped with a savoury meat sauce, making a substantial but inexpensive winter main-course dish.

Serves 6

6 oz (175 g) raw lamb or beef, minced

2 oz (50 g) streaky bacon with the rinds removed

1 lb (450 g) calabrese or purple-sprouting broccoli

2 onions

1 clove garlic

3 tablespoons vegetable oil

2 teaspoons finely chopped parsley

2 teaspoons finely chopped marjoram

4 bay leaves

1 tablespoon flour

1 tablespoon tomato purée

1 tablespoon mushroom ketchup

¼ pint (150 ml) stock

salt and freshly ground black pepper

Peel and finely chop the onions. Mince the bacon. Peel and crush the garlic.

Heat the oil in a heavy pan. Add the onion and cook over a low heat, stirring every now and then, until it is soft and transparent. Raise the heat, add the meat and bacon and stir over a high heat until the meat is browned. Add the herbs, bay leaves and garlic, mix in the flour, stir for a further minute and then mix in the tomato purée, mushroom ketchup and stock. Season with salt and pepper, bring to the boil, cover tightly and cook for 20 minutes over a low heat, stirring every now and then to prevent sticking, until the meat is tender. Remove the cover and continue to stir until the mixture is fairly dry and most of the liquid has been absorbed. Remove the bay leaves.

Cook the calabrese or broccoli in boiling salted water until it is just tender and drain it well. Arrange the vegetables in a serving dish and spoon over the sauce.

Calabrese and Ham Quiche

The quiche can be eaten hot, warm or cold and makes an excellent picnic dish.
Serves 6

1 *partially baked* 10 *inch (25 cm) quiche case (see page 4)*
8 *oz (225 g) ham*
8 *oz (225 g) calabrese*
1 *large onion*
1 *oz (25 g) butter*
3 *eggs*
½ *pint (300 ml) single cream*

3 *oz (75 g) Cheddar cheese, grated*
1 *oz (25 g) Parmesan cheese, grated*
salt and freshly ground black pepper
pinch ground nutmeg

Cook the calabrese in boiling salted water until just tender and drain well. Thinly slice the calabrese unless the heads are very thin. Peel and thinly slice the onion. Melt the butter in a frying pan, add the onion and cook over a low heat, stirring, until the onion is soft and transparent. Mix together the Cheddar and Parmesan cheeses. Cut the ham into thin strips. Beat the eggs until smooth and mix in the cream and half the cheese. Season the custard with salt, pepper and a pinch of nutmeg.

Arrange the onion in the bottom of the quiche shell and cover with the calabrese and ham. Pour over the custard, sprinkle over the remaining cheese and bake in a moderate oven (350°F. 180°C.

Reg. 4) for about 30 minutes or until the filling is set and the top is golden brown.

Pasta with Broccoli Spears and Tuna Fish

Serves 6

1 lb (450 g) purple-sprouting broccoli or calabrese

1 tin (7 oz, 200 g) tuna fish

1 lb (450 g) pasta shells or macaroni

salt and freshly ground black pepper

3 tablespoons olive or vegetable oil

1 lb (450 g) tomatoes

2 cloves garlic

4 anchovy fillets

1 tablespoon finely chopped parsley

Cover the tomatoes with boiling water for 2 minutes, drain well, slide off the skins and discard the core and seeds. Purée the tomato flesh in an electric blender or food processor. Drain and finely chop the anchovy fillets. Drain the tuna and flake the flesh.

Heat the oil in a saucepan, add the tomato purée, garlic and anchovies, season with pepper and cook over a moderate heat for 10 minutes. Mix in the tuna.

Cut the broccoli or calabrese into thin lengthwise slices, cook it in a little boiling salted water until it is just tender and drain well.

Cook the pasta in boiling salted water for about 12 minutes, or until just tender, and drain well.

Combine the pasta and broccoli or calabrese in a saucepan with the butter and toss lightly until the butter has melted. Turn into a serving dish and top with the tomato sauce. Sprinkle over the parsley before serving.

Broccoli or Calabrese with Chicken in a Rich Cheese Sauce

Chicken and broccoli or calabrese go exceptionally well together. In this dish the greens are lightly cooked, slices of cooked chicken are placed on top of them, a rich cheese sauce is poured

over and the dish is then baked in the oven to allow the top to become a gorgeous bubbling golden brown.
Serves 6

12 oz (350 g) cooked chicken
1 lb (450 g) purple-sprouting
   broccoli or calabrese
2 oz (50 g) butter
2 tablespoons flour
½ pint (300 ml) milk
4 tablespoons stock
4 tablespoons single cream
3 oz (75 g) grated Gruyère
   cheese

½ oz (15 g) finely grated
   Parmesan cheese
1 egg yolk
salt and freshly ground black
   pepper
pinch nutmeg
3 tablespoons fresh white
   breadcrumbs

Cook the broccoli or calabrese in boiling salted water until it is just tender and drain well. Cut the cooked chicken into thin strips. Arrange the greens in a lightly buttered baking dish and arrange the chicken on top of the vegetables.

Melt 1½ oz (35 g) butter in a saucepan. Add the 2 tablespoons of flour and mix well. Gradually blend in the milk, stirring continually over a medium high heat until the sauce comes to the boil and is thick and smooth. Add the stock and cream, mix in three-quarters of the cheese and stir over a low heat until the cheese has melted. Season the sauce with salt, pepper and nutmeg. Beat the egg yolk, add it to the sauce and stir over a low heat until the sauce is rich and satiny.

Pour the sauce over the chicken and vegetables and top with the breadcrumbs and the remaining cheese. Dribble over ½ oz (15 g) melted butter and bake for 20 minutes in a moderate oven (350°F. 180°C. Reg. 4). Finish the dish under a hot grill for a couple of minutes so that the topping becomes a rich golden colour.

Chicken with Calabrese and Almonds

Serves 4

12 oz (350 g) cooked chicken
1 lb (450 g) calabrese
1 teaspoon grated onion

2 oz (50 g) butter
2 tablespoons flour
½ pint (300 ml) chicken stock

4 oz (100 g) grated Cheddar
  cheese
salt and freshly ground black
  pepper
pinch each ground nutmeg and
  mace

¼ pint (150 ml) single cream
3 tablespoons dry sherry
4 tablespoons double cream
1 oz (25 g) flaked almonds

Cook the calabrese in boiling salted water until just tender and drain well. Very thinly slice the chicken meat.

Melt the butter in a saucepan. Add the onion and flour and mix well. Gradually add the chicken stock, stirring continually over a medium high heat until the sauce comes to the boil and is thick and smooth. Add the cheese, season with salt, pepper, nutmeg and mace and continue to stir until the cheese has melted. Add the single cream and sherry and mix well.

Arrange the calabrese in a shallow dish, lightly buttered. Place the chicken on top of the calabrese. Whip the double cream until thick and fold it into the sauce. Spread the sauce over the chicken and calabrese and sprinkle over the almonds. Bake in a moderate oven (350°F. 180°C. Reg. 4) for about 20 minutes until the dish is hot through and the almonds are a light golden brown.

Carrots

If I use the name 'love philtre' or 'honey underground' you might be hard put to believe I was talking about that common or garden vegetable the carrot, and yet 'love philtre' was the early nickname given to carrots because they were thought to raise sexual desire, and 'honey underground' was the Celtic name given to carrots because of their sweet, almost sugary flavour. Whether or not the popular belief that the eating of carrots really does help one see in the dark is true I have not been able to discover, but I imagine that one would have to eat an enormous amount of carrots to make any discernible difference in one's night sight. In any case this seems to be a slightly dangerous practice because too high an intake of carotid (the cause of the colouring of not only carrots but the yolks of eggs and the flesh of mangoes) is said to cause jaundice.

The carrot is actually native to Britain and to many parts of Europe but in its wild state the root is white and fairly tasteless, and it wasn't until around the sixteenth century that it was introduced into Britain as a garden vegetable. One of the plant's special features is its attractive green foliage, which was so fancied by the ladies of Charles I's court that they wore it as a decoration, and although I haven't yet turned up at a wedding with a spray of carrot leaves in my buttonhole I have added the leaves, with great success, to stocks.

Two of the great advantages of this root vegetable are its availability all the year round and its great storing capacity which, in medieval times, made it a must on the menu of any winter banquet. These features contributed to the tradition of boiled beef and carrots in both Britain and, later, the new Americas. Indeed carrots still thrive as a popular everyday vegetable in casseroles and stews.

Undoubtedly the best carrots of all are the small early ones with a sweet and tender flavour and a satisfactory crunch to their flesh. These young carrots also have the advantage of not needing to be peeled and since much of their mineral goodness lies close to the skin this is obviously important from the nutritional point of view. When you are using older carrots that do have to be peeled, don't throw away the skins but put them to good use by adding them to stocks in order to provide colour, flavour and goodness. (Carrot peelings as well as the other peelings and trimmings from prepared vegetables can be stored in a refrigerator, in a polythene bag, for quite a few days until they are needed.)

Over the centuries carrots have been continually improved until they now appear in all shapes and sizes, from the traditional long variety to blunt-ended roots, specially developed so that they do not pierce supermarket polythene bags.

One of the joys of carrots is their versatility. Combined with meat or poultry in a stew they take on the flavour of the main ingredient and they do not lose any of their charm or texture by being cooked for a long time. Small carrots, on the other hand, especially if they are newly pulled, need only a short cooking time and should be served while still crisp and crunchy. Raw grated carrots are delicious in salads, and thinly sliced carrots, or matchstick-thin strips of carrot, can be invaluable in a great many dishes. For most of the recipes in this book which incorporate carrots, the roots are sliced lengthwise or on the diagonal and the slices should be really wafer thin.

And one last word on this particular vegetable: whereas so many other vegetables are said, and indeed do, tend to cause wind, the carrot for some reason is believed to have the opposite effect and for years was used medicinally as a 'breaker of wind'.

A Summer Soup of Carrots and Lovage

A light and delicate soup with a good flavour, the vegetables giving an interesting texture.
Serves 6

3 *carrots*
12 *young and tender stalks of*
    lovage
1 *small onion*
½ *tablespoon olive or vegetable oil*
1 *medium tin (14 oz, 392 g)*
    tomatoes

2½ *pints (1500 ml) well-*
    flavoured chicken stock
¼ *pint (150 ml) red wine*
few marjoram leaves
2 *bay leaves*
salt and pepper

Peel and finely chop the onion. Heat the oil in a large saucepan, add the onion and cook over a low heat until the onion is soft and transparent. Add the tomatoes and mix well. Add the stock, wine, marjoram and bay leaves, bring to the boil and simmer for 20 minutes. Remove the bay leaves. Sieve the soup to remove the tomato seeds or put it through a fine food mill.

Remove the tops and leaves of the lovage (reserve a few leaves for garnishing the soup). Cut the stalks into really thin matchstick strips. Peel the carrots, slice them, lengthwise, as thinly as possible and then cut into matchstick strips.

Put the soup into a clean pan, bring to the boil, add the lovage and carrots and cook over a moderately high heat for about 10 minutes or until the vegetables are just tender but still retain a slight crispness. Season if necessary and garnish with finely chopped lovage leaves.

A Pâté of Carrots and Gammon with a Cucumber and Yoghurt Sauce

Another of these sensitive and delicate vegetable pâtés. This time the base is carrots, which give a delicious golden-orange colour to the pâté which is spiked with small pieces of gammon to give an attractive pink contrast to the carrots. Serve the pâté with hot toast and with a well-flavoured sauce such as a home-made tomato sauce, a garlic mayonnaise or with the yoghurt and cucumber in the recipe. If you do grow dill yourself do freeze some for the winter.

Serves 6

8 *oz (225 g) gammon*
8 *oz (225 g) carrots*
1½ *oz (40 g) white bread with*
    the crusts removed

2 *eggs*
2 *tablespoons very finely chopped*
    parsley
1½ *oz (40 g) melted butter*

salt and freshly ground black
    pepper
small pinch each ground mace and
    cayenne pepper
2 bay leaves
1 carton yoghurt (5 fl. oz, 150 ml)

½ small cucumber
1 teaspoon French Dijon
    mustard
1 teaspoon fresh or frozen finely
    chopped dill

Clean the carrots and cook them in salted water until they are tender. Purée the carrots through a fine food mill, in an electric blender or in a food processor. Remove the rind from the gammon and cut the flesh and fat into *very* small dice. Soak the bread in a little warm water until it is soft and squeeze out the excess water. Beat the eggs until smooth. Add the bread, eggs, parsley and melted butter to the carrots and mix really well. Add the gammon and season with salt, pepper, mace and cayenne, remembering that more seasoning is needed for a dish that is to be served cold than one that is to be served hot.

Line a terrine with several strips of well-buttered foil, leaving the ends of the foil hanging out over the edge of the terrine. Pack the pâté firmly into the terrine, fold over the strips of foil, top with the bay leaves and cover the terrine with another two thicknesses of foil. Stand the terrine in a *bain marie* of hot water and bake the pâté in a moderate oven (350°F. 180°C. Reg. 4) for about 1½ hours until it has set firm. Leave it to cool, refrigerate until set even firmer and chilled, and then remove the pâté from the terrine by pulling it up with the ends of the foil. Turn the pâté upside down on a serving dish and gently remove the foil.

Peel and coarsely grate the cucumber and put it into a colander or sieve. Sprinkle over some salt and leave the cucumber to 'sweat' for 20 minutes. Press firmly to get rid of excess water and pat dry with kitchen paper.

Add the mustard to the yoghurt, mix in the cucumber and dill and season with salt and ground pepper.

Serve the sauce with the pâté.

A Brawn of Pig's Trotters, Carrots and Parsley

Brawns look attractive and are not difficult to make, although they do take time. In this recipe I have used pig's trotters instead of the more conventional pig's head and combined the meat with a little ham, sliced carrots and plenty of finely chopped parsley. A little ground coriander gives an unusual flavour to the jelly. Shops that sell ham off the bone will usually sell a ham bone at a very reasonable price.

Serves 4 as a main course or 6 as a first course

2 *pig's trotters*	*salt and freshly ground black*
6 *oz (175 g) ham*	*pepper*
1 *ham bone*	½ *teaspoon ground coriander*
1 *onion*	*bouquet garni including 3 bay*
1 *carrot*	*leaves, parsley, sage, thyme and*
1 *stick celery*	*marjoram*
½ *pint (300 ml) dry white wine*	1 *tablespoon white wine vinegar*
1 *stock cube*	12 *oz (350 g) carrots*
water	4 *tablespoons finely chopped parsley*

Wash and roughly chop the onion, the single carrot and celery stalk, wash the pig's trotters and place the vegetables and trotters in a saucepan with the ham bone, white wine, bouquet garni, vinegar, stock cube and enough water to cover the ingredients. Season with salt and pepper, add the coriander, bring slowly to the boil, cover tightly and simmer very slowly (the water should only just be moving) for about 1½ hours or until the meat is falling off the trotters. Drain off the stock, leave it to cool and refrigerate overnight.

Remove the skin from the trotters and cut the meat, including the jellied tendons, off the trotters. Cut the meat in very, very small dice.

Skim off the fat from the surface of the stock and check how well the stock has set; if it has not set really firm you will have to add a little gelatine powder at a later stage. Combine the stock and the meat from the trotters, bring to the boil and boil over a high heat until the liquid is reduced to at least half.

Peel the carrots and cook them in salted water until they are just tender. Drain and cut them into thin slices. Very finely chop the ham.

Strain off the liquid from the meat, remove any scum from the surface and check seasoning. If the stock did not set firmly, stir in ½ teaspoon of gelatine dissolved in 1 tablespoon of warm water.

Place a layer of carrots in the bottom of a pudding basin.

Cover with a generous sprinkling of the parsley and then with a layer of the pig's trotters mixed with the ham. Continue with the layers until the ingredients have been used up and pour over just enough stock to cover the ingredients. Chill the brawn in the refrigerator until it is set firm and serve with new potatoes and a salad or with hot toast as a first course. A mayonnaise flavoured with mustard also goes well with this dish.

Tartlets Filled with Salmon, Carrots and Celery in a Wine-flavoured Sauce

I used salmon for this recipe but you could just as well use a good-quality white fish (poached in a *court bouillon*) or some lightly cooked and sliced scallops.
Serves 6–8

8 *tartlet cases made with the quiche pastry (see page 4)*
12 *oz (350 g) cooked salmon, white fish or scallops*
1 *lb (450 g) carrots*
4 *sticks celery*
2 *oz (50 g) butter*
2 *tablespoons flour*
½ *pint (300 ml) good chicken stock*

¼ *pint (150 ml) dry white wine*
pinch dried tarragon, or
  1 *teaspoon finely chopped fresh tarragon*
4 *tablespoons double cream*
salt and freshly ground black pepper

Peel and thinly slice the carrots and cook them until they are just tender. Trim the celery stalks and cut them into thin slices. Cook the celery in boiling salted water until it is just tender (the water from both these vegetables can be used for making stock). Flake the fish.

Melt the butter in a saucepan. Add the flour and mix well. Gradually add the stock, stirring continually over a medium high heat until the sauce comes to the boil and is thick and smooth. Add the wine and tarragon, season with salt and pepper and simmer for 5 minutes. Add the cream, salmon, carrots and celery and mix well. Divide the filling between the tartlet cases and heat through in a moderate oven (350°F. 180°C. Reg. 4) for about 15 minutes.

✓ Belly of Pork Slowly Cooked with Carrots and Parsley

In this recipe the pork and vegetables are slowly cooked in butter. The fat from the pork is absorbed by the carrots and the meat becomes deliciously tender.
Serves 4

1¼ lb (550 g) belly of pork
    with the bones removed
1 lb (450 g) carrots
1 onion
2 oz (50 g) butter

3 tablespoons finely chopped
    parsley
salt, pepper and ground nutmeg
4 tablespoons well-flavoured stock

Cut the pork into very thin strips. Peel and thinly slice the carrots. Peel and chop the onion.

Melt 1 oz (25 g) butter in a sauté pan. Arrange layers of onion, carrot and pork in the pan, sprinkling the layers with parsley and seasoning them with salt, pepper and nutmeg. Pour in the stock. Dot the remaining butter over the top and cover with a double circle of foil, pressing down so that the ingredients are well compacted. Cover with a lid and cook over a very, very low heat for 1½ hours. Invert the pan on to a serving plate so that the ingredients come out like a round cake, and sprinkle with a little more parsley just before serving.

Cauliflower

This is another ancient plant grown thousands of years ago in the East. It was then gradually introduced into the Mediterranean area, and finally brought to England at the end of the sixteenth century. Like cabbage, cauliflower is very often overcooked (and, indeed, it is a difficult vegetable to get exactly right as the stalk and the 'curds', or florettes, require a different cooking time). On the whole I favour the practice of dividing up the florettes before cooking them and then steaming them rather than immersing them in water but if you do like to cook your cauliflowers whole, they should always be cooked with the stem end down and in just enough boiling salted water to cover the stalk so that the stalk cooks in the water and the head steams in the vapour that rises.

Once again I despair at the waste which so often accompanies the preparation and cooking of cauliflower. Those green leaves have a valuable use and goodness which should not be overlooked and, if you strip off the leaf and then cut the white vein into fairly thick lengths, it can be cooked and served exactly like asparagus, making an excellent vegetable in its own right. Raw or blanched florettes of cauliflower are delicious in salads or to serve as part of a dish of *crudités* with a garlic mayonnaise, and there are a hundred variations on the classic theme of cauliflower cheese.

On good land in fairly warm conditions (they do not like frost) cauliflowers can be grown almost all the year round and they need not be large to be delicious. If you buy your cauliflowers from a greengrocer examine them carefully to make sure there is no discolouration or bruising because once a head has been damaged no amount of careful cooking will disguise the impaired colour and flavour.

If you are particularly fond of this vegetable then you may like to know that you are in good company. The French Comtesse du Barry (murdered in the French Revolution) also found them very much to her taste and such was her influence that many dishes incorporating cauliflower were named after her with *crème du Barry*, a rich cream of cauliflower soup, still being a popular winter dish on many restaurant menus.

Spaghetti and Cauliflower with a Carbonara Sauce

Carbonara is a classic Italian sauce to serve with spaghetti. If the pasta is combined with lightly cooked cauliflower you introduce an interesting texture and flavour, making this a delicious and delicate dish. You can serve it as a fairly substantial first course or as a light lunch or supper dish accompanied with a salad or some crisply cooked French beans.
Serves 6

6 oz (175 g) ham
1 lb (450 g) spaghetti
1 medium cauliflower
salt

1½ oz (40 g) butter
1 small tin asparagus tips
6 fl. oz (175 ml) double cream
freshly ground black pepper

Trim the cauliflower and steam it over boiling water until it is just tender. Reserve the water and use it to cook the pasta in, adding a little salt. Bring the liquid to the boil, add the pasta and cook over a high heat for about 15–20 minutes until the pasta is tender. Drain the pasta and divide the cauliflower into florettes.

Cut the ham into thin strips. Drain the asparagus. Heat the butter in a large saucepan. Add the ham and asparagus, season with plenty of pepper and heat through. Add the cream, cauliflower and pasta and mix lightly, tossing the pan over a medium heat until the ingredients are hot through. Turn on to a serving dish and serve at once.

Mussels with Cauliflower in a Light Curry Sauce

Both cauliflower and shellfish such as mussels go well with a light curry sauce. This is an excellent and unusual combination and makes a marvellously subtle and pleasant dish for a starter or main course.
Serves 6–8

2 quarts (2400 ml) mussels
1 small cauliflower
2 shallots
¼ pint (150 ml) dry white wine
1 oz (25 g) butter
1 tablespoon flour

1 teaspoon ground cumin
½ teaspoon ground coriander
½ teaspoon ground turmeric
black pepper
4 tablespoons double cream
a little cayenne pepper

Scrub the mussels removing their beards and any dirt and barnacles. Peel and finely chop the shallots. Steam the cauliflower until it is just tender (be careful not to overcook it), leave to cool and then divide into florettes.

Put the wine and shallots into a large saucepan and bring gently to the boil. Add the mussels, cover tightly and cook over a high heat, shaking the pan, for about 5 minutes until the mussels have opened. Remove the mussels and strain the cooking liquid through a fine sieve. Take the mussels out of their shells discarding any that have not opened.

Melt the butter in a saucepan. Add the flour, cumin, coriander, turmeric and pepper and mix well. Gradually add the cooking liquid, stirring continually over a medium high heat until the sauce comes to the boil and is thick and smooth. Simmer, stirring from time to time, over a low heat, for five minutes.

Whip the cream until thick. Add the mussels and cauliflower to the sauce and mix lightly, trying not to break up the cauliflower too much. Fold in the whipped cream and divide the mixture between 6 or 8 small dishes. Sprinkle over a little cayenne and brown quickly under a hot grill.

Chicken and Cauliflower Soufflés with a Wine and Herb Sauce

Unlike most soufflés these do not subside soon after you remove them from the oven. They are really more like a mousse than a soufflé but they are marvellously feather-light and have the most subtle flavour. Instead of the wine sauce you could serve them with a home-made tomato sauce.

The easiest way to make this dish is in an electric food processor but it can also be made very satisfactorily with the use of a food mill.

Serves 6

12 oz (350 g) raw chicken
1 small cauliflower (8 oz, 225 g)
1 small onion
3 oz (80 g) butter
3 tablespoons brandy
2 oz (50 g) ground almonds
3 eggs, separated
salt and freshly ground black pepper
pinch ground nutmeg
3 tablespoons flour
½ pint (300 ml) good chicken stock
¼ pint (150 ml) dry white wine
1½ tablespoons finely chopped parsley
½ tablespoon finely chopped chervil
½ pint (300 ml) double cream

Remove the outside green leaves of the cauliflower. Divide the cauliflower into florettes and steam over boiling water until the florettes are just tender. Purée the cauliflower through a fine food mill. (This can be done in an electric food processor.)

Chop the chicken, mince it through the fine blades of a mincing machine and then force it through a fine food mill to produce a purée. (This can also be done in an electric food processor.)

Peel and finely chop the onion. Melt 1½ oz (40 g) butter in a saucepan, add the onion and cook over a low heat, stirring to prevent sticking, until the onion is soft and transparent. Force the onion and butter through a fine food mill to produce a purée. (This can also be done in an electric food processor.)

Combine the chicken, cauliflower and onion purée, add the brandy and mix well. Season with plenty of salt, pepper and nutmeg and beat in the ground almonds and the egg yolks, one by one, so that the mixture is light and smooth.

Oil 12 ramekin dishes or 8 larger individual pudding moulds.

Beat the egg whites until stiff, add half the purée and mix lightly. Fold in the rest of the purée and turn the mixture into the ramekin dishes or moulds, filling them about two-thirds full.

Place the soufflés in a roasting pan, fill the pan half full with hot water and bake them in a moderately hot oven (375°F. 190°C. Reg. 5) for about 25 minutes until they are risen and firm to touch.

Melt the remaining 1½ oz (40 g) butter in a small heavy pan, add the flour and mix well. Gradually add the chicken stock, stirring all the time over a medium high heat until the sauce comes to the boil and is thick and smooth. Season with salt, pepper and a touch of nutmeg and simmer for 4 minutes. Add the wine, parsley and chervil and continue to simmer for a further 3 minutes. Gradually add the cream, beating the sauce over a low heat, until hot through.

Turn the cooked soufflés out on to a heated serving plate, coat the soufflés with the sauce and serve the remaining sauce separately.

I present the soufflés on a bed of cooked, chopped and buttered spinach, with just a little lemon juice added, and serve them with rice.

Cauliflower with a Sauce of Chicken and Onion

A lovely autumn dish that looks as attractive as it tastes. Care must be taken not to overcook the cauliflower. I use the hot curry paste made by that marvellous firm Elsenham.
Serves 4

8 oz (225 g) uncooked chicken
   breast
1 medium cauliflower
1 large onion
2 oz (50 g) butter

1 teaspoon hot curry paste
1 tablespoon flour
½ pint (300 ml) milk
salt

Peel and chop the onion. Cut the chicken breast into ¼ inch (¾ cm) thick strips.

Melt the butter in a saucepan. Add the onion and cook over a low heat until the onion is soft and transparent. Add the chicken and stir over a medium heat until the flesh just loses its opaque quality. Add the curry paste and flour and mix well. Gradually blend in the milk, stirring continually over a medium high heat until the sauce comes to the boil and is thick and smooth. Season with salt, lower the heat and simmer the sauce for 10 minutes.

Steam the cauliflower until it is just tender. Place the cauliflower in a serving dish and cut it neatly into four. Pour over the sauce and serve at once.

Minced Beef with Cauliflower

Another dish of layered vegetables with a rich meat sauce and a topping of cheese; aromatic and marvellously warming for a winter's evening.
Serves 6

1 *lb (450 g) minced lean raw beef*
1 *large cauliflower*
1 *large onion*
2 *rashers streaky bacon*
8 *oz (225 g) carrots*
1 *stalk celery*
2 *tablespoons olive oil or vegetable oil*
1 *medium tin (14 oz, 392 g) tomatoes*

2 *teaspoons tomato purée*
6 *fl. oz (175 ml) dry white wine*
salt, freshly ground black pepper
1 *teaspoon ground cumin*
1½ *oz (40 g) butter*
2 *tablespoons flour*
¾ *pint (450 ml) milk*
pinch ground nutmeg
2 *oz (50 g) grated Parmesan cheese*
2 *eggs*

Peel and very finely chop the onion. Remove the bacon rinds and mince the bacon. Peel and grate the carrot. Very finely chop the celery.

Heat the oil in a saucepan. Add the onion, bacon and meat and cook over a moderately high heat, stirring, until the meat is lightly browned. Add the grated carrot, celery, tomatoes, tomato purée and white wine, season with salt and pepper and mix in the cumin. Bring to the boil and simmer gently for 45 minutes, tightly covered. Mix well to break up the tomatoes.

Meanwhile steam the cauliflower until it is *just* tender. Break up the cauliflower into florettes. Layer the cauliflower and meat sauce in a lightly buttered casserole dish.

Melt the butter in a saucepan, add the flour and mix well. Gradually blend in the milk, stirring continually over a medium high heat until the sauce comes to the boil and is thick and smooth. Add half the grated cheese and season the sauce with salt, pepper and a pinch of nutmeg. Beat the eggs, add them to the sauce, beating well to blend smoothly. Pour the sauce over the casserole, sprinkle the remaining cheese over the dish and bake in a moderately hot oven (375°F. 190°C. Reg. 5) for 30 minutes until the dish is really hot through and the custard topping is golden brown.

Cauliflower and Turnip with a Well-flavoured Meat Sauce

One can get very bored with cauliflower cheese but few cookery books ever suggest how one can use this vegetable to make an alternative form of main course. This recipe does just that, combining the flavour and texture of lightly steamed cauliflower with the subtleness of young white turnips and topping the combination with a really well-spiced and rich meat sauce. Serves 4

8 oz (225 g) raw minced beef
1 small cauliflower
3 small white turnips
1 onion
2 cloves garlic
3 tablespoons olive or vegetable oil

4 tablespoons tomato juice
1 tablespoon mushroom ketchup
6 crushed coriander seeds
salt and freshly ground black pepper

Divide the cauliflower into florettes. Peel the turnips and cut them into thick matchstick strips about ¼ inch (¾ cm) wide.

Peel and finely chop the onion. Crush the garlic cloves. Heat the oil in a small saucepan. Add the onion and garlic and cook over a medium high heat until the onion is slightly browned. Raise the heat, add the meat, and cook over a high heat, stirring, until the meat is well browned. Add the tomato juice, mushroom ketchup and coriander seeds and season with salt and pepper. Cover and cook over a low heat, stirring every now and then, for about 30 minutes or until the meat is tender.

Steam the cauliflower until just tender. Cook the turnip in

boiling, salted water for about 5 minutes until just tender and drain well.

Combine the cauliflower and turnip in a heated serving dish and spoon over the sauce, which should be slightly on the dry side.

Cauliflower Cheese with Macaroni, Ham and Ginger

Cauliflower cheese tends to bring memories of nursery food to mind; this version, however, is a most sophisticated version of the old favourite. Fresh ginger root (you can use ground ginger if the root is not available) and a topping of ginger nuts mixed with cheese and mustard give the dish an unusual and deliciously crisp golden-brown topping, and make it a main course I would happily serve for a dinner party.
Serves 6

1 *medium cauliflower*
4 *oz (100 g) macaroni*
4 *oz (100 g) ham*
4 *tomatoes*
1 *inch (2½ cm) fresh ginger root (or use 1 teaspoon ground ginger)*
1 *onion*
1 *clove garlic*
2 *oz (50 g) butter*
2 *tablespoons flour*
wine glass of dry white wine

¼ *pint (150 ml) good chicken stock*
¼ *pint (150 ml) milk*
3 *oz (75 g) Cheddar cheese, grated*
3 *tablespoons double cream*
5 *ginger nut biscuits*
1½ *teaspoons French Dijon mustard*
salt and freshly ground black pepper

Divide the cauliflower into florettes and chop the tough stalk into dice. Cook the cauliflower in boiling salted water until it is *just* tender, drain it well and place it in a fireproof serving dish. Cook the macaroni until just tender, drain it well and combine it with the cauliflower. Add the ham, cut into thin strips. Cover the tomatoes with boiling water for 2 minutes, drain them, slide off their skins and cut them into slices. Arrange the tomato slices on top of the cauliflower.

Cabbages

PLATE 3

Courgettes

PLATE 4

Peel and very finely chop the onion. Peel the ginger and cut it into small pieces and squeeze it through a garlic press. Peel the garlic and squeeze it through a garlic press.

Heat the butter in a pan, add the onion, ginger and garlic and cook over a very low heat, stirring to prevent sticking, for about 10 minutes or until the onion is really soft. Add the flour and mix well. Gradually blend in the wine, stock and milk, stirring continually over a medium heat until the sauce comes to the boil and is thick and smooth. Add half the cheese and continue to cook over a medium heat for 3 minutes, stirring all the time. Season with salt and pepper. Lower the heat and mix in the cream.

Pour the sauce over the tomatoes.

Crush the biscuits with a rolling pin into fairly fine crumbs, mix them with the mustard and remaining cheese. Sprinkle the mixture over the top of the dish and bake in a moderate oven (350°F. 180°C. Reg. 4) for 20 minutes. Finish under a hot grill for a few minutes until the topping is bubbling, crisp and golden brown.

Celery and Celeriac

The flavouring properties of celery have been recognized from the time when man first began to think about the taste of food rather than just the necessity of eating. The Egyptians gathered it wild and used it as a flavouring ingredient for soups and stews. The Romans, besides using it in their cookery and wearing the leaves in a wreath around their heads after a particularly violent orgy to help dispel a hangover, fed their poultry on celery to give the flesh of chickens, geese and ducks a good flavour. In England too the wild celery, smallage, was used as a flavouring herb until the seventeenth century when Italian gardeners began growing celery as a garden vegetable and it was imported into England.

The taste of celery is a pronounced one. If it is to be included in a dish as a flavouring ingredient it should be used with discretion, but it also makes a fine vegetable in its own right and can be chosen to great advantage as one of the main ingredients for a dish of meat, poultry or fish and vegetables. The trimmings from the stalks are an excellent additive to stocks and the leaves, finely chopped, make an interesting alternative to finely chopped parsley as a garnish for both hot and cold dishes.

Unfortunately good celery is not all that easy to grow in the amateur garden, as it needs a rich soil and has to be banked up in order to blanch the stems. Celery also requires a climate with a definite touch of frost in it to produce those really deliciously crisp and white stems. There are self-blanching varieties available and I find these perfectly satisfactory for flavouring and cooking with, although their stems do not have the quality that makes them really suitable for cold dishes or for serving raw with cheese.

Much easier to grow is the ugly but invaluable celeriac (turnip-rooted celery) which is grown for its bulbous root rather than for the stalks. The stalks and leaves (especially the leaves), which have a strong celery flavour, can be used in casseroles and stews, in stocks or soups, but it is the root which is the really important part of this plant. In the root you have a pleasantly mild celery flavour and the most exquisite texture, which make it excellent material for both salads and cooked dishes. Celeriac discolours once it is peeled so that the raw flesh, peeled and cut into matchstick lengths, or coarsely grated, should be dropped into cold, salted water to which some lemon juice has been added as soon as it has been prepared. Lemon juice should also be added to the water in which celeriac is to be cooked.

Celeriac was introduced into Britain in the eighteenth century when its merits were sensibly recognized, and it became a vegetable especially popular on account of its storing properties. For some reason (perhaps because of its ugliness) its popularity waned and it is only now that the bulbous roots are beginning to find their way back into the shops once more. Buy them when you see them and store the roots in a cool dark place or in the bottom of your refrigerator where they will keep in good condition for at least two weeks.

Celery and Cider Soup

Serves 6

1 *head celery*
1 *large carrot*
1 *onion*
1 *oz (25 g) butter*
1½ *pints (900 ml) good stock*
  (or 2 chicken stock cubes)

¾ *pint (450 ml) dry cider*
salt and freshly ground black
  pepper
3 *tablespoons double cream*

Remove the leaves of the celery, reserving a few of the tenderest for garnish. Clean and chop the celery stalks. Peel and finely chop the carrot and onion. Melt the butter in a saucepan, add the vegetables and cook over a low heat, stirring to prevent sticking, until all the fat has been absorbed and the vegetables are transparent. Add the stock and cider, season with salt and pepper, bring to the boil and simmer until the vegetables are quite tender. Purée the vegetables through a fine sieve, in a liquidizer or through a food mill and return the purée to a clean pan.

Heat the soup through, check seasoning and add the cream just before serving. Garnish with finely chopped celery leaves.

Note: If the soup is too thick it can be thinned down with a little more stock.

Celery and White Fish Rémoulade

I make this dish, a really first-class starter for the summer, with huss when I can get it but it can equally well be made with any other firm-fleshed white fish. You can also, if you wish, make it with prawns or with thinly sliced scallops.
Serves 4

8 *oz (225 g) huss or other
    firm-fleshed white fish or
    shellfish*
1 *head celery*
court bouillon *or chicken stock*
¼ *pint (150 ml) home-made,
    stiff mayonnaise*
salt and freshly ground black
    pepper

*few drops Worcestershire and
    Tabasco sauce*
1 *teaspoon French Dijon
    mustard*
4 *tablespoons double cream*
1 *tablespoon finely chopped
    parsley*

Remove the leaves and any tough fibres from the celery stalks and cut the stalks into very thin sticks about 1½ inches (4 cm) long. Cook the sticks in boiling salted water for about 15 minutes until they are just tender but still crisp. Drain the celery and leave it to cool (use the cooking water for stock).

Cover the fish with cold *court bouillon* or chicken stock, bring slowly to the boil and simmer for about 10 minutes or until the fish is just tender. Remove any skin and bones from the fish, coarsely flake the fish and leave it to cool.

Flavour the mayonnaise with a little Tabasco and Worcestershire sauce and mix in the mustard. Whip the cream until thick and lightly fold it into the mayonnaise. Add the celery and fish to the mayonnaise mixture, add salt and pepper if necessary and form into a neat loaf shape on a serving dish. Sprinkle with parsley, cover very lightly with cling film and chill well before serving with hot French bread and butter, with thin slices of buttered brown bread or with hot toast.

You can also serve this dish as a light main course in the summer with a green or mixed salad.

Celery with Mayonnaise Wrapped in Smoked Salmon

Smoked salmon is a real luxury but serving it with a filling does make a little stretch further and the combination of the flavours of the celery and salmon is a memorable one.
Serves 4

4 *slices smoked salmon*
1 *small head of celery*
salt
$\frac{1}{4}$ *pint (150 ml) mayonnaise*
1 *tablespoon tomato purée*
  (preferably home-made,
  page 247)

few drops Worcestershire and
  Tabasco sauce
$\frac{1}{4}$ *pint (150 ml) double cream*

Trim off the leaves and root of celery and cut the stalks into very thin matchstick strips about $1\frac{1}{2}$ inches (4 cm) long. Blanch the sticks in boiling salted water for 5 minutes until just tender, drain well and leave to cool. Combine the mayonnaise with the tomato purée, add a few drops of Worcestershire and Tabasco sauce and mix well. Whip the cream until stiff and fold it into the mayonnaise mixture. Add the celery and mix lightly.

Place some of the mayonnaise mixture on each of the slices of smoked salmon and roll them up neatly. Garnish with very thin slices of lemon and serve with thin slices of buttered brown bread.

Beef Salad with Celery and Carrots

Such a good dish for the summer and perfect for a buffet party in the garden—I use shin beef for this, simmering it gently with stock, vegetables and herbs until it is really tender and then using the resulting stock as a base for a revitalizing home-made consommé. Serve the beef salad with a rice or potato salad and a plain green salad.
Serves 8

1 *lb (450 g) cooked shin beef (or you can use lean, leftover cooked beef or tongue)*
12 *oz (350 g) carrots*
4 *large sticks celery*
6 *tablespoons olive or vegetable oil*
2 *tablespoons white wine vinegar*
1 *teaspoon French Dijon mustard*

salt and freshly ground black pepper
2 *teaspoons finely chopped capers*
1 *tablespoon finely chopped chives*
1 *tablespoon very finely chopped parsley*

Peel the carrots, cut them into thin lengthwise slices and then into thin matchstick strips. Remove the leaves and any tough fibres from the celery and cut the stalks into thin matchstick strips about 2 inches (5 cm) long.

Plunge the vegetables into boiling salted water and cook them for about 5 minutes until they are just tender but still retain a crisp quality. Drain well and leave to cool.

Cut the meat into thin slices and then into thin matchstick strips. Combine the oil, vinegar and mustard and mix well. Season with salt and pepper and mix in the finely chopped capers, chives and parsley. Add the meat and vegetables to the dressing, toss lightly, turn on to a serving dish and chill before serving.

Salad of Duck with Celery, Orange and Walnut

Boiled duck is best for making this rather dramatic summer salad. Only half the duck is used for this dish so it is remarkably economical. The other half could go towards making the salad of duck, French beans and oranges on page 132.

To cook the duck place it, with the giblets, in a large saucepan. Add some onion, carrots, herbs and seasonings, cover it with cold water, adding a little red wine if you have some and a chicken stock cube to give extra flavour. Bring to the boil, cover and simmer gently, as you would a boiled chicken, for about 1–1½ hours until the legs of the duck are beginning to come away from the body.
Serves 4

½ cooked duck
1 head celery
4 black olives
3 tablespoons olive or sunflower oil
1½ tablespoons white wine vinegar
2 teaspoons finely chopped,
    shelled, walnuts
1 cabbage lettuce

1 bunch watercress
1 orange
¼ pint (150 ml) mayonnaise
salt and freshly ground black
    pepper
1 tablespoon finely chopped
    chives or parsley

Remove the meat from the bones and cut the duck into thin strips. Trim the celery, remove any tough outer stalks and cut the celery into thin matchstick strips. Remove the stones from the olives and finely chop the flesh. Combine the oil with the vinegar and walnuts and season with salt and pepper. Add the duck and celery to the dressing and leave to marinate in the refrigerator for about 30 minutes.

Shred the lettuce leaves. Remove the tough stalks from the watercress. Peel and thinly slice the orange, remove the pips and cut each slice into four.

Surround a shallow serving dish with the shredded lettuce. Place the watercress in the centre, top with the orange pieces and spoon over the mayonnaise as neatly as possible. Arrange the duck and celery on top of the mayonnaise and sprinkle over the finely chopped chives or parsley.

Quick-fried Beef with Celery and Oyster Sauce

An extremely quickly fried meat and vegetable dish with a rich oyster sauce. Chinese oyster sauce can be bought from Chinese supermarkets or a good delicatessen shop. If you have a Chinese *wok* use it for this kind of quickly cooked dish; if not, then use a heavy frying pan and make sure it is really hot before you add the ingredients.

Always assemble and prepare the ingredients for this kind of a dish before you begin to use them as quick cooking is the essence of success.

Serves 4

12 oz (350 g) rump or chuck
   steak
1 head celery
2 cloves garlic
½ inch (1½ cm) fresh ginger root
1 large onion
1 dried red chilli pepper
   (optional)

3 carrots
1 tablespoon Chinese oyster sauce
1 tablespoon tomato purée
6 tablespoons chicken stock
4 tablespoons olive or vegetable oil

Chill the steak in the deep freeze for about 30 minutes to make it easier to slice.

Cut the celery, including the leaves, into very thin slices (leave the head whole to do this and slice right through the stalks). Peel the garlic and cut them into thin slivers.

Peel and very finely chop the ginger root. Peel the onion, cut it into very thin slices and divide into rings. Finely chop the red chilli. Peel the carrots and cut them into wafer-thin slices.

Cut the beef into wafer-thin slices against the grain and then into thin matchstick strips.

Combine the oyster sauce, tomato purée and stock and mix well.

Heat the oil in a *wok* or frying pan. When the oil is smoking add the onion, garlic, ginger, chilli and carrots and cook over a high heat, tossing the pan or stirring the ingredients all the time to prevent them browning. Cook the vegetables for 1 minute and then add the celery and cook over a high heat for a further 2 minutes. Push the vegetables to the side of the pan, add the meat and continue to cook over a high heat, turning the meat, until the meat is browned on all sides. Add the oyster sauce mixture and mix well. Lower the heat and cook for a further 2 minutes or until the meat is just tender — overcooling will toughen the meat.

Serve as quickly as possible with rice.

Stovey Chicken

A deliciously simple and tender dish of chicken with celery, potatoes and onions.

Serves 6–8

A 3 lb (1350 g) chicken
2 large onions
2½ lb (1125 g) potatoes
6 sticks celery
2 rashers streaky bacon
2 oz (50 g) butter
salt

freshly ground black pepper
pinch ground nutmeg
2 tablespoons finely chopped
  parsley
1 pint (600 ml) good chicken
  stock

Remove the skin from the chicken, cut the flesh from the bones and then cut it into thin slices. Peel and slice the onions and divide them into rings. Peel and slice the potatoes. Remove any tough fibres and leaves from the celery and cut the rinds from the bacon rashers. Mince the celery and bacon through the coarse blades of a mincing machine or finely chop them in an electric food processor.

Melt the butter in a heavy frying pan. Add the chicken and cook over a high heat, tossing the pan, for about 3 minutes. Remove the chicken with a slotted spoon. Layer the potatoes, onions, chicken slices, celery and bacon in a well-buttered casserole, seasoning the layers with a little salt, pepper and nutmeg and sprinkling them with a little parsley. Finish the layers with potatoes, pour over the stock and dribble over the remaining butter from the pan. Cover with buttered greaseproof paper, put on a tight-fitting lid and cook in a moderate oven (300°F. 150°C. Reg. 2) for 2 hours or until the potatoes are really tender.

Gammon Steaks with a Vegetable Sauce

A combination of celery, turnip and carrots and the addition of some Dijon mustard to this vegetable sauce makes it an excellent accompaniment to gently cooked gammon steaks.

Serves 4

4 *gammon steaks*
1 *small onion or shallot*
1 *small head celery*
1 *small white turnip*
1 *large carrot*
1 *chicken stock cube*
2 *oz (50 g) butter*
1 *tablespoon vegetable oil*
1½ *tablespoons flour*

½ *pint (300 ml) milk*
1 *teaspoon French Dijon*
   mustard
1 *tablespoon double cream*
salt and freshly ground black
   pepper
1 *tablespoon finely chopped*
   parsley

Peel and finely chop the onion or shallot. Trim and thinly slice the celery stalks. Peel the turnip and carrot and cut them into small dice.

Cover the vegetables with cold water, add the stock cube and bring to the boil. Cover and cook over a medium heat until the vegetables are tender. Drain off and reserve the stock.

Heat the butter and oil in a large heavy pan. Add the gammon steaks and cook gently for about 5 minutes a side (the time will depend on the quality and thickness of the steaks) until the gammon is tender. Transfer the steaks to a heated serving dish and keep warm.

Add the flour to the juices in the pan and mix well. Gradually blend in ¼ pint (150 ml) of the stock and the milk and cook over a medium heat, stirring all the time, until the sauce comes to the boil and is thick and smooth. Add the vegetables and the mustard and season with salt and pepper. Simmer for 3 minutes, mix in the cream and parsley and pour the sauce over the steaks.

A Salad of Mixed Cold Meats and Celeriac

This is a really excellent summer salad and a useful dish to have for a buffet party. Ham, garlic sausage and tongue are mixed with blanched celeriac, tomatoes and green pepper in a mustardy mayonnaise. The texture of the celeriac makes a good contrast to the meat ingredients and the chopped tomatoes give a rosy tone to the dressing.
Serves 4–6

4 *oz (100 g) garlic sausage*
2 *slices tongue*
2 *slices ham*

1 *lb (450 g) celeriac*
2 *teaspoons lemon juice*
1 *green pepper*

3 *tomatoes*
¼ *pint (150 ml) mayonnaise*
2 *teaspoons French Dijon*
   mustard

2 *tablespoons double cream*
salt and freshly ground black
   pepper
1 *cos lettuce*

Have ready a bowl of cold water to which you have added 1 teaspoon of lemon juice. Peel the celeriac, cut it into thin slices and then into very thin matchstick strips (they really should not be much bigger than matchsticks) dropping the sticks into the water as soon as they have been cut to prevent the vegetable turning brown.

Drain the celeriac and plunge it into boiling salted water to which the second teaspoon of lemon juice has been added and blanch the celeriac for 2 minutes. Drain it, plunge it into cold water and drain again.

Remove the core and seeds from the green pepper and cut the flesh into thin strips. Cut the meat into thin strips. Cover the tomatoes with boiling water for 2 minutes and drain them. Slide off the skins, remove the core and seeds and chop the flesh.

Combine the mayonnaise with the mustard and cream, season with a little salt and pepper and mix well.

Add the tomatoes to the mayonnaise and mix well. Add the celeriac, pepper and meat and toss lightly.

Wash the lettuce and arrange the leaves, with the stalks towards the centre, around a shallow, round serving dish. Pile the salad into the centre of the dish.

Celeriac and Carrots with Ham in a Dijon Mayonnaise

A dish that can be served as an hors d'oeuvre or as a main-course salad on a bed of crisp lettuce leaves.

Serves 4

6 *oz (175 g) ham in one piece*
2 *young celeriac roots*
2 *teaspoons lemon juice*
2 *carrots*
6 *fl. oz (175 ml) mayonnaise*

2 *tablespoons double cream*
3 *teaspoons French Dijon*
   mustard
1 *tablespoon finely chopped*
   parsley

Peel the celeriac, cut the flesh into thin slices and then into matchstick strips about 1 inch (2½ cm) long. As soon as the strips are prepared, drop them into cold water to which the lemon juice has been added to prevent them discolouring.

Peel the carrots, cut them into thin slices and then into thin matchstick strips the same length as the celeriac.

Blanch the celeriac in boiling salted water for 2 minutes and drain well. Blanch the carrots in boiling salted water for 4–5 minutes (they should be tender but still crisp) and drain well. Leave the vegetables to cool.

Cut the ham into thin slices and then into matchstick strips the same size as the vegetables.

Add the cream and mustard to the mayonnaise and mix well.

Lightly fold the celeriac, carrots and ham into the mayonnaise, pile on to a serving dish, sprinkle over the parsley and serve as soon as possible so that the vegetables do not become limp.

A Salad of Sweetbreads with Mayonnaise and Celeriac

Sweetbreads are usually sold trimmed but they do need to be soaked in cold water before being blanched and cooked. This is an exceptionally delicate and delicious dish for a hot summer's day. Serve it with the accompaniment of a rice salad and a salad of mixed lettuce leaves in a vinaigrette dressing.
Serves 4

1 *lb (450 g) sweetbreads,*
   trimmed
4 *tablespoons olive oil*
2 *teaspoons lemon juice*
salt and freshly ground black
   pepper
white wine

1 *root celeriac*
½ *pint (300 ml) home-made*
   mayonnaise
1 *teaspoon French Dijon mustard*
2 *firm, ripe tomatoes*
1 *tablespoon finely chopped celery*
   leaves

Wash the sweetbreads in cold water and then soak them in cold water, changing the water twice during the process, for 2 hours. Drain well and carefully pull off as much as you can of the filament that surrounds them without tearing the flesh.

Immediately blanch the sweetbreads in boiling salted water for 15 minutes and then plunge them straight into cold water. Drain them well and leave to cool. Remove any filaments still left on the sweetbreads and marinate them in the olive oil and 1 teaspoon lemon juice with a light seasoning of salt and pepper. Leave the sweetbreads to marinate for 2 hours.

Place the sweetbreads in a saucepan and pour over just enough wine to cover. Bring to the boil and simmer gently for 30 minutes. Drain off the wine (this can be added to stocks or soups), put the sweetbreads on to a plate, cover with a second plate and weight down. Leave the sweetbreads to cool. Drain off any liquid and cut the sweetbreads into thin slices.

Peel the celeriac, cut it quickly into thin slices and then into thin matchstick strips and plunge them into boiling salted water to which 1 teaspoon of lemon juice has been added. Cook the celeriac for about 20 minutes until it is just tender and drain well. Leave it to cool.

Add the mustard to the mayonnaise and mix well. Add the celeriac to the mayonnaise and mix lightly without breaking up the celeriac.

Thinly slice the tomatoes (peel them if the skins seem tough by covering the tomatoes with boiling water for 2 minutes and then draining off the water and sliding off the skins). Arrange the slices of tomatoes on a serving plate, cover with the slices of the sweetbreads and then top with the mayonnaise and celeriac. Garnish the dish with finely chopped leaves of celery and serve chilled.

A Salad of Mussels, Celeriac and Potatoes

This is one of the best summer salads in my collection. The fresher the mussels are the better they will be and if you can pick them yourself (they are to be found in great numbers around many of our coasts) take advantage of a trick I was told by a Cornish fisherman: as soon as you get your mussels home place them in a bucket, cover them with cold water, sprinkle a large handful of oatmeal into the water, and leave them in a cool place for up to 24 hours. Not only will the oatmeal be

absorbed into the mussels and almost double their size but it will also help to rid them of any impurities there may be.
Serves 6

3½ quarts (4200 ml) mussels
4 shallots
1 sprig thyme
6 sprigs parsley
¼ pint (150 ml) dry white wine
1 root celeriac
salt and freshly ground black
    pepper

2 lb (900 g) new, waxy potatoes
few drops lemon juice
5 tablespoons olive or sunflower oil
2 tablespoons white wine vinegar
½ teaspoon French Dijon mustard
1 tablespoon mixed finely chopped
    parsley and chives

Scrape off any barnacles from the mussels and scrub them with a scrubbing brush. Pull out the beard which protrudes from the shell.

Peel and finely chop the shallots. Place the shallots, thyme, and parsley sprigs in a large saucepan. Add the mussels, pour over the white wine, season with pepper and cook over a high heat, shaking the pan every now and then, until the shells have opened.

Lift out the mussels, strain the liquid and discard the herbs and shallots. Remove the mussels from their shells as soon as they are cool enough to handle. Check the mussels to see that no beards have been left attached to them.

Boil the potatoes in their skins until just tender. Remove the skins and slice the potatoes as soon as they are cool enough to handle. Peel the celeriac root, cut the flesh into matchstick strips, blanch them for 2 minutes in boiling salted water to which a little lemon juice has been added and drain them well.

Pour the mussel liquid over the potatoes and leave to cool.

Combine the oil, mustard and vinegar, season with a little salt and pepper and mix in the chopped parsley and chives.

When the potatoes and celeriac have cooled, arrange the potatoes neatly around a flat serving dish. Place the celeriac in the centre, top the celeriac with the mussels and pour over the dressing.

Serve well chilled with a green salad.

Chicken with Celeriac in a Tuna Fish Sauce

The tuna sauce, a mixture of pounded tuna fish and home-made mayonnaise, is one that is usually served with cold veal. It goes well with chicken and this dish makes a really good centre-piece for a buffet lunch party. The chicken can be served in a ring of rice or small pasta, dressed while still hot with a vinaigrette and then allowed to get cold.
Serves 6–8

1 *medium chicken*
1 *carrot*
1 *stalk celery*
1 *onion*
salt and freshly ground black pepper
$\frac{1}{2}$ *lemon*
$\frac{1}{4}$ *pint (150 ml) dry white wine*
1 *chicken stock cube*

6 *sprigs parsley*
1 *tin (7 oz, 200 g) tuna fish*
3 *anchovies*
1 *celeriac root*
2 *teaspoons lemon juice*
$\frac{3}{4}$ *pint (450 ml) home-made mayonnaise*
green olives for garnishing

Peel and roughly chop the carrot. Roughly chop the celery including the leaves. Wash the onion and cut it into quarters leaving the skin on. Quarter the lemon half. Place the chicken in a saucepan, add the vegetables, lemon, wine and stock cube, season with salt and pepper and add enough water to cover the chicken. Bring to the boil, cover and simmer for about 1 hour until the chicken is just tender. Remove from the heat, leave to stand for 5 minutes and then remove the chicken and leave it to get cold. (The stock can be used to make delicious soups.)

Mince the parsley. Drain the tuna and anchovies. Pound the parsley, tuna and anchovies to a paste in a mortar. Add the pounded mixture to the mayonnaise, mix until smooth and season lightly with salt and pepper.

Peel the celeriac, cut it into thin slices and then into matchstick strips, dropping the strips, as soon as they have been cut, into cold water to which the lemon juice has been added. Drain the strips and plunge them immediately into boiling salted water and boil over a high heat for 4 minutes until the strips are just tender but still crisp. Drain them well and leave them to cool.

Carve the flesh from the breast, legs and wings of the chicken into very thin slices. Arrange the celeriac and chicken on a shallow serving dish and spoon over the tuna mayonnaise. Garnish with slices of green olives.

Courgettes (Zucchini)

While gardeners all over the world have been spending the last hundred years or so trying to produce larger cauliflowers, more prolific bean plants, plumper peas, champion cabbages and larger and larger leeks, one great revolution has taken place among the vegetables now gaining popularity which indicates that, in some areas at least, small in the kitchen is beautiful. Once we grew marrows for their size and then moaned because they were watery and lacking in flavour. Now we grow the miniature courgettes, flavoursome and succulent and crisp, for their taste rather than their size and we are gradually learning to scorn a courgette that has grown to more than about $1\frac{1}{2}$ inches (4 cm) in width. Fortunately from the taste point of view, although perhaps not for garden-produce shows and harvest festivals, those giant, waterblown marrows have become a thing of the past and it is possible to buy tender young courgettes almost all the year round these days.

Courgettes (also called zucchini) are an admirable vegetable, a good tenderizer and a satisfactory absorber of other flavours. They are easily grown in the amateur garden and their only problem is that, in a good year when water and sun are both plentiful, they grow so fast that it is sometimes difficult to catch them when they are small enough. (Courgettes or zucchini, like any other marrow, will swell to a prodigious size if left unpicked.) In the height of their season they must be picked every day and it is useful to know that the flowers, great golden blooms, are also good food value. When the courgettes are in their first bloom, at about 6 inches (15 cm), the flowers should still be in good condition; they make a delicious golden soup, can be deep fried in batter as a vegetable and are, I am told, delicious if chopped, cooked in butter with lemon and seasoning and served in the middle of half an avocado pear.

Courgettes are, in fact, yet another example of the progress of horticulture. They have been developed so as not, like marrows, to get too large but instead to produce a large number of fruits on one stem. In the same way as runner beans, courgettes seem to thrive on hard culling – the more you pick the more you get in the future. Lightly cooked in butter and seasoned generously with salt and freshly ground black pepper, the flesh is fresh-tasting and delicious. Courgettes can be served raw in salads and, cooked with meat, poultry or fish, they have a chameleon quality which absorbs the flavour of the main ingredient as well as helping to tenderize it if necessary.

If you buy courgettes from a greengrocer make sure their colour is bright green and their flesh is firm and crisp, not flabby or soft. Always slice courgettes from the flower end to prevent any bitterness tainting their flesh. Store courgettes in the bottom of the refrigerator where they will retain their crispness for a week or even longer.

Courgettes Cooked with Mushrooms

One of those vegetable dishes which can well stand as a first course in their own right.
Serves 4

1 lb (450 g) small firm
  courgettes
4 oz (100 g) firm button
  mushrooms
2 oz (50 g) butter
½ teaspoon each finely chopped
  chervil and basil
salt and freshly ground black
  pepper

¼ pint (150 ml) double cream
2 oz (50 g) fresh white
  breadcrumbs
1½ oz (40 g) finely grated
  Cheddar cheese
1½ teaspoons vegetable oil

Remove the stems from the courgettes and cut the flesh into slices. Very thinly slice the mushrooms. Melt the butter in the frying pan, add the courgettes and mushrooms, sprinkle with the herbs, season with salt and pepper and cover with a lid. Cook gently, over a low heat, shaking the pan every now and then, for 15 minutes.

Gently mix in the cream and turn the vegetables into a shallow baking dish. Combine the breadcrumbs and cheese and sprinkle the mixture over the vegetables, dribble over the oil and put under a hot grill for a few minutes until the topping is crisp and golden brown.

Gougère with Courgettes and Ham

This is a marvellous variation on the choux pastry theme. A savoury choux pastry with cheese has the addition of puréed courgettes and ham; the dough is then shaped in a ring and the resulting light and well-flavoured pastry makes an excellent first course or main course. You can fill the centre of the ring with a savoury meat or fish sauce or with a well-flavoured home-made tomato sauce and, as a main course, the only other accompaniment you need is a green or mixed salad.
Serves 4–6

4 oz (100 g) ham
1 lb (450 g) courgettes
5 oz (150 g) butter
¼ pint (150 ml) water
10 oz (275 g) plain flour
2 oz (50 g) Parmesan cheese

salt and freshly ground black
    pepper
pinch cayenne pepper
4 eggs, separated
2 oz (50 g) Gruyère cheese,
    grated

Thinly slice the courgettes. Melt 1 oz (25 g) butter in a saucepan, add the courgettes, cover tightly, and cook them over a low heat, shaking the pan to prevent sticking, for about 20 minutes or until the courgettes are soft. Purée the courgettes through a fine food mill or in an electric blender or food processor. Mince or finely chop the ham.

Combine the remaining butter with the water in a medium-sized saucepan and heat until the butter has melted. Bring to the boil, mix in the courgette purée and then add the flour, all at once, and beat hard, off the heat, until the mixture is thick and smooth and comes away from the sides of the pan. Leave to cool for about 10 minutes. Fold in the Parmesan cheese and season the mixture with salt, pepper and cayenne.

Beat the egg yolks until smooth and add them, a little at a time, to the courgette mixture, beating after each addition of yolk, until the mixture is smooth and shining.

Oil a baking sheet and dust it with flour. Draw a circle on the sheet round a dinner plate and another circle 2 inches (5 cm) inside that.

Beat the egg whites until stiff. Fold the egg whites into the courgette mixture as lightly as possible and then spoon the mixture on to the sheet in between the two circles. Sprinkle over the Gruyère cheese and bake in a moderately hot oven (375°F. 190°C. Reg. 5) for about 30 minutes until well risen and firm to touch. Slide on to a circular serving dish and serve hot or cold.

Courgette and Chicken Quiche

The combination of vegetables and chicken, ham or bacon in a quiche is one that has almost infinite varieties. This variation is one that is especially good and makes a light, pleasant main course for a summer meal.
Serves 6

1 *partially baked* 10 *inch* (25 cm) *quiche case (see page 4)*	3 *eggs*
	½ *pint (300 ml) single cream*
6 *oz (175 g) cooked chicken*	2½ *oz (65 g) Cheddar cheese, grated*
12 *oz (350 g) courgettes*	
1 *onion*	1 *oz (25 g) Parmesan cheese, grated*
4 *oz (100 g) streaky bacon*	
1 *oz (25 g) butter*	*salt and freshly ground black pepper*

Cut the courgettes into thin slices. Peel and slice the onion and divide it into rings. Remove the rinds from the bacon and cut the rashers into thin strips. Cut the chicken into thin strips.

Melt the butter in a heavy frying pan. Add the bacon and onion and cook over a low heat until the onion is soft and transparent. Add the courgettes and continue to cook over a low heat, stirring every now and then, until the courgettes are just tender.

Beat the eggs until smooth and mix in the cream. Add the cheese and season with salt and pepper.

Arrange the courgettes, bacon and onion in the bottom of the quiche case and top with the strips of chicken. Pour over the custard and bake in a moderate oven (350°F. 180°C. Reg. 4) for about 30 minutes or until the filling is set and golden.

Serve hot or cold with a salad.

Moussaka with Courgettes and Tomatoes

When courgettes mature in the garden they all seem to mature at once and suddenly, after having longed for them to arrive, you find yourself with more than you feel you can cope with. This is an excellent way of using quite a large number of courgettes for a dish.
Serves 6

1 *lb (450 g) minced raw lamb*
1½ *lb (675 g) courgettes*
1 *large onion*
2 *rashers streaky bacon*
8 *oz (225 g) carrots*
1 *stalk celery*
4 *tablespoons olive or vegetable oil*
1 *medium tin (14 oz, 392 g) tomatoes*
2 *teaspoons tomato purée*
6 *fl. oz (175 ml) dry white wine*

salt and freshly ground black pepper
pinch of ground nutmeg
pinch oregano
4 *tablespoons flour*
1½ *oz (40 g) butter*
¾ *pint (450 ml) milk*
2 *oz (50 g) grated Parmesan cheese*
2 *eggs*

Peel and very finely chop the onion. Remove the bacon rinds and mince the bacon. Peel and grate the carrot. Very finely chop the celery.

Heat 2 tablespoons of the oil in a saucepan. Add the onion, bacon and meat and cook over a moderately high heat, stirring, until the meat is lightly browned. Add the carrots, celery, tomatoes, tomato purée and white wine, season with salt, pepper and nutmeg and mix in the oregano. Bring to the boil and simmer gently for 30 minutes, tightly covered. Mix well to break up the tomatoes.

Peel and thinly slice the courgettes without peeling them. Sprinkle the slices with salt and leave them to 'sweat' in a colander. Dry the slices well, sprinkle them lightly with 2 table-spoons of flour and fry them lightly, on both sides, in the remaining oil. Drain off excess oil.

Layer the courgettes and meat sauce in a casserole dish, leaving enough room for another sauce to go on the top.

Melt the butter in a saucepan, add the remaining flour and mix well. Gradually blend in the milk, stirring continually over a medium high heat until the sauce comes to the boil and is thick and smooth. Add half the grated cheese and season the sauce with salt and pepper. Beat the eggs, add them to the sauce, beating to blend well, and pour the sauce over the casserole. Sprinkle over the cheese, bake the dish in a moderately hot oven (375°F. 190°C. Reg. 5) for 30 minutes until the dish is really hot through and the top is golden brown.

A Leg of Lamb Roasted on a Bed of Vegetables

Although it is so tender, young lamb can be slightly lacking in flavour. In this recipe the leg is roasted on a delicious combination of vegetables which become a marvellously soft and aromatic accompaniment to the meat and also pervade it with a most evocative taste. Please do not serve mint sauce with the meat as that would only spoil the flavour. Lamb cooked in this way is also delicious cold and if there are any of the vegetables left over as well they can be puréed and flavoured with a little lemon juice to make a very good sauce to go with the cold meat.
Serves 8

1 *leg lamb (about 4 lb, 1800 g)*   3 *cloves garlic*
2 *onions*   2 *sprigs rosemary*
4 *courgettes*   *salt and freshly ground black*
6 *ripe tomatoes*   *pepper*
4 *tablespoons olive or vegetable oil*   *a wine glass of red wine*

Peel and slice the onions. Slice the courgettes. Cover the tomatoes with boiling water and leave them to stand for

2 minutes. Drain off the water, slide off the skin of the tomatoes and cut them into thick slices. Arrange the onions in a roasting pan. Cover with the courgettes and then with the tomatoes, and pour over half the oil.

Peel the garlic cloves and cut them into very thin slivers. Using a small, sharp-pointed knife make very small slits all over the lamb. Insert a garlic sliver and a few leaves of fresh rosemary into each slit. Sprinkle the rest of the garlic and a few leaves of rosemary over the vegetables, place the leg on top of the vegetables and season with salt and pepper. Pour the remaining oil over the meat and roast in a hot oven (450°F. 230°C. Reg. 8) for 10 minutes, then lower the heat to moderate and continue to cook for a further 30 minutes, basting the lamb and vegetables every now and then with the juices from the pan. Pour over the wine and continue to cook for a further 20–30 minutes depending on how pink you like your meat to be.

Remove the lamb on to a serving dish. Remove the vegetables from the pan with a slotted spoon, spoon off any excess fat from the juices in the pan and serve the juice separately as a gravy.

Rack of Lamb Tenderized with Baby Courgettes

Young lamb should always be tender but in this recipe the action of cooking the lamb smothered in courgettes gives the meat a texture that is really deliciously succulent. The flavour is extremely subtle and, all in all, it makes a really spectacular dinner-party main course.
Serves 4

A rack of lamb with 8 *small
cutlets, trimmed, with the top
of the bones chined*
1 *lb (450 g) courgettes*

*salt and freshly ground black
pepper*
2 *sprigs fresh thyme*
2 *tablespoons olive or vegetable oil*

Cut the courgettes into ½ inch (1½ cm) thick slices. Roast the lamb in a hot oven (425°F. 220°C. Reg. 7) for 10 minutes until the outside is nicely browned. Place the lamb in a casserole just large enough to take the lamb and the courgettes. Smother the lamb with the slices of courgettes, season with salt and pepper, top with the sprigs of thyme and pour over the oil. Cover tightly and braise in a moderate oven (350°F. 180°C. Reg. 4) for 1 hour. Remove the lamb from the dish, cut it into cutlets, arrange the cutlets on a serving dish, surround them with the slices of courgettes and pour over the juices from the casserole.

Serve the lamb with baby new potatoes and carrots dripping with country butter. No gravy is necessary as the meat and courgettes make their own juice.

Chicken with Courgettes

Soy sauce and almonds give this dish an Eastern flavour. Serve it with rice and a green vegetable such as runner beans or cabbage.
Serves 6

1 *small chicken*	6 *spring onions*
1 *tablespoon cornflour*	12 *oz (350 g) courgettes*
3 *tablespoons soy sauce*	3 *tablespoons vegetable oil*
1 *teaspoon brown sugar*	4 *oz (100 g) split, blanched*
salt and freshly ground black	*almonds*
pepper	4 *tablespoons chicken stock*

Cut the chicken off the bones and then cut the flesh into thin strips. Combine the cornflour, soy sauce and sugar in a bowl, season with salt and pepper, add the chicken strips and mix well so that the chicken flesh is coated with the sauce.

Trim the spring onions and cut them into thin, lengthwise strips. Thinly slice the courgettes.

Heat the oil in a Chinese *wok* or large heavy frying pan. Add the almonds and cook over a medium heat until they are golden brown. Remove the almonds with a slotted spoon and drain them on kitchen paper.

Add the chicken strips to the oil and cook over a high heat, stirring, until they are browned on all sides. Add the spring onions and courgettes and continue to cook over a medium heat, stirring every now and then, until the chicken, courgettes and onions are tender. Add the stock, mix well, check the seasoning, mix in the almonds and heat through until boiling hot. Pour in the cornflour mixture and stir gently until the sauce is shiny and slightly thickened. Do not overcook as this will ruin the texture of the courgettes.

Wafer-thin Slices of Pork with Carrots and Courgettes

This is really a combination of Chinese, Indian and French cookery with the subtle flavour of Eastern spices, vegetables cooked in the Chinese manner and a rich sauce enlivened with port. Part of the charm of this dish is its presentation, which is very decorative indeed, and although it does use port the small quantity of meat makes it an inexpensive dish.

In order to get the meat cut thinly enough it should be chilled in the freezer for about 30 minutes before cutting.
Serves 4

12 oz (350 g) boned belly of pork	salt and freshly ground black
6 cardamoms	pepper
1 teaspoon coriander seeds	7 fl. oz (200 ml) chicken or beef
1 stick cinnamon	stock
2 tablespoons vegetable oil	¼ pint (150 ml) port
1 clove garlic	1 tablespoon flour
1 onion	1 oz (25 g) butter, softened
3 carrots	1 tablespoon tomato chutney
4 small courgettes	3 tablespoons single cream

Peel and finely chop the garlic and onion. Peel the carrots and cut them into very thin lengthwise slices. Cut the courgettes into very thin lengthwise slices. Chill the belly of pork in the freezer for 30 minutes, cut it into very thin, wafer-like and almost transparent slices (they should resemble very thin slices of streaky bacon) and remove the skin.

Heat the oil in the frying pan. Add the cardamoms, coriander, and cinnamon and cook over a high heat, stirring, until the cardamoms turn brown and start to pop. Remove the spices with a slotted spoon. Add the onions and garlic to the oil and cook over a moderate heat, stirring, until the onions are soft and transparent. Add the carrots and continue to cook over a moderate heat until the carrots are just tender (the length of time will depend on the thickness of the slices and the age of the carrots), stirring to prevent browning. Remove the carrots with a slotted spoon and arrange them with the wide ends of the slices towards the centre of a circular serving dish. Remove the onions with a slotted spoon and sprinkle them over the carrots. Keep the carrots and onions warm.

Add the courgettes to the oil in the pan, cover and cook over a medium heat, shaking the pan to prevent browning, for about 5 minutes or until the courgettes are just tender. Arrange the slices of courgette in between the slices of carrot, cover with foil and keep warm.

Add the slices of belly of pork to the juices in the pan and brown them quickly on both sides over a high heat. Pour over the stock, season with salt and pepper, bring to the boil, cover and simmer gently for about 15 minutes or until the pork is tender. Remove the slices of pork from the pan with a slotted spoon and arrange them in the centre of the vegetables.

Add the port to the stock, bring to the boil and boil for 2 minutes to reduce the liquid slightly. Mix the flour and softened butter to a smooth paste and mix in the tomato chutney. Add this mixture to the stock and port and stir over a high heat until the sauce is thick and smooth. Check the seasoning, add the cream, heat through without boiling and pour the sauce over the meat.

Courgette and Tomato Sauce to Serve with Grilled Meat or Poultry

I first made this sauce to go with grilled steaks and then found it so delicious I have continued to serve it with grilled meat, poultry and fish of all kinds. It freezes well and can also be used as the basis for a light summer soup. Green peppercorns can be bought in jars or tins from a good delicatessen.
Serves 4

8 oz (225 g) courgettes
1 onion
1 green chilli pepper (or use half a dried red chilli)
2 cloves garlic
1 lb (450 g) golden or red tomatoes

1 tablespoon olive or vegetable oil
¼ pint (150 ml) dry white wine
½ teaspoon chopped oregano
salt
1 teaspoon green peppercorns
1½ oz (40 g) butter
2 teaspoons lemon juice

Cut the courgettes into small dice. Peel and chop the onion. Chop the chilli. Peel and chop the garlic. Cover the tomatoes with boiling water for 2 minutes. Drain well, slide off the skins, cut out the core and chop the flesh.

Heat the oil in a saucepan. Add the onion, chilli and garlic and cook over a low heat until the onion is soft and transparent. Add the courgettes and tomatoes, bring to the boil, mix in the wine and oregano, season with salt, add the peppercorns, cover tightly and simmer for 30 minutes. Remove the lid, increase the heat and cook over a high heat, stirring, for about 5 minutes or until most of the liquid has evaporated. Beat in the butter and lemon juice and check the seasoning before serving.

Cucumbers

Those who discuss such matters can never agree whether it is the skin of the cucumber or the seeds which may cause indigestion to those eating cucumbers and I have yet to find out the truth in this question. A report I read recently maintained that there was no truth in either theory and no reason to believe that cucumbers are indigestible at all. Others maintain that, providing the skin and seeds are removed and the sliced cucumber is sprinkled with salt, left to 'sweat' and then drained, there would be no after-effects. Frankly I find myself dubious about this question of indigestion and I am certainly convinced that, as a cooked vegetable, cucumber has no ill effects at all.

In Britain cucumbers have had an up-and-down career. They were brought first by the Romans but, for some reason, never gained any popularity at all except amongst the very poor. Then, in the sixteenth century, they were reintroduced from India and from then on maintained a position of some standing as a salad ingredient although according to Mrs Beeton, 'It is a cold food'. She considered the cucumber to be more suitable for serving as a preserved sweet. Dr Johnson was also pretty disparaging about the fruit and maintained it should be 'sliced, dressed with pepper and vinegar and then thrown out as good for nothing'.

It always surprises me that more use is not made of cooked cucumbers because, although their taste is light, their texture is excellent and there are times during the year when, if you grow your own cucumbers, they become almost embarrassingly prolific or, if you have to buy them, they are very reasonably priced indeed. The Romans, who really were the most imaginative cooks, boiled cucumbers with brains, honey, cumin and other ingredients, and at one time in England it was a popular ingredient to serve with boiled mutton.

There are many varieties of cucumber in the seed catalogues these days. Our favourite remains 'Telegraph Improved', which can be grown in a greenhouse or frame, and we also grow a certain amount of the tougher-skinned ridge varieties which are hardier, easy to grow and which, providing the weather is reasonable, can be grown out of doors. All cucumbers like a rather humid atmosphere and should therefore not be grown side by side with tomatoes. If you are still concerned about the indigestion question you can grow Suttons 'Burpless Tasty Green' cucumbers which are small but sweet and very crisp.

Cucumbers should always be cut from the flower end of the fruit (this prevents them turning bitter) and if you do pare off the skin it can be used as a face pack to clarify the skin or as yet another ingredient for the stock pot.

Prawn and Cucumber Soup

So often the problem with prawns (delicious as they can be) is that, since they are sold cooked on the whole, they tend to become overcooked and tough when they are combined in made-up dishes. This is something that has to be watched and in this soup, based on the idea of a Japanese lobster-and-cucumber soup, the problem does not really arise because hot stock is poured over the prawns rather than the shellfish being cooked in the stock. It is important in a soup of this type to use, whenever possible, a home-made stock rather than one made with water and stock cubes.
Serves 6

8 oz (225 g) peeled, cooked
  prawns
2 small cucumbers
4 oz (100 g) very firm button
  mushrooms

¼ pint (150 ml) water
salt and white pepper
2¼ pints (1350 ml) good
  chicken stock
6 thin slices of lemon rind

Very thinly slice the mushrooms. Bring the water to the boil, season it with salt and drop in the sliced mushrooms. Boil the mushrooms for 5 minutes and drain well.

Peel and very thinly slice the cucumbers. Bring the stock to the boil. Divide the mushrooms, prawns and cucumbers between six heated soup bowls, pour over the stock and float a thin piece of lemon rind in each bowl. Serve at once.

Prawn Cocktail with Cucumber and a Little Curry Flavouring

Serves 6

1 *lb (450 g) peeled, cooked*
  prawns
1 *cucumber*
4 *tender sticks celery*
3 *tablespoons mayonnaise*
1 *teaspoon curry paste*
1 *teaspoon tomato ketchup*

4 *tablespoons double cream*
few drops Worcestershire and
  Tabasco sauce
salt and freshly ground black
  pepper
1 *lettuce heart*

Peel and dice the cucumber and put it into a colander. Sprinkle with salt and leave the cucumber to 'sweat' for 20 minutes. Drain off excess liquid and pat dry with kitchen paper.

Remove, and reserve, the leaves from the celery and cut the stalks into thin slices.

Combine the mayonnaise with the curry paste and tomato ketchup, mix in the cream, season with salt and pepper and mix in a few drops of Worcestershire and Tabasco sauce.

Add the prawns, cucumber and celery to the mayonnaise mixture and mix lightly.

Finely shred the lettuce and divide it between six glass goblets. Spoon over the prawn cocktail, garnish with finely chopped celery leaves and chill before serving with slices of buttered brown bread.

Curried Eggs with Cucumber

A mild and attractive-looking curry dish which you can serve with rice as a main course or on its own as a first course.
Serves 4 as a main course or 8 as a first course

2 *cucumbers*
8 *eggs, hard-boiled*
2 *onions*
1 *small red chilli pepper (fresh or dried)*
1 *large clove garlic*
1 *oz (25 g) butter*
1 *tablespoon vegetable oil*

1½ *tablespoons curry paste*
small wine glass dry white wine
¼ *pint (150 ml) chicken stock*
1 *tablespoon mango chutney*
pinch each ground cumin and coriander
salt
¼ *pint (150 ml) single cream*

Peel the cucumbers, cut them in half, lengthwise, and scoop out the seeds. Cut the flesh into small dice, place them in a colander, sprinkle them with salt and leave them to 'sweat' for 30 minutes. Shake the colander to get rid of excess liquid and pat the cucumber dry on kitchen paper.

Peel and thinly slice the onions and divide them into rings. Very finely chop the chilli pepper and garlic. Heat the butter with the oil in a heavy pan. Add the onion, chilli and garlic and cook over a low heat until the onion is soft and transparent. Add the curry paste and mix well. Add the cucumber, mix well, cover and cook over a low heat for 15 minutes. Add the wine, stock, chutney, cumin and coriander, and season with salt and pepper and continue to cook for a further 10 minutes.

Shell and halve the eggs and place them cut side down in a serving dish. Add the cream to the vegetables, combine well and pour the mixture over the eggs. Cover with foil and heat through in a moderate oven (350°F. 180°C. Reg. 4) for 15 minutes.

Serve with poppadums.

Cucumber and Salmon Quiche

This is a most excellent and delicious quiche – pale green and a gentle pink with the golden glow that epitomizes a good quiche. It is a good way to use up left over cooked salmon.
Serves 6

1 *partially baked 10 in. (25 cm) quiche case (see page 4)*
2 *cucumbers*
8 *oz (225 g) cooked salmon*
2 *medium-sized onions*

1 *oz (25 g) butter*
1 *oz (25 g) Parmesan cheese*
1 *oz (25 g) Gruyère cheese*
salt, white pepper and a pinch of cayenne pepper

3 eggs   2 oz (50 g) grated Cheddar
½ pint (300 ml) single cream   cheese

Peel the cucumbers and cut the flesh into small dice. Place the cucumber in a colander, sprinkle it with salt and leave it to 'sweat' for at least 30 minutes. Shake the colander to remove excess liquid and pat the cucumber dry with kitchen paper. Peel and very thinly slice the onions and divide them into rings. Remove any bones and skin from the salmon and flake the flesh. Beat the eggs with the cream until smooth. Mix in the Cheddar and Parmesan cheese and season with salt, pepper and a touch of cayenne.

Melt the butter in a heavy frying pan, add the onions and cook over a low heat, stirring every now and then, until the onions are soft and transparent and most of the butter has been absorbed. Leave to cool.

Arrange the onions in the bottom of the cool, half-baked, quiche case and cover with the diced cucumber and salmon. Pour over the egg and cream mixture and top with the grated Gruyère cheese.

Bake the quiche in a moderately hot oven (375°F. 190°C. Reg. 5) for about 25 minutes or until the quiche is puffed and golden brown.

Serve hot or cold with a salad and, if you like, potatoes and a green vegetable.

Prawns, Cucumber and Apple Salad Served on a Poppadum

The contrast here between the cool smoothness of the salad and the crisp, slightly peppery flavour of the poppadum is both unusual and delightful.
Serves 6

8 oz (225 g) peeled, cooked   1 teaspoon curry paste
  prawns   2 tablespoons double cream
½ large cucumber   6 fl. oz (175 ml) mayonnaise
1 crisp eating apple   4 leaves fresh mint
1 small dill-pickled cucumber   6 poppadums
1 teaspoon lemon juice   oil for frying

Add the lemon juice, curry paste and cream to the mayonnaise and mix well. Finely chop the mint. Peel the cucumber, cut it in half, remove the seeds with a spoon and cut the flesh into small dice. Peel the apple, remove the core and cut the flesh into small dice. Cut the dill-pickled cucumber into small dice.

Add the mint, cucumber, apple, prawns and dill-pickled cucumber to the mayonnaise and mix lightly.

Fry the poppadums in about $\frac{1}{2}$ inch ($1\frac{1}{2}$ cm) very hot oil (press them flat with a spatula as they begin to swell), turning them once, until they have puffed to about twice their original size and are crisp and golden brown. Drain them on kitchen paper and leave them to cool.

At the last minute place a poppadum on each serving plate and spoon salad over half each poppadum. Serve at once.

Strawberry and Cucumber Salad
Serves 4

$\frac{1}{2}$ *cucumber*
$\frac{1}{2}$ *lb (225 g) strawberries*
1 *carton (5 fl. oz, 150 ml)*
    yoghurt
1 *small clove garlic*
$\frac{1}{2}$ *teaspoon English mustard*

2 *teaspoons lemon juice*
1 *teaspoon finely chopped chives*
    or spring onion tops
salt and pepper
1 *teaspoon finely chopped mint*

Peel the cucumber and cut into thin slices. Place cucumber slices in a colander, sprinkle generously with salt and leave for 1 hour to draw out the excess liquid. Shake slices well and pat dry on kitchen paper.

Hull and slice the strawberries. Combine the yoghurt with the garlic (peeled and squeezed through a garlic press), the mustard and lemon juice and mix well. Add the chives, season with pepper and gently fold in the cucumber and strawberries. Turn into a serving dish, sprinkle with the chopped mint and chill well before serving.

Note: This goes really well with a chicken roasted with plenty of fresh rosemary and some lemon juice and butter.

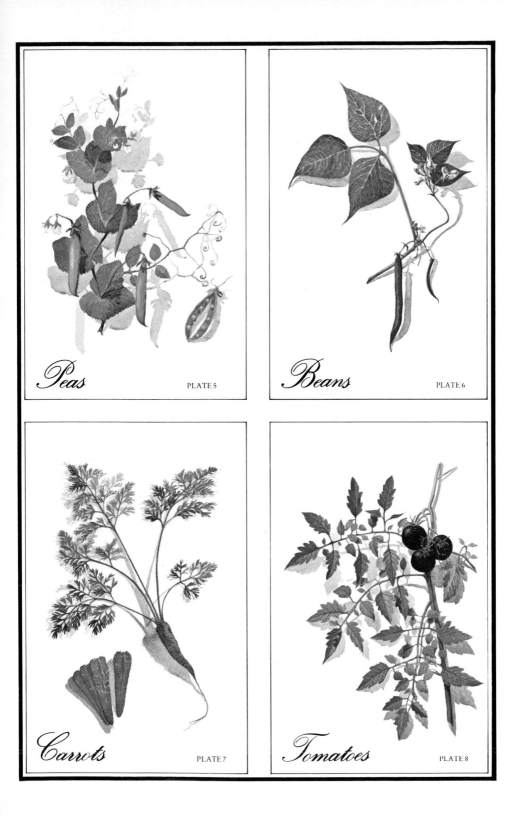

Peas   PLATE 5

Beans   PLATE 6

Carrots   PLATE 7

Tomatoes   PLATE 8

Ridge Cucumber

PLATE 9

Salmon Steaks with Cucumber and Cream

Salmon, when it is fresh and in season and not dried out from the freezer, is such a delicate and perfect fish that I feel it is a shame to mask its flavour with a strong mayonnaise or other robust sauce. In this dish the taste of the salmon is complemented by a sauce made by cooking it gently in a mixture of cucumber and cream – the effect is very special indeed and the pale pink, cream and transparent green of this dish make it a delight to look at. Serve the dish with new potatoes and some really young green beans. You can also make this dish from pollock, brill or cod steaks but the flavour and colour effects will not be as sensational as they are if you use salmon.

Serves 6

6 *salmon steaks*	½ *pint (300 ml) double cream*
2 *small cucumbers*	*salt and freshly ground black*
6 *bay leaves*	*pepper*
2 *oz (50 g) butter*	2 *tablespoons dry Vermouth*

Remove the skin from the cucumbers, cut them in half and scoop out the seeds with a small spoon. Cut the cucumbers into ½ inch (1½ cm) thick slices, place them in a colander, sprinkle them with salt and leave them to 'sweat' for at least 30 minutes. Shake well and pat them dry on kitchen paper.

Arrange the salmon steaks in a well-buttered baking dish and top each steak with a bay leaf and the remaining butter cut into small pieces. Surround the steaks with the pieces of cucumber and pour over the Vermouth and cream. Season with salt and pepper, cover tightly with foil and bake in a moderately hot oven (375°F. 190°C. Reg. 5) for about 30 minutes (remove the foil half-way through the cooking time, baste the steaks with the cream and return the foil again) or until the salmon is *just* cooked. Serve the steaks from the dish they were cooked in.

Chicken Breasts with Cucumber

A delicate dish which goes well after a hearty first course. Serve it after a rich salad *niçoise* in summer or a substantial vegetable soup in winter.

Serves 4

E

2 *chicken breasts*
1 *large or 2 small cucumbers*
1 *shallot*
5 *oz (150 g) butter*
flour

salt and freshly ground black
  pepper
¼ *pint (150 ml) red wine*
¼ *pint (150 ml) chicken stock*

Slice each chicken breast in half through the length of the breasts. Beat the breasts between two sheets of greaseproof paper to flatten them. Peel the cucumber, cut it in half lengthwise and scoop out the seeds with a small spoon. Slice the cucumber into ¾ inch (2 cm) thick slices. Peel and finely chop the shallot.

Melt 1 oz (25 g) butter in a frying pan. Add the cucumber and cook over a low heat, stirring to prevent sticking, for 10 minutes. Arrange the cucumber on a heated serving dish. Dust the chicken breasts lightly with a little seasoned flour.

Add 2 oz (50 g) of butter to the juices in the pan. Add the chicken breasts and cook them over a low heat for 15 minutes or until tender. Remove the chicken with a slotted spoon and arrange them on the bed of cucumber. Add the shallot to the juice in the pan and pour in the wine. Bring to the boil and cook over a high heat for 1 minute. Add the stock and continue to boil until the sauce is reduced to about half the quantity. Add the remaining butter, season with salt and pepper and pour the sauce over the chicken and cucumber.

Cucumber with Spiced Meat Balls and Tomato Sauce

The taste of cooked cucumber is a subtle and delicate one and makes a good contrast to the rich flavour of these meat balls. Although meat balls are an economical dish it is a mistake to try to make them from inferior-quality meat as both their flavour and texture will be impaired.
Serves 6

1 *large cucumber*
1½ *lb (675 g) lean minced beef*
  (chuck is good for this)
1 *small onion*
1 *clove garlic*

1 *egg*
1 *oz (25 g) fresh white*
  breadcrumbs
salt and freshly ground black
  pepper

pinch each ground cumin and   *¾ pint (450 ml) chicken stock*
   coriander   *½ pint (300 ml) home-made*
small pinch allspice   *tomato purée (see page 247)*
oil for frying

Peel and very finely chop the onion. Peel and crush the garlic. Combine the onion, garlic, beef and breadcrumbs, add the egg, season with salt and pepper and add the cumin, coriander and allspice. Mix really well and then form into small balls.

Peel the cucumber and cut it into 1 inch (2½ cm) cubes. Combine the cucumber and stock and cook for about 15 minutes or until the cucumber is just tender.

Heat ½ inch (1½ cm) oil in a heavy frying pan. Add the meat balls and fry over a high heat, turning every now and then, for about 20 minutes or until the balls are crisply browned and cooked throughout. Drain the meat balls on kitchen paper.

Drain off the liquid from the cucumbers, combine the cucumbers and meat balls on a serving dish and pour over the tomato purée.

Lamb Stew with Cucumbers Topped with Roasted Almonds
Serves 4

1½ lb (675 g) lean lamb   *2 tablespoons tomato purée*
1½ cucumbers   *4 tablespoons good stock*
2 onions   *salt and freshly ground black*
2 cloves garlic   *pepper*
3 medium-sized tomatoes   *¼ pint (150 ml) yoghurt*
2 oz (50 g) butter   *1 tablespoon finely chopped mint*
1 tablespoon oil   *leaves*

Cut the lamb into ¾ inch (2 cm) cubes. Peel the cucumbers and cut them into ¾ inch (2 cm) cubes, sprinkle with salt and leave for 1 hour. Peel and chop the onions. Peel and finely chop the garlic. Cover the tomatoes with boiling water for 2 minutes, drain and slide off the skins. Remove the core and chop the flesh of the tomatoes.

Drain off the liquid from the cucumber and pat the cubes dry with kitchen paper. Melt the butter with the oil in a heavy frying pan. Add the onion and garlic and cook over a low heat, stirring to prevent sticking, for about 5 minutes until the onions are soft and transparent. Raise the heat, add the lamb and brown the cubes of lamb on all sides. Lower the heat, add the cucumber and continue to cook for 2 minutes.

Add the tomatoes, tomato purée and enough stock to cover, bring to the boil, season with salt and pepper, cover and simmer over a low heat for about 1 hour or until the lamb is tender.

Strain off the liquid from the pan and put it into a large saucepan; boil over a high heat until the liquid is reduced and syrupy. Remove from the heat, beat in the yoghurt and mix in the mint. Add the meat and vegetables, mix lightly and adjust the seasoning. Turn on to a serving dish and serve with rice or potatoes and a tomato salad.

Fennel

Those who have a weight problem might be interested to know that Florentine fennel (grown for its bulbous base rather than its leaves) was said by the Romans to have slimming properties; and like so many other vegetables it was also thought to have been an aphrodisiac. Whether these two claims are in fact true I cannot pretend to know for sure but I can say that this bulb is a well-worthwhile growing addition to the garden. The crisp leaves of the bulb have a fresh taste with a slight hint of aniseed and a marvellous texture, and the feathery leaves can be used in the same way as the fennel herb to flavour many fish dishes. The fleshy leaves can be used raw in salads or cold dishes and they are also delicious braised or boiled as a vegetable.

Florentine fennel, providing you have a reasonably good season, is easy to grow and can be lifted from about September onwards. To use the plant for cooking, trim off the feathery leaves and any tough base to the bulb and cut the leaves into thin slices. In some recipes, to remove a little of the strong aniseed flavouring, the leaves are blanched before being incorporated in a cooked dish. Traditionally fennel is a herb or vegetable to serve with fish but it also goes well with chicken and pork and is a really invaluable flavouring ingredient to grow in the garden. It is also appearing much more frequently in the greengrocer's these days but make sure, if you buy the bulbs, that they are firm, unblemished and crisp.

Cream of Green Pepper and Fennel Soup

One of the most delicious and subtle soups I have ever made. It can be served hot or ice cold, is a beautiful pale green in colour and has a delicate, most memorable flavour.
Serves 4–5

2 green peppers
1 fennel bulb
1 onion
1½ tablespoons oil
3 oz (75 g) ground almonds

2 pints (1200 ml) good chicken
  stock
salt and freshly ground black
  pepper
¼ pint (150 ml) single cream

Remove the core and seeds from the peppers and chop the flesh. Thinly slice the fennel bulb including any feathery green leaves. Peel and chop the onion.

Heat the oil in a heavy saucepan. Add the onion, fennel and pepper and cook over a low heat until the vegetables are soft and the onion is transparent. Add the almonds and stock, bring to the boil, season with salt and pepper and simmer for about 30 minutes or until the vegetables are all tender. Strain off and reserve the stock and purée the vegetables through a fine food mill, in an electric liquidizer or food processor and return the purée to a clean pan. Add the stock and cream and heat through without boiling. Taste for seasoning and serve hot or leave to cool and then chill in a refrigerator until ice cold.

Fennel Soup with Bacon

A delicious cream of vegetable soup that is topped with crunchy snippets of crisply fried bacon.
Serves 5–6

1 lb (450 g) fennel
1½ oz (40 g) butter
1 pint (600 ml) milk
1 pint (600 ml) good chicken
  stock

salt and freshly ground black
  pepper
5 rashers streaky bacon
¼ pint (150 ml) single cream

Trim the fennel roots and cut them into thin slices. Blanch the fennel in boiling salted water for 15 minutes and drain well. Melt the butter in a heavy saucepan, add the fennel and cook over a low heat, stirring every now and then to prevent sticking, until the fennel is soft. Purée the fennel through a fine food mill, in an electric blender or in a food processor.

Put the fennel purée into a clean pan, add the milk and stock, season with salt and pepper, bring to the boil and simmer for 10 minutes. (If the purée is too thick you can thin it with a little more milk.)

Remove the rinds from the bacon and chop the rashers finely. Fry the bacon until crisp without using any extra fat. Drain it on kitchen paper.

Add the cream to the soup and heat through without boiling. Sprinkle some crumbled bacon over each bowl just before serving.

Smoked Haddock with Fennel and Celery

Serves 4

1½ *lb (675 g) smoked haddock*	2½ *tablespoons flour*
3 *stalks celery*	1 *tablespoon grated Parmesan*
1 *head fennel*	*cheese*
2 *bay leaves*	*freshly ground black pepper*
1 *pint (600 ml) milk*	*pinch ground nutmeg*
2½ *oz (65 g) butter*	

Place the haddock in a shallow pan. Add the milk and bay leaves and cook over a low heat for about 15 minutes until the haddock is just tender. Drain off, discard the bay leaves and reserve the milk. Remove any skin and bones from the fish and coarsely flake the fish.

Trim the celery stalks and cut them into ½ inch (1½ cm) thick slices. Trim the fennel and thinly slice the flesh. Cook the fennel and celery in boiling salted water for about 15 minutes or until they are just tender.

Melt the butter in a saucepan. Add the flour and mix well. Gradually blend in the milk, stirring continually over a medium high heat until the sauce comes to the boil and is thick and smooth. Add the cheese, season with pepper and nutmeg and continue to stir over a low heat for a further 3 minutes. Place the fish in a lightly buttered baking dish, cover with the vegetables and pour over the sauce. Bake in a moderate oven (350°F. 180°C. Reg. 4) for 15 minutes or until the top of the dish is bubbling and golden.

Fish Steaks with Fennel and Tomatoes

A dish with a Provençal flavour to it. I find it an excellent way to cook steaks of pollock or other inexpensive fish as the vegetables give the somewhat uninteresting taste of the fish a delicious and robust flavouring. The dish can be served cold if the fish does not contain any bones.
Serves 4

4 *steaks of pollock or other white*   3 *tablespoons olive or vegetable oil*
  fish   *sprig of marjoram and thyme*
1 *lb (450 g) fennel*   3 *bay leaves*
1 *lb (450 g) tomatoes*   *freshly grated rind of ½ lemon*
1 *large onion*   *salt and freshly ground black*
2 *or 3 courgettes*   *pepper*

Remove any discoloured parts from the fennel and trim off the base and any green leaves from the top. Cut the fennel into thick slices lengthwise. Peel and finely slice the onion and divide it into rings. Cover the tomatoes with boiling water for 2 minutes, remove the skins and roughly chop the tomatoes. Cut the courgettes into ½ inch (1½ cm) thick slices.

Heat the oil in a heavy pan. Add the onion and cook over a low heat until it is soft and transparent. Add the fennel in a layer and cover with the courgettes and tomatoes. Season with salt and pepper to taste, sprinkle over the lemon rind and add the herbs. Cover tightly and cook over a very low heat for 45 minutes.

Arrange the fish steaks in a shallow baking dish. Smother the fish with the vegetables, cover tightly with foil and bake in a moderate oven (350°F. 180°C. Reg. 4) for about 30 minutes or until the fish is just tender.

Mussels with Tomatoes, Onions, Fennel and Peppers

An aromatic dish that makes a substantial main course for four people. Start the meal with a robust pâté, go on to the mussels and finish with fresh fruit, cheese and salad and what more could you want? A light dry white wine can be served throughout the meal.
Serves 4

2 quarts (2400 ml) mussels
¼ pint (150 ml) water
bouquet garni
2 onions
4 large tomatoes

1 bulb fennel
1 green pepper
1 oz (25 g) butter
1 tablespoon vegetable oil
freshly ground black pepper

Scrub the mussels, pulling out their beards and removing dirt and barnacles. Put the water and bouquet garni into a large saucepan and bring to the boil. Add the mussels, cover tightly and cook over a high heat, shaking the pan, for about 5 minutes, until the mussels have opened. Peel and finely chop the onions. Cover the tomatoes with boiling water for 2 minutes, drain them and then slide off the skins. Remove the cores and seeds and chop the flesh of the tomatoes. Trim the fennel and cut it into very, very thin slices. Remove the core and seeds of the pepper and cut the flesh into very, very thin strips.

Heat the oil with the butter in a heavy pan. Add the onion, fennel and pepper and cook, stirring, over a medium heat until the vegetables are soft and transparent. Add the tomatoes and cook for a further 10 minutes. Remove the mussels from their shells and add the mussels to the pan, cover and turn up the heat to high and cook, shaking the pan every now and then, for about 3 minutes or until all the mussels have been heated through. Season with pepper.

Transfer the mussels and the sauce to four serving dishes and serve at once.

Chicken Breasts with Vegetables

Serves 4

2 *chicken breasts*
1 *tablespoon sweet paprika*
1 *teaspoon lemon juice*
salt and white pepper
1 *carrot*
1 *large onion*
1 *large bulb fennel*

2½ *oz (65 g) butter*
2½ *fl. oz (75 ml) good brown*
   stock or consommé
2½ *fl. oz (75 ml) Madeira*
½ *pint (300 ml) single cream*
2 *tablespoons finely chopped*
   parsley

Cut each chicken breast in half lengthwise with the grain, making four flat slices. Place the slices in between two sheets of greaseproof paper and beat them lightly to flatten and tenderize the breasts. Sprinkle the breasts with ½ teaspoon lemon juice and season them with the paprika and a little salt and white pepper.

Peel the carrot and cut it into thin matchstick strips. Peel and chop the onion. Trim the fennel, cut it into thin slices and divide into rings.

Melt the butter in a heavy fireproof casserole. Add the carrot, onion and fennel and cook over a low heat, stirring every now and then to prevent sticking for about 15 minutes until the vegetables are soft. Place the chicken breasts on the bed of vegetables, cover them tightly with a piece of buttered grease-proof paper, tightly cover the casserole and cook in a hot oven (400°F. 200°C. Reg. 6) for about 8 minutes or until the breasts are *just* cooked through. Drain off the juices from the casserole and arrange the vegetables, with the chicken breasts on top, on a heated serving dish.

Return the casserole to the top of the stove. Add the stock or consommé and Madeira to the juices in the pan and cook over a high heat for 5 minutes to reduce the liquid. When the liquid is syrupy add the cream and continue to cook over a high heat for a few minutes until the sauce has thickened. Remove from the heat, season with salt and pepper and add the remaining ½ teaspoon of lemon juice.

Pour the sauce over the chicken and vegetables, sprinkle with parsley and serve with a risotto of rice made in chicken stock, with the addition of some peas or finely chopped green pepper.

Lamb Chops with Fennel, Carrots and Cumin

Meaty lamb chops are bedded on cumin-flavoured vegetables and cooked in tomato juice to make a succulent and satisfying dish.
Serves 6

6 *lamb chops*
1 *fennel bulb*
2 *large onions*
3 *carrots*
salt and freshly ground black
  pepper

3 *tablespoons vegetable oil*
½ *teaspoon cumin seeds*
½ *pint (300 ml) tomato juice*

Peel and thinly slice the onions. Peel the carrots and cut them into sticks about ¼ inch (¾ cm) thick. Trim the fennel bulb and slice the flesh.

Heat the oil in a heavy frying pan. Add the chops and cook them over a high heat until they are browned on both sides. Remove the chops with a slotted spoon, lower the heat and add the onions, carrots and fennel to the juices in the pan. Season with plenty of salt and pepper, add the cumin seeds and continue to cook over a low heat, stirring every now and then to prevent sticking until the oil has been absorbed into the vegetables.

Place the vegetables in a thick layer in a casserole and top with the chops. Pour over the tomato juice, cover tightly with a double thickness of foil and then with a lid, and bake in a moderate oven (350°F. 180°C. Reg. 4) for 45 minutes.

Serve with minted new potatoes or with mashed or sauté potatoes.

Beef Stew with Onions and Fennel

A rich and hearty stew that has the addition of an aromatic mixture of herbs, cheese and garlic to finish it off.
Serves 6

2 *lb (900 g) stewing beef*
8 *oz (225 g) lean bacon*
1 *lb (450 g) onions*
1 *lb (450 g) fennel bulb*
2 *tomatoes*
4 *cloves garlic*
4 *tablespoons vegetable oil*
¾ *pint (450 ml) good beef stock*
bouquet garni
¾ *pint (450 ml) red wine*
salt and freshly ground black
   pepper

pinch allspice
1 *oz (25 g) butter*
2 *tablespoons flour*
3 *tablespoons tomato purée*
1 *teaspoon mixed basil and*
   oregano
2 *tablespoons finely chopped*
   parsley
1 *oz (25 g) Parmesan cheese*
few drops Tabasco sauce

Cut the beef into 1½ inch (4 cm) cubes. Remove the rinds from the bacon and cut the rashers into ¼ inch (¾ cm) thick strips. Blanch the bacon in boiling water for 2 minutes and drain well. Peel and very thinly slice the onions. Trim the fennel bulb and cut it into thin slices. Cover the tomatoes with boiling water for 2 minutes, drain them, slide off the skins, remove the cores and seeds and chop the flesh.

Heat the oil in a large, heavy frying pan. Add the bacon and cook over a low heat for 3 minutes. Transfer the bacon to a casserole dish, raise the heat, add the beef to the oil in the pan and cook over a high heat, stirring, until the meat is browned on all sides. Remove the meat to the casserole, lower the heat, and add the onion and fennel to the juices in the pan, stirring them over a low heat until the onion is soft and transparent. Pour in the wine and bring it to the boil, scraping the pan to incorporate all the flavour. Boil for 3 minutes and then pour the vegetables and wine into the casserole. Add the tomatoes, 2 garlic cloves (peeled and crushed), stock, bouquet garni and allspice, and season with salt and pepper. Mix the ingredients, cover them with two layers of foil and then with the lid of the casserole and either cook the casserole over a very low heat on top of the stove or in a medium oven (300°F. 150°C. Reg. 2) for about 2 hours, stirring every now and then—the meat should be very tender and the length of cooking time will depend on the quality of the meat.

Discard the bouquet garni and remove the meat and vegetables to a clean serving dish with a slotted spoon and keep warm. Return the liquid to the heat, bring to the boil and boil fast for

5 minutes. Check the seasoning and then blend in the flour mixed to a smooth paste with the butter, stirring continually until the gravy is thick and smooth.

Crush the remaining 2 garlic cloves through a garlic press and combine them with the tomato purée, basil, oregano and 1 tablespoon of parsley, Parmesan cheese and a few drops of Tabasco. Mix until smooth and then stir the mixture into the gravy. Pour the gravy over the meat and vegetables, mix lightly and sprinkle with the remaining parsley before serving.

Note: Like most stews this one benefits from being made a day or two before it is required. Cook the stew but do not thicken the gravy, leave it to cool and then refrigerate until about 30 minutes before the stew is to be served. Bring it gently to the boil on top of the stove and then continue as above. The stew can also be frozen once it is cooked.

Potatoes Cooked with Florentine Fennel or Parsnips

A marvellous combination that goes well with any meat or poultry dish. If fennel is not available you can substitute parsnips instead.
Serves 4

1½ lb (675 g) potatoes   salt and freshly ground black
1 large fennel root   pepper
2 oz (50 g) butter

Wash the potatoes and boil them in their skins until they are just tender. Leave to cool.

Remove any tough outer leaves of the fennel, trim off the base and cut off any feathery green leaves from the top. Cut the root into thin strips and boil them in salted water until they are just tender—about 15 minutes. Drain the fennel well.

Heat the butter in a large, heavy frying pan, add the potatoes and fennel, season with salt and pepper and cook, shaking the pan over a medium heat, until the vegetables are hot through and the butter has been absorbed.

French Beans

Early instructions to the first settlers of America suggested cooking all forms of green beans until 'they be mashed between the fingers' or stewing them with other ingredients until they lost all their flavour. It is not to be wondered at, therefore, that for a long time dried beans were more popular in the States than fresh ones. It was from the French that both the British and the Americans discovered the art of cooking fresh beans when they were young for only just long enough to tenderize them, and now some of the best beans are grown in California and exported during the winter months.

In America French beans are known as 'snap' beans for the very good reason that when they are at their perfect prime of life they should cleanly break in half with a sharp snapping sound, being crisp, crunchy and firm without any strings or tough edges. The same thing really applies to the cooked beans, which should be so lightly cooked that they retain their essential crispness, freshness and bright-green colouring. If the beans are to be served cold (one of their nicest forms and an essential part of that so delicious dish, salad *niçoise*) they should be plunged into very cold water (preferably iced water) as soon as they have been cooked and drained.

French beans are not as easy to grow as their rather suburban cousin the runner bean and they are very much affected by wind and draughts but if you can get them going they will bear fruit prodigiously from July until the end of the summer and make an excellent subject for freezing. Like runner beans they must be picked daily and, in my book anyway, the smaller and thinner they are the better they taste—I like them the thickness of matchsticks and not much longer than an adult's middle finger.

As a combination-salad ingredient French beans make an excellent subject with their crisp, garden freshness adding great attraction to the dish. They soak up a good vinaigrette in an admirable way and also go well with mayonnaise, providing a good texture contrast to the blandness of that particular sauce.

Cook French beans with a sprig of savory if you have it, don't flood them in water, make sure the water is absolutely on the boil when they are added (except when cooking frozen beans which I have found to be better if added, frozen, to a small quantity of cold water—about 4 tablespoons for 8 oz, 225 g beans) and always add a generous pinch of salt to the cooking water—a touch of cooking soda will help to preserve the colour for salad dishes.

Look out for the varieties of purple French beans: they turn green when cooked, make an attractive addition to the garden and *must* be picked when small and thin. They also have an excellent flavour. If you are as fond of this vegetable as I am, try to stagger your plantings so that you get about three or four harvests throughout the late summer.

One of the nicest ways of cooking these beans (a French practice) is to drop them into boiling water for just about 4 minutes, drain them well and then put them into the juices that surround a roast joint for about the last 15 minutes of cooking time; they will soak up the juice and flavour from the meat and make a delicious partner to it. Another simple method is to stew them gently in some melted butter so that they virtually cook in their own juices and if you want to jazz them up you can garnish them with some crisply fried, crumbled bacon or some slivered almonds which have been crisply roasted in a hot oven for a few seconds only.

If the beans are to be used for a salad dish you have to decide between looks and flavour; for the best flavour they should be marinated in a vinaigrette dressing as soon as they have been cooked but this has the disadvantage of robbing them of that fresh, bright-green colouring; the alternative method is to cool them quickly in ice-cold water, drain them well and then dress them when they are completely cold.

If beans are used in a cooked dish add them for only the last 10 minutes of the cooking time as overcooking destroys their texture.

A Salad of Crab and French Beans

A good way to serve white, frozen, crab meat. If you make the dish from a fresh crab the brown meat can be used to make a rich and delicious soup.

Serves 4 as a main course

8 oz (225 g) white crab meat
8 oz (225 g) French beans
1 cos lettuce
½ cucumber
2 tomatoes
2 hard-boiled eggs
3 tablespoons olive oil

1 tablespoon white wine vinegar
½ teaspoon French Dijon mustard
salt and freshly ground black
  pepper
1 small onion
6 black olives

Wash, dry and roughly shred the cos lettuce and arrange the leaves in a shallow serving dish. Peel the cucumber and cut it into 2 inch (5 cm) lengths and then into thick sticks. Cook the beans in boiling salted water for about 6 minutes until they are just tender but still nice and crisp. As soon as they are cooked, plunge them into cold water to prevent them cooking any further. Drain the beans and leave them to cool.

Cover the tomatoes with boiling water for 2 minutes, drain off the water, slide off the skins and cut the tomatoes into quarters. Cut the olives off the stones into thin slices. Peel and quarter the hard-boiled eggs. Peel and slice the onion and divide into rings.

Arrange the cucumber, tomatoes and eggs around the edge of the dish and place the beans in the centre. Put the crab meat on top of the beans. Combine the oil, vinegar and mustard, season with salt and pepper and mix well. Pour the vinaigrette over the crab and beans and garnish with black olives and raw onion rings.

A Salad of Cooked Duck, French Beans and Oranges

Serves 4

½ cooked duck
1 lb (450 g) French beans
2 oranges

4 stuffed olives
½ teaspoon French Dijon mustard
4 tablespoons olive or sunflower oil

1 *tablespoon white wine vinegar*　　2 *teaspoons each finely chopped*
salt and freshly ground black　　　　*parsley and chives*
　pepper

Cook the beans in boiling salted water until just tender, plunge them into cold water and drain well. Peel and thinly slice the oranges across the segments. Cut the duck meat into thin matchstick strips. Thinly slice the stuffed olives.

Combine the mustard, oil and vinegar, season with salt and pepper and mix well. Add the parsley and chives.

Arrange the slices of orange around the outside of a shallow serving dish. Place the beans in the centre and top with the strips of duck. Pour over the dressing and serve chilled with a potato or rice salad.

A Savoury Rice Salad with Ham, Tongue and French Beans

This is an adaptation of that delicious rice side-salad which is always popular in the summer. By adding ham, tongue and French beans to the basic recipe you come up with a fresh-tasting summer main course that needs little preparation or cooking.
Serves 4

8 *oz (225 g) long-grain or*　　　　3 *spring onions*
　Patna rice　　　　　　　　　　　1½ *teaspoons coriander seeds*
6 *oz (175 g) ham or cooked,*　　　*pinch ground nutmeg*
　lean bacon　　　　　　　　　　　6 *tablespoons olive or sunflower oil*
6 *oz (175 g) cooked tongue*　　　　2 *tablespoons white wine vinegar*
8 *oz (225 g) French beans*　　　　　2 *tablespoons chopped blanched*
1 *inch (2½ cm) piece of ginger*　　　*almonds*
　root　　　　　　　　　　　　　　4 *dried apricots*
1 *tablespoon sultanas*　　　　　　　*salt and freshly ground black*
1 *tablespoon seedless raisins*　　　　*pepper*

Wash the rice, put it into a saucepan with a teaspoon of salt and cover it with twice the quantity of cold water as the quantity of rice. Bring slowly to the boil, stir once, cover very tightly and cook over a low heat for 20 minutes without raising the lid.

Remove the rice from the heat and fluff it up with two forks to let air into the grains. Cover again and leave to stand for 10 minutes.

Pound the coriander to a powder in a pestle and mix it with the oil and vinegar. Season with nutmeg, salt and pepper, and then pour the dressing over the rice while it is still warm. Mix well and leave to cool.

Cut the ham and tongue into thin matchstick strips about 1 inch (2½ cm) long or into very small dice. Peel and grate the ginger root. Soak the sultanas and raisins in a little warm water until they swell up, and drain off the excess liquid. Cook the French beans in a little boiling salted water for about 5 minutes until they are tender but still crisp and plunge them immediately you have drained them into ice-cold water. Drain them well again.

Roast the almonds in a hot oven for about 1 minute until they are crisp and golden. Very finely chop the dried apricots. Trim and chop the spring onions.

Add all the ingredients to the rice salad, mix lightly, check the seasoning and pile the salad on to a serving dish. Top with the roasted almonds and serve well chilled.

Delano Salad

This is a salad for special summer parties when you should use top-quality fillet or entrecôte steak, cooking it until it is moist, still rare and succulent and using it to give the flavour and luxury of good-quality meat in a small quantity. This is romantic food to serve with flagons of well-chilled rosé on a scrubbed trestle table in the garden.

Serves 4

1 lb (450 g) under-cooked fillet, entrecôte or top roast of beef

1 lb (450 g) new potatoes

8 oz (225 g) cooked French beans

1 lb (450 g) firm, ripe tomatoes

1 hard-boiled egg

¼ pint (150 ml) vinaigrette dressing

1 tablespoon finely chopped chives

1 tablespoon finely chopped parsley

Wash the potatoes and boil them in their skins until tender. Drain and leave to cool. Cut the meat into thin julienne strips (cut the meat into very thin slices against the grain and then cut the slices into thin matchstick strips). Cover the tomatoes with boiling water for 2 minutes, drain off the water and slide off the tomato skins. Remove the core and cut the flesh into thin strips. Peel the potatoes if necessary and cut them into thin slices.

Arrange the beans in a circle around the outside of a shallow circular serving dish, place the potato slices in overlapping circles in the centre and top the potatoes with the beef. Place the thin slices of tomato over the beans. Finely chop the white of egg and sprinkle it over the beans and tomato. Rub the hard-boiled egg yolk over the beef strips.

Make the vinaigrette dressing and add the finely chopped parsley and chives. Pour the dressing over the salad and chill it well before serving.

Serve the salad with a rice and green salad and with plenty of crisp, hot French bread.

Lambs' Tongues on a Bed of French Beans with an Aromatic Sauce of Carrots and Madeira

Lambs' tongues are delicious with a soft almost silky texture and a light pleasant flavour. They are cooked like an ox tongue but for a much shorter period and should be skinned while still warm.
Serves 6

6 *lambs' tongues*
1 *lb (450 g) French beans*
1 *onion*
1 *carrot*
1 *chicken stock cube*
bouquet garni
salt and freshly ground black pepper
pinch allspice

2 *shallots*
12 *oz (350 g) carrots*
1½ *oz (40 g) butter*
1 *tablespoon sultanas*
1 *tablespoon tomato purée*
3 *tablespoons Madeira (or medium dry sherry)*
1 *tablespoon finely chopped parsley*

Cover the tongues with cold water and leave them to soak for 1 hour. Drain the tongues, cover with cold water, bring to the boil and drain. Return the tongues to the saucepan and add the onion, washed and quartered but not peeled, the carrot scrubbed and roughly chopped, the stock cube and the bouquet garni. Cover with cold water, season with salt, pepper and a pinch of allspice, bring slowly to the boil and simmer very gently for about 1 hour or until the tongues are tender when pierced with a fork. Remove the tongues with a slotted spoon and, as soon as they are cool enough to handle, strip off the skins. Strain the stock.

Top and tail the beans and cook them in the boiling stock until they are just tender. Drain and reserve the stock.

Peel and finely chop the shallots. Peel and finely chop the carrots. Melt the butter in a small pan. Add the shallots and carrots and cook over a low heat, stirring every now and then to prevent sticking, until the butter has been absorbed into the vegetables. Add ½ pint (300 ml) reserved stock (you may have to use water and some stock cube to make up the required quantity) and mix in the tomato purée and sultanas. Season with salt and pepper, add the Madeira or sherry and simmer until the carrots are just tender and the sauce is thick and glossy.

Thinly slice the tongues and arrange the slices on the beans. Pour over the sauce, cover with foil and heat through in a moderate oven (350°F. 180°C. Reg. 4) for about 15 minutes.

Sprinkle over the parsley and serve the dish with rice and a green vegetable.

Kohlrabi

I remember causing a sensation when I took some kohlrabi to my local harvest festival one year. Few in Cornwall had seen them before and their strange shape produced smiles from even the most dedicated at the service. They are indeed strange-looking vegetables, members of the cabbage family deriving their name from the German *Kohl* or cabbage, with bulbous roots growing above the ground from which leaves shoot out at intervals. Trimmed for cooking, with the leaves removed, they look like green or purplish sputniks and completely removed from any other vegetable form.

Kohlrabi is a native of the East and was brought to Europe by way of the Silk Route in the Middle Ages. It became a popular vegetable of Germany, Hungary and Austria although it was not until recently that the vegetable began to catch on in Britain. Perhaps it is the strange shape of the kohlrabi that makes the housewife avoid the roots; whatever the reason it should be rectified because the flavour of the kohlrabi has a lot to recommend it and its texture too has an indefinable nutty grain that is really delicious. What is more, this is one of the easiest vegetables to grow in the garden, requiring little care once it is in the ground and maturing surprisingly early providing it is quickly grown in good soil, making it a most useful root vegetable for the summer months.

Kohlrabi are rich in minerals; Mrs Beeton recommended them as being 'wholesome, nutritious and very palatable'. The roots should be harvested when they are still quite young, from the size of large ping-pong balls to tennis balls – if the roots are left too long in the ground they tend to become woody and tough.

A lot of the goodness of the roots lies close to the surface, under the skin, so the skins should be removed as thinly as possible or after the vegetable has been steamed or boiled. The leaves can be cooked like spinach and make a pleasant green vegetable and the roots can be cooked and served cold in mayonnaise or as a salad ingredient, puréed and flavoured with salt, pepper and nutmeg, sliced and added to stews, casseroles and braised dishes or used in place of any recipe that incorporates young turnips.

Kohlrabi are often to be seen in the better greengrocer shops these days and are well worth buying—they should be good value for your money providing you don't buy any that are too large. White as well as green roots are on sale.

Steak and Giblet Pie with Kohlrabi

This makes a very good pie indeed and one with an unusual flavour. The kohlrabi emerge crisp and with that special nutty flavour that is so subtle and the giblets provide a marvellously rich and aromatic gravy for the meat.
Serves 6–8

12 oz (350 g) shortcrust pastry	1 chicken stock cube
(see page 4)	bouquet garni
8 oz (225 g) stewing beef	salt and freshly ground black
1 lb (450 g) poultry giblets	pepper
(gizzards and hearts)	pinch allspice
1 lb (450 g) kohlrabi	1 tablespoon finely chopped parsley
2 onions	few drops Worcestershire or
1 carrot	Harvey's sauce

Put the giblets into a saucepan. Add 1 onion and the carrot, washed and roughly chopped but not peeled, season with salt and pepper and add the bouquet garni and stock cube. Cover with water, bring to the boil, stir well, cover tightly and simmer for 2 hours. Drain off the stock, remove the vegetables and bouquet garni and cut the giblets into small pieces. Cut the beef into small cubes. Peel the kohlrabi and cut it into slices and then into thin sticks. Put the giblets, steak and kohlrabi into a pie dish and add 1 onion, peeled and finely chopped. Sprinkle over the parsley and Worcestershire sauce, and season with salt, pepper and a little allspice. Pour over enough of the strained stock to cover the ingredients.

Roll out the pastry, damp the edges of the dish and press the pastry down firmly, and bake in a moderately hot oven (375°F. 190°C. Reg. 5) for 45 minutes.

Kohlrabi with Ham

Serves 6

1½ lb (675 g) kohlrabi
6 oz (175 g) ham
4 tomatoes
2 oz (50 g) butter
2 tablespoons flour
½ pint (300 ml) chicken stock
2 teaspoons French Dijon mustard
½ pint (300 ml) single cream

1 egg
4 oz (100 g) grated Cheddar
  cheese
salt and freshly ground black
  pepper
pinch of ground nutmeg
2 oz (50 g) fresh white
  breadcrumbs

Wash the kohlrabi, remove the tops and side shoots and parboil the roots in boiling salted water for 20 minutes. Cool and slide off the skins. Cut the kohlrabi into thin slices.

Chop the ham. Cover the tomatoes with boiling water for 2 minutes and slide off the skins. Cut the tomatoes into fairly thick slices.

Melt the butter in a saucepan. Add the flour and mix well. Gradually add the stock, stirring continually over a medium high heat until the sauce comes to the boil and is thick and smooth. Add the mustard and mix well. Beat the egg with the cream and gradually add the mixture to the sauce, stirring continually without allowing the sauce to boil. Mix in half the cheese and continue to stir, without boiling, until the cheese has melted. Season with salt, pepper and a touch of nutmeg.

Layer the kohlrabi slices and the ham with cheese sauce between the layers and reserving about a quarter of the sauce for the top.

Cover the top of the dish with the tomato slices, pour over the remaining sauce and sprinkle with the remaining cheese mixed with the breadcrumbs. Bake in a moderately hot oven (400°F. 200°C. Reg. 6) for 30 minutes.

A Stew of Shin of Beef and Kohlrabi

Larger kohlrabi need a relatively long cooking time and therefore make a good combination with shin of beef. The dish can be made in a pressure cooker or slow, electric cooker.
Serves 4

12 oz (350 g) shin of beef
1 lb (450 g) kohlrabi
flour
salt and freshly ground black
    pepper
1 teaspoon paprika
1 onion

3 tablespoons vegetable oil
¼ pint (150 ml) dry white wine
½ pint (300 ml) stock
1 teaspoon mushroom or walnut
    ketchup
1½ tablespoons finely chopped
    parsley

Peel the kohlrabi and cut them into finger-thick sticks. Cut the beef into thin sticks about ¼ inch (¾ cm) thick. Coat the beef in flour seasoned with salt, pepper and paprika. Peel and chop the onion.

Heat the oil in a flameproof casserole. Add the onion and cook over a low heat until the onion is soft and transparent. Raise the heat, add the meat and cook over a high heat until the meat is browned on all sides. Add the wine and stock, stirring well to make sure all the sediment from the bottom of the pan is absorbed into the gravy. Mix in the kohlrabi and ketchup, bring to the boil, cover tightly and cook over a very low heat for about 1½ hours (stir every now and then to ensure that the ingredients are not sticking to the bottom of the dish) until the meat is really tender.

Adjust the seasoning, mix in the parsley just before serving, and serve the dish with boiled rice or puréed potatoes.

Leeks

One of the vegetables I have most respect for (especially at the end of winter when the choice is a bit thin) is the leek. I have never succeeded in growing enough of them for my needs. Leeks must surely be one of the most versatile of vegetables; their taste is far more subtle than that of onions, they are far more elegant in appearance, are virtually non-fattening and, as far as I am concerned, too delicious to relegate to the position of a mere accompaniment to a main course. The flavour of leeks is such that they can easily stand in their own right as hot or cold first courses, they form one of the best major ingredients for a nourishing winter soup and give a marvellous flavouring to a quiche or an old-fashioned covered pie.

The Egyptians were dedicated leek-eaters, the Romans were so conscious of their value that they almost certainly introduced the plant to England but, strangely enough, the leek has never, despite its long history, been all that popular in Britain. The Welsh, it is true, believe they are good for the voice and for some reason *wear* the plant in their buttonholes on St David's Day (a custom I have always found rather curious), but when it comes to eating the vegetable it is difficult to find more than a handful of recipes which make anything special of leeks. Once you have got cock-a-leekie soup out of the way or read how to smother the poor things in a tasteless white sauce, it is left to the French, Italians and Portuguese to bring out the merits of *Allium porrum* and to the Chinese and Japanese to cut them into thin slices and cook them extremely lightly in a combination of meat or fish and vegetables or to float them, almost raw, in delectable and delicate bowls of clear soup.

Leeks are easy to grow from seed, they need well-dug soil and some rich manuring, and it is worth getting the seedlings transplanted by about the beginning of June. Some seed catalogues actually suggest lifting and storing the plants in the late autumn but, unless you actually need the ground for winter vegetables, I find it is just as well to leave them where they are as you can then use them as required. They can be eaten from about the time they have reached an inch (2½ cm) in diameter (like so many vegetables they are usually left too long before being picked) and these mini leeks have a really wonderful texture and a very light flavour. If you like leeks as much as I do and the Egyptians did and you grow your own, it is well worth staggering the planting so that when they have grown you will be able to take your pick, finding exactly the right size for your requirements. Use the smaller thin leeks for serving cold or for slicing into salads and the larger ones for braising and stewing and for soups and pies.

One of the drawbacks of the leek is its capacity to retain dirt and grit within its tightly furled leaves when it is lifted from the ground. Don't be tempted to massacre the stalk to remove the dirt (unless you want to slice the leeks anyway). There is an almost magic formula for removing any earth. Trim off the coarse outer leaves and the ragged ends at the top – don't remove all the green leaf from the top, as some people do, because these contain a lot of the flavour – then stand the leeks, green end down, in a jar or bowl of cold water for at least 2 hours; this will release all the dirt and a quick final wash in more cold water should result in clean, grit-free vegetables.

Leeks also retain a lot of water when they are boiled, so avoid this by draining them, green end down, in a colander for at least 10 minutes after they have been cooked.

Take care not to overcook your leeks. The length of time you cook them obviously depends on the thickness of the stalks but check them every now and then with a carving fork and remove them from the heat as soon as the leeks reach a point of acceptable tenderness – as with all vegetables I like my leeks to retain just a touch of crispness to them.

Devon Winter Soup

Just as good today as it was when a man came home from a dark rainy night after beating the tax on a barrel or two of rum and brandy. This is my version.
Serves 6

3 *leeks*
1 *large onion*
2 *carrots*
½ *lb (225 g) peeled potatoes*
2 *oz (50 g) butter or chicken fat*
2½ *pints (1500 ml) chicken stock*

salt and white pepper
1 *bunch parsley*
¼ *pint (150 ml) milk*
¼ *pint (150 ml) double cream*
pinch paprika

Clean and chop the leeks, removing most of the dark-green part. Peel and chop the onion and carrots. Roughly chop the peeled potatoes.

Melt the butter in a large heavy pan. Add the leeks, onion, carrot and potato and cook over a low heat, stirring to prevent sticking, until the leeks and onions are soft and transparent and all the butter is absorbed. Add the stock and mix well. Bring to the boil, season with salt and pepper and simmer, covered, for 20 minutes or until the vegetables are soft. Purée the soup through a sieve, a fine good mill or in an electric liquidizer and return to a clean pan.

Remove the stalks of the parsley (use the stalks for the stock pot) and very finely chop the leaves. Add the parsley to the soup with the milk, heat through and blend in the cream. Heat without boiling and serve at once with a pinch of paprika on top.

Note: Enrich the soup by adding ½ inch (1½ cm) cubes of cooked mackerel, some crab meat, a few prawns or some mussels.

Pork and Vegetable Soup

Another of those quickly made but very delicious and sustaining meat and vegetable soups which makes an excellent starter for a late autumn or winter meal. You can use cabbage instead of the spinach but the important ingredient in this soup is the pork, which should be cooked just enough to be tender but should not be allowed to overcook and therefore toughen.
Serves 6

8 oz (225 g) lean pork	8 oz (225 g) spinach
4 leeks	2 carrots
3 oz (75 g) firm button	1 inch (2½ cm) green ginger root
mushrooms	2½ pints (1500 ml) chicken stock

Cut the pork into very thin matchstick strips. Clean the leeks and slice them very thinly. Very thinly slice the mushrooms. Chop the spinach. Peel the carrots and cut into very, very thin slices. Peel and grate the ginger root.

Bring the stock to the boil and add the carrots and mushrooms. Cook over a low heat until the soup returns to the boil. Add the pork and cook over a medium heat for 5 minutes. Add the spinach and leeks and continue to cook for a further 5 minutes or until the meat is tender. Divide between six bowls and sprinkle with a little grated raw ginger before serving.

Crab with Leeks

An excellent hot-weather first course similar to the Continental way of doing leeks in a vinaigrette sauce but with the added bonus of white crab meat mixed with mayonnaise.
Serves 4

4 oz (100 g) white crab meat	salt and freshly ground black
8 young leeks	pepper
3 tablespoons olive oil	2 hard-boiled eggs
1 tablespoon lemon juice	½ pint (300 ml) mayonnaise
½ teaspoon made English mustard	

Clean the leeks and cook them in boiling salted water until just tender. Drain well and leave standing upside down in a colander for 15 minutes. Arrange the leeks on a shallow serving dish.

Combine the olive oil with the lemon juice and mustard in a screw-topped jar. Season with salt and pepper and shake to mix well. Pour the dressing over the leeks and chill for 1 hour in a refrigerator.

Separate the egg yolks from the whites and chop the white part. Add the egg white and the crab meat to the mayonnaise and mix lightly. Pile the mayonnaise mixture on top of the chilled leeks and garnish with the egg yolks rubbed through a coarse sieve.

Serve with slices of buttered brown bread or with hot French bread.

Scallops with Leeks in a Rich Sauce

Scallops, leeks and bacon: what better combination could one wish for? This is a very superior dish indeed. You could serve it as a first course but I prefer it as the *pièce de résistance* of the meal with an accompaniment of miniature new potatoes and a salad of tomatoes, lightly cooked skinned broad beans, plenty of chopped parsley and a scattering of finely chopped raw onions. Serves 4

6–8 *good scallops*
6 *medium-sized leeks*
6 *oz (175 g) bacon*
1½ *oz (40 g) butter*
1 *tablespoon olive or vegetable oil*
¼ *pint (150 ml) dry white wine*

1 *tablespoon flour*
¼ *pint (150 ml) double cream*
2 *egg yolks*
salt and freshly ground black
  pepper
pinch of ground mace

Clean the leeks and cut them into ½ inch (1½ cm) thick slices. Remove the black vein from the scallops and separate the red coral from the white flesh. Cut the white flesh into thin slices. Remove the rinds from the bacon and cut the rashers into ½ inch (1½ cm) wide strips.

Heat the butter and oil in a heavy frying pan. Add the bacon and cook over a low heat until the bacon is tender. Add the leeks and continue to cook over a low heat until the leeks are soft. Add the white slices of scallop and cook gently for 2 minutes. Add the white wine and raise the heat so that the wine bubbles for 1 minute.

Beat the egg yolks with the cream until the mixture is smooth. Add the red coral to the scallops and leeks, sprinkle over the flour and stir lightly. Add the cream and egg mixture, season with salt, pepper and a pinch of mace and stir gently over a low heat until the sauce is thickened and smooth. Serve as soon as possible.

Quiche of Leeks and Chicken

A delicate and delicious quiche which can be served hot, warm or cold and which makes a useful picnic dish.
Serves 6

1 *partially baked* 10 *inch (25 cm) quiche case (see page 4)*
1½ *lb (675 g) leeks*
8 *oz (225 g) cooked chicken*
1 *onion*
2 *oz (50 g) butter*
3 *eggs*
½ *pint (300 ml) single cream*

2 *oz (50 g) Cheddar cheese, grated*
1 *oz (25 g) Parmesan cheese, grated*
salt and freshly ground black pepper
pinch ground nutmeg

Trim and thoroughly clean the leeks and cut them into thin slices. Cut the chicken into thin strips. Peel the onion, cut it into thin slices and divide it into rings. Melt the butter in a heavy frying pan, add the leeks and onion rings and cook over a very low heat, stirring to prevent sticking, until the leeks and onion are soft, tender and transparent.

Beat the eggs until smooth and mix in the cream and the Cheddar and Parmesan cheese. Season the custard with salt, pepper and nutmeg.

Arrange the leeks, onion and chicken in the quiche case, pour over the custard and bake in a moderate oven (350°F. 180°C. Reg. 4) for 30 minutes or until the filling is set and the top is golden.

Fish Pie with Leeks

A wonderful combination that is light but satisfying and which, depending on the quality of the fish you use, can be served at anything from the simplest of suppers to the most sophisticated of dinner parties.
Serves 5–6

1 *lb (450 g) white fish (cod, coley, pollock, haddock, brill etc.) or salmon*

4 *large leeks*
1 *small onion*
2 *bay leaves*

¾ *pint (450 ml) milk*
salt and freshly ground black
  pepper
4 *oz (105 g) butter*
2 *tablespoons flour*
1 *oz (25 g) Parmesan cheese*

3 *oz (75 g) Cheddar cheese*
2 *egg yolks*
pinch cayenne pepper
1½ *lb (675 g) potatoes*
2 *tablespoons double cream*

Clean and trim the leeks and cut them into ½ inch (1½ cm) thick slices. Peel and slice the onion. Place the fish in a shallow saucepan with the onion, bay leaves and milk, bring slowly to the boil and cook gently until the fish is tender. Drain off the liquid and discard the onion and bay leaves. Remove the skin and the bones from the fish and roughly flake the flesh.

Melt 1½ oz (40 g) butter in a heavy frying pan. Add the leeks and cook them, covered, over a low heat, stirring every now and then, until the leeks are tender and the butter has been absorbed.

Melt 2 oz (50 g) butter in a saucepan. Add the flour and mix well. Gradually add the milk in which the fish was cooked, stirring continually over a medium high heat until the sauce is thick and smooth. Add the Parmesan and Cheddar cheese and stir over a low heat until the cheese has melted. Add the egg yolks and beat until the sauce is satiny.

Add the leeks and fish to the sauce, season with cayenne, salt and pepper and mix lightly. Turn the mixture into a lightly greased pie dish.

Peel and roughly chop the potatoes and cook them in boiling salted water until just tender. Mash the potatoes until smooth, add the remaining ½ oz (15 g) butter and the cream and season with salt and pepper. Beat to a smooth purée and spread the mixture over the fish pie. Bake in a moderately hot oven (375°F. 190°C. Reg. 5) for about 20 minutes until the potato topping is golden and the pie is hot through.

Chicken, Ham and Leek Pie

Leek pies were once an everyday part of Cornish and French peasant life. Recipes vary but the basic ingredient of leeks remains the same, with their smooth texture and subtle taste producing a light and aromatic pie to be served as a main course.

In this recipe I combine the leeks with some leftover cooked chicken and some ham to make a dish that is just a little more substantial.
Serves 4

8 oz (225 g) cooked chicken
4 oz (100 g) cooked ham or
   bacon
8 oz (225 g) leeks
4 oz (100 g) butter
1 medium onion
1 teaspoon flour

¼ pint (150 ml) double cream
salt and freshly ground black
   pepper
pinch ground nutmeg
1 lb (900 g) frozen puff pastry
1 small egg, beaten

Peel and slice the onion. Clean and slice the leeks. Dice the chicken and ham or bacon.

Melt half the butter in a large frying pan. Add the onion and cook over a low heat until it is soft and transparent. Add the remaining butter and leeks and continue to cook over a low heat for 15 minutes until the leeks are soft and limp. Gently stir in the flour, cream, chicken and ham or bacon and season with salt, pepper and a pinch of ground nutmeg.

Roll out the pastry to ⅛ inch (½ cm) thickness and cut out of it two large circles. Place one circle on a greased baking sheet and spread the leek mixture over the pastry leaving about 1 inch (2½ cm) of pastry around the rim. Brush the rim with beaten egg and cover with the second circle of pastry. Press the edges firmly together, brush with beaten egg, flute the edges with the back of a fork and cut a slit in the centre of the pie.

Bake the pie in a hot oven (450°F. 230°C. Reg. 8) for 15 minutes then lower the heat to moderate (350°F. 180°C. Reg. 4) and continue to cook for a further 20 minutes.

Pork with Cider and Leeks

Serves 4

4 pork chops
2 cloves garlic
1 teaspoon fresh rosemary

salt and freshly ground black
   pepper
2 teaspoons English mustard

Leeks

PLATE 10

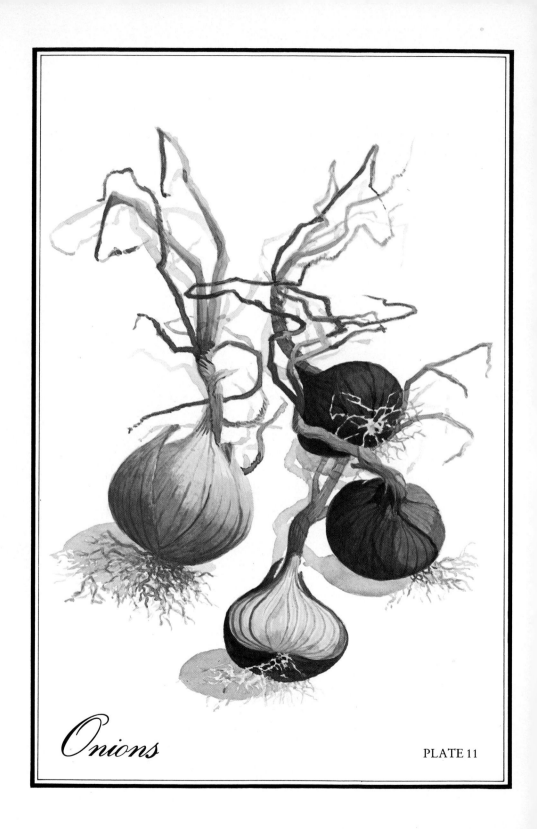

Onions

PLATE 11

$\frac{3}{4}$ lb (350 g) young leeks
$\frac{1}{2}$ pint (300 ml) dry cider
4 tablespoons double cream

2 oz (50 g) fresh breadcrumbs
1 oz (25 g) grated Cheddar
  cheese

Peel the garlic and crush the clovers with the rosemary and a generous seasoning of salt and pepper. Mix the mustard into the seasonings.

Remove any excess fat from the pork and chop the fat up finely. Rub the chops with the seasoning mixture on both sides. Put the pork fat in a heavy frying pan and cook over a medium high heat for 5 minutes until the fat has melted. Remove any remaining pieces of fat, add the chops and cook over a high heat until nicely browned on both sides. Arrange the chops in a fireproof baking dish.

Clean the leeks and cut them in half lengthwise. Arrange the leeks over the chops, pour over the cider and cream and top with the breadcrumbs and grated cheese. Cover with foil and bake in a moderate oven (350°F. 180°C. Reg. 4) for 1 hour. Remove the foil for the last 10 minutes of cooking time to brown the top.

Pork Chops Marinaded and Cooked with Potatoes and Leeks

This is an advance on the rather Provençal dish of chops cooked with potatoes. It makes an excellent dish for a cold winter's day and the combination of vegetables with the meat means that you can get away with having four small chops for four servings
Serves 4

4 pork chops
1 clove garlic
6 fl. oz (175 ml) white wine
2 tablespoons cider vinegar
2 bay leaves
1 stalk parsley
sprig each thyme and marjoram
4 crushed juniper berries
salt

freshly ground black pepper
4 rashers lean bacon
4 leeks
1$\frac{1}{2}$ lb (675 g) potatoes
1 shallot or small onion
1 tablespoon vegetable oil
2 tablespoons finely chopped
  parsley

F

Peel and finely chop the shallot and garlic. Combine the garlic, shallot, white wine, cider vinegar, herbs and juniper berries in a small saucepan, season with salt and pepper, bring to the boil, simmer for 5 minutes and then remove from the heat and leave to cool. Place the chops in a shallow dish, pour over the marinade and leave the chops to marinade in a refrigerator for 24 hours, turning them when you think about it.

Strain off the marinade and scrape the herbs off the chops. Remove the rinds from the bacon.

Peel and thinly slice the potatoes. Clean and slice the leeks. Arrange half the potatoes and half the leeks in a shallow baking dish.

Heat the vegetable oil in a heavy frying pan, add the chops and cook them very quickly over a high heat until they are browned on both sides. Drain off all excess fat and arrange the chops on top of the vegetables. Cover with the remaining vegetables, pour over the strained marinade and top with the bacon. Cover tightly with a double layer of foil and bake in a slow oven (275°F. 140°C. Reg. 1) for about 2½ hours.

Remove the foil, carefully spoon off as much of the fat from the vegetables as you can and scatter over the parsley.

This dish doesn't require any extra vegetables but I like to follow it with a separate course of a crisp salad to counteract the richness of the pork.

Lettuce

I always find myself in a spot when asked to recommend varieties of lettuce for growing in the garden or, for that matter, for buying in the shops. The trouble is I change my own mind so frequently on this matter. Sometimes I have an orgy of using those crisp 'Iceberg' type lettuce that crackle as you crunch them; for periods I favour the slightly bitter 'Webb's Wonder' or 'Batavia'; I have bursts of enthusiasm for the long-leaved 'Cos' and often yearn for the sweet, tender leaves of 'lamb's lettuce'. At last I have solved those problems by growing a small quantity of a number of different varieties in the garden at the same time and my idea of the perfect green salad has now emerged as a combination of no less than three different types of lettuce, shredded and combined with a little shredded seakale beet or spinach leaves and a little shredded sorrel, dressed with a slightly sharp vinaigrette to which some finely chopped chives have been added.

Lettuces have a long history although no one seems to know exactly where the practice of eating them originated. They figure strongly in the mythological world and when Adonis was killed by a boar, Aphrodite was said to have laid him on a bed of lettuce leaves like some weird and wonderful salad ingredient. The Romans, those great gourmets, ate cooked lettuce with eggs to whet their appetites before really getting stuck into a meal and for the Hebrews lettuces became an important feature of their annual dish of Paschal lamb. The milky juice from the lettuce stalk was purported to be sucked by dragons to soothe their over-excited nerves in the spring and it has always been suggested that this juice had narcotic properties – remember the effect it had on the rabbits in Beatrix Potter's *The Tale of the Flopsy Bunnies*? They all went to sleep after eating lettuce, and even Mrs Beeton regarded it as a vegetable 'conducive to repose ... a cooling summer vegetable, not very nutritive but serving as a corrective, or diluent of animal food'.

As every gardener knows, the trouble about growing lettuces is that they all come at once. One day you are still waiting for the hearts to swell and the leaves to crisp up and the next moment you are inundated with more plants than you can possibly cope with. This is the moment to cook with lettuce, producing a number of really delicious dishes that have a subtle and unusual flavouring. The leaves can be used as a casing for stuffed ingredients, they are delicious braised and they make an excellent light, summer soup. Thinly shredded lettuce leaves make an attractive garnish for cold foods and the leaves are a good background for many cold first courses.

Wash lettuces as little as possible, dry them carefully and gently and store the cleaned lettuce in a polythene bag in the bottom of the refrigerator. Limp lettuce can be refreshed by being plunged into cold water to which a lump of coal has been added. I don't know why this works but the effect can be almost miraculous.

Lettuces made their appearance on the British eating scene in about the fourteenth century but those grown in country gardens were, in the beginning, considered to be fare for the poor rather than the aristocracy. Catherine Parr (Henry VIII's wife) sent to Holland for any lettuce she required and it is only in the last fifty years, when slimming has for some people become a compulsive part of British life, that the lettuce has really gained the favour it deserves. Now I would like to see it used more as a vegetable instead of just a salad ingredient as it has a lot to contribute to modern-day cooking.

Scallops, Bacon and Lettuce with a Whipped Cream Topping

Scallops go well with bacon, bacon goes well with lettuce, so if you combine all three the chances are you must come up with something good. This is a really lovely dish and one that I find ever popular as a first course for the dinner parties I give at home. It is quick to make and light enough not to take the edge off one's appetite for the rest of a leisurely meal.

The secret of this particular recipe lies in whipping the cream with egg yolks, floating this mixture over the top of the scallops and their partner ingredients and then quickly browning the result under a hot grill.

Serves 6

12 scallops
6 oz (175 g) thinly cut streaky bacon with the rinds removed
1 large or 2 small lettuces
1 onion or 2 shallots
2 oz (50 g) butter
1 tablespoon vegetable oil

salt and freshly ground black pepper
2½ fl. oz (75 ml) dry white wine
½ pint (300 ml) double cream
2 egg yolks
cayenne pepper

Remove the coral from the scallops and set them to one side. Remove and discard any black vein from around the shellfish. Cut the scallops in half horizontally.

Cut the streaky bacon into very thin strips. Wash, dry and finely shred the lettuce. Peel and very finely chop the onion or shallot.

Heat the butter and oil in a large, heavy frying pan. Add the onion and cook over a low heat, stirring every now and then to prevent sticking, until the onion is soft and transparent. Add the main body of the scallops and cook over a medium heat until the scallops lose their opaque look. Add the corals and cook for a further 2 minutes. Mix in the lettuce, stir over the heat for 2 minutes until the lettuce has softened, season with salt and pepper and mix in the wine. Bring to the boil, continue to boil over the heat for 1 minute and remove from the heat. Keep the scallops mixture warm.

Beat the cream until it begins to thicken. Add the egg yolks and continue to beat until the cream and egg yolks are stiff and light.

Divide the scallop mixture between six shallow dishes. Top with the whipped cream mixture, sprinkle with a little cayenne pepper and grill under a hot flame until the top forms a golden-brown crust.

Serve at once with hot French bread and butter.

Place the lettuces in a shallow casserole dish and spread the peas over them. Spread the meat and onion over the peas and pour over the liquid from the pan. Add the crushed juniper berries and bay leaves, cover tightly with a double thickness of foil and braise in a moderate oven (350°F. 180°C. Reg. 4) for 1½ hours or until the meat is tender. Taste for seasoning before serving and remove the bay leaves.

A Curry of Minced Beef and Lettuce

Minced beef (*kheema*) and lettuce curries are very popular in the East and this is an excellent way of using lettuces when they all come at once and it is quite impossible to eat them all in salads. Serves 4

1 *lb (450 g) minced stewing beef*	3 *tablespoons vegetable oil*
2 *cos or cabbage lettuces*	1 *tablespoon tomato purée*
2 *onions*	1 *tablespoon ground coriander*
3 *cloves garlic*	1 *teaspoon each ground turmeric,*
1 *inch (2½ cm) fresh ginger root*	*cumin, chilli and garam masala*
12 *oz (350 g) tomatoes (or use*	*salt*
tinned tomatoes)	

Peel and finely chop the onions. Peel and very finely chop the garlic and ginger. Cover the tomatoes with boiling water for 2 minutes, drain and slide off the skins. Remove the core and seeds from the tomatoes and chop the flesh (or chop the tinned tomatoes). Wash, dry and roughly chop the lettuces.

Heat the oil in a heavy frying pan. Add the onions, garlic and ginger and cook over a low heat, stirring, until the onions are soft and transparent. Raise the heat, add the meat, and stir until the meat is browned on all sides. Add the tomatoes, tomato purée and spices and cook, stirring occasionally over a medium heat, for 10 minutes. Add the lettuce, season with salt, and cook over a low heat, stirring now and then until the meat is tender – this will take between about 30 and 40 minutes depending on the quality of the meat. The curry should be slightly on the dry side and should not be cooked with a lid on.

Serve it with rice and curry accompaniments. The dish is even more delicious if you mix in some yoghurt and chopped mint at the last minute before serving.

A Summer Casserole with Chicken and Bacon

Lettuce added to this casserole gives it a light and summery texture and the ingredients are layered so that the flavour of the chicken and bacon impregnates the vegetables.

Serves 4

6 oz (175 g) raw chicken
6 oz (175 g) lean bacon
1½ lb (675 g) new potatoes
3 onions
1 large cabbage lettuce

2 oz (50 g) butter
salt and freshly ground black pepper
6 tablespoons good stock
1 teaspoon lemon juice

Peel and thinly slice the potatoes. Peel and thinly slice the onions. Shred the lettuce. Coarsely mince or finely chop the bacon and chicken.

Melt 1½ oz (35 g) butter in a saucepan, add the onions and cook over a low heat until they are soft and transparent.

Butter a shallow casserole dish. Arrange half the potatoes in the bottom of the dish, cover with half the lettuce and half the onions and then spread over the combined chicken and bacon. Season with salt and pepper. Top with the remaining lettuce, onions and then with the potatoes, arranging them in a neat overlapping layer. Pour over the stock mixed with the lemon juice and dot with the remaining butter cut into very small pieces. Cover the dish tightly with foil and bake in a moderate oven (350°F. 180°C. Reg. 4) for 30 minutes. Remove the foil and continue to bake for a further 20 minutes until the potatoes are brown and the ingredients are tender.

Lettuce Leaves Stuffed with a Ham Filling

Another delicate and unusual dish with a flavouring of lemon and of green peppercorns.

Serves 4

8 oz (225 g) ham
8 outside leaves from cos lettuces
1 medium onion
finely grated rind of ½ lemon
2 thick slices of white bread

2 eggs
1 teaspoon green peppercorns
salt
¼ pint (150 ml) chicken stock
¼ pint (150 ml) double cream

Mince the ham. Peel and mince the onion. Remove the crusts from the bread, soften the bread in a little warm water and squeeze out excess water. Beat the eggs. Crush the peppercorns with a fork. Wash 8 large cos lettuce leaves and blanch them in boiling water for 3 minutes. Drain the leaves well and pat them dry on kitchen paper.

Combine the ham, onion, bread, lemon rind, eggs and peppercorns and mix them until smooth. Season with a little salt and divide the stuffing between the lettuce leaves. Roll up the leaves into neat parcels so that the filling is entirely enclosed and place the rolls in a shallow, lightly buttered baking dish. Pour over the stock, cover tightly with foil and bake in a moderate oven (350°F. 180°C. Reg. 4) for 45 minutes. Remove the lettuce parcels and place them on a heated serving dish. Add the cream to the cooking liquid, test for seasoning and pour the sauce over the leaves.

Onions

There is so much to say about the family of *Allium cepa* (onions) that it is difficult to know quite where to start but it must certainly be true to say that unless you 'know your onions' you have no possible chance of coming anywhere near to making a good cook. In some form or another one of the many members of this pungent vegetable family plays an important role in a vast number of everyday and haute cuisine dishes. Onions themselves provide a lubricating ingredient and give flavour to almost any meat, poultry or fish dish; garlic is both a tenderizer and the magic ingredient of some of the best food in the world; leeks give a smooth texture and a milder flavour to soups, casseroles and a number of dishes where they form the basic ingredient; shallots are a must in many classic sauces and marinades, and spring onions, chives and Welsh onions are invaluable as a salad ingredient and garnishing material.

Although they have no great food value, onions have always rated extremely highly in the culinary world. They also have a medicinal quality that is still being researched and, in the case of garlic especially, supposed magical properties. The herbalist Culpeper thought a lot of the onion family and made it sound like a 'cure all'. 'The onion itself', he said, 'did provoke appetite, increase thirst, ease the bowels, help the bites of mad dogs, increase sperm and kill worms in children.' Of garlic he reported, 'It performs almost miracles in phlegmatic habits of body. It wonderfully opens the lungs and gives relief in asthmas' and of leeks, 'when being applied warm, help the piles.'

There is some confusion as to where onions actually originated as they were certainly in fairly wide usage before any records were ever kept. The Babylonians thought them a symbol of perfection (a circle around which one can travel for eternity), the Egyptians worshipped them and buried bunches of onions with their mummies. By the beginning of the Christian era onions had reached a height of such sanctity that the people were forbidden to eat them. Like so many other vegetables onions were also thought to have aphrodisiac qualities (a belief supported by Alexander the Great who put great faith in their powers and in parts of India where women are forbidden to prepare the vegetables as it is thought their powers might encourage them towards infidelity).

In the kitchen garden onions play a great part and in the smaller garden they can be planted in the borders to help encourage other plants and keep them free from pests. They are particularly helpful in a rose bed. With careful planning it is possible to produce one form or another of the onion to be harvested all the year round, with the small spring onions coming first and the leeks and Welsh onions carrying on through the winter months. Providing weather conditions are reasonably favourable both shallots and onions are easily dried for storage and their flavour actually intensifies during the winter months.

When you are cooking with any of the members of the onion family remember that much of the flavour lies in the outer leaves, so use these to flavour soups and stock. The outer, brown, skin of a dried onion is invaluable in both flavouring and colouring stock, giving it a rich golden colour, and the trimmed leaves of leeks also add a delicious flavouring to chicken stock.

Garlic also increases in taste when it is dried so if you grow it yourself you will find you can use the freshly picked, mild and delicious cloves with a surprisingly lavish hand.

Onions

Centuries ago it was usual for onions to be eaten raw and they formed an important feature in a peasant diet when they were eaten on bread with cheese, tomatoes or merely a sprinkling of coarse olive oil. These onions, however, probably had a more mild flavour than most grown today and it is worth growing some red and yellow onions for the purpose of serving them raw as both a garnish and flavouring ingredient for cold dishes and salads. Both varieties are easy to grow.

As they are biennials most onions these days are grown from sets and although these are obviously more expensive to buy than the seeds, they do save space, and providing you can grow enough for your use throughout the year they certainly represent a considerable saving as onions, like all other vegetables, are no longer the cheap commodity they once were. For good value look out for 'Giant Zittau' for winter storage, 'Autumn Spice' for an early crop, Suttons 'Long-keeping' for a good red variety and Suttons 'Solidity' for an onion that is highly resistant to bolting.

The success of storing onions depends to a great extent on the conditions when they were harvested. They must be left in the ground until their tops have yellowed and died back and lifted when the weather is fine enough to allow them to be laid out and dried in the sun. Onions that have bolted should be used at once with the central, hard, core removed and if it should happen to be a year in which this happens to a large part of your crop, you can chop up the best of the flesh and store it in the deep freeze.

Shallots

Shallots produce clusters of bulbs in the same way as garlic and, in a good year, they can be very prolific indeed. Their flavour is stronger and slightly sharper than that of onions and this is why they are used so much for the making of many sauces. Like onions they are usually grown from sets rather than seeds and they are dried in the same way. On the whole I have found them more reliable to dry than onions providing that you take care to separate the bulbs before laying them out on racks or stringing them up.

Spring Onions

The most popular of these is the 'White Lisbon' variety and for a regular supply they should be planted at monthly intervals providing either the thin pullings popular for salads or, if left to mature, the larger white bulb which can be pickled or used whole in stews and casseroles. They grow easily and the tops can be substituted for chives if these are not available. Whole spring onions play a great part in Far Eastern cookery; usually they are cut into lengthwise strips and added for the last few minutes of cooking time so that they impart flavouring to a dish but still preserve their fresh green colouring. Spring onions are also known as 'Scallions' or 'Chipples'.

Welsh Onions

I find these a most useful addition to the garden since they continue to grow throughout the winter, providing thick pickings which are similar to spring onions and which can be used like chives. They are a perennial plant and can be increased by division and replanting in the spring or autumn and, if you are cramped for space, they look attractive in a rock garden.

Chives

Chives are mainly used as a garnishing for both hot and cold dishes although in some classic recipes such as Vichyssoise soup they do constitute an important flavouring ingredient in their own right. Again chives are easy to grow (although they are a perennial it is worth bringing on new clumps each year as in my experience they tend to decrease in size if left in the same ground for too long) and as they don't take up much room they can be grown in pots or window boxes. The more you snip off the tops with scissors the more vigorous will be their growth during the summer months and they make an excellent addition to almost any salad dish. Finely chopped chives also freeze well.

Garlic

Single cloves of garlic should be planted in rows about 15 inches apart with some 6 inches in between each clove. They grow well in a reasonable summer and provide a great saving if, like me, you rely heavily on their flavour to impart an interest to a wide variety of dishes. Plant the cloves in the autumn or very early spring and harvest the bulbs in late July or early August. Dry them in the same way as shallots but do not divide up the cloves. Use the fresh bulbs soon after they have been lifted.

Chicken and Spring Onion Soup with Mushrooms

Soups, to my way of thinking, divide into three categories: there are the cold, fresh soups of summer which should be served in ice-cold glass bowls; the rich, aromatic and hearty soups of winter which restore both one's sense of humour and one's vigour after a hard day's work in cold weather; and the light sophisticated soups that fall outside both these groups. This recipe is of the third group; it is light, subtle and an excellent starter to a good evening meal. Its origins are Japanese, it is quick to make and I think very good indeed to sup. Serves 4

8 oz (225 g) raw chicken
6 spring onions
2 oz (50 g) firm button mushrooms

1¼ pints (750 ml) good chicken stock
1 inch (2½ cm) fresh ginger root

Cut the meat into very thin matchstick strips. Remove the outer leaves of the spring onions and slice them very thinly. Very thinly slice the button mushrooms.

Heat ¼ pint (150 ml) of the chicken stock to boiling point. Add the chicken and cook over a medium high heat for about 2 minutes or until the chicken is *just* tender. Strain the chicken and add the stock to the remaining chicken stock.

Divide the cooked chicken, spring onions and mushrooms between four heated serving bowls. Heat the stock to boiling point. Squeeze the peeled ginger root through a garlic press to extract the juice. Add the ginger juice to the stock and pour the boiling liquid over the ingredients in the bowls. Serve at once.

Chipples (Spring Onions) with Egg Sauce

A tasty and simply made inexpensive first course which, despite its simplicity, is very good indeed.
Serves 4

1 *bunch spring onions*	*salt and freshly ground black*
3 *hard-boiled eggs*	*pepper*
2 *ripe romatoes*	*butter*
1½ *oz (40 g) butter*	4 *slices toasted brown bread*
2 *tablespoons flour*	*few drops Worcestershire sauce*
½ *pint (300 ml) milk*	

Trim the spring onions and divide each one in half lengthwise. Chop the hard-boiled eggs. Slice the tomatoes.

Melt the butter in a small saucepan. Add the flour and mix well. Gradually blend in the milk, stirring continually over a medium high heat until the sauce comes to the boil and is thick and smooth. Season with salt and pepper, simmer for 3 minutes and then lightly fold in the chopped eggs.

Butter the toast and arrange slices of tomato on the toast. Top with the spring onions and sprinkle with a drop or two of Worcestershire sauce. Pour over the egg sauce and serve at once.

New Potatoes, Chipples, Parsley and Cream

A delicious way to serve new potatoes with cold meat or a simple dish like grilled lamb chops.
Serves 4

12 *oz (350 g) peeled and cooked*	*salt and freshly ground black*
new potatoes	*pepper*
8 *spring onions*	2 *tablespoons finely chopped*
1 *oz (25 g) butter*	*parsley*
4 *tablespoons single cream*	

Cut the cooked potatoes into small dice. Chop the spring onions. Heat the butter in a frying pan, add the spring onions and cook over a low heat until transparent. Add the potatoes and continue to cook, shaking the pan to prevent sticking, until the potatoes are golden brown on all sides.

Add the cream, season with salt and pepper and heat through. Stir in the finely chopped parsley and serve at once.

Cockle and Onion Pie

This makes an inexpensive supper dish.
Serves 4

8 oz (225 g) fresh cockles
1 large onion
1 oz (25 g) butter
2 tablespoons flour
¾ pint (450 ml) milk
2 tablespoons finely chopped
    parsley

salt and freshly ground black
    pepper
1 lb (450 g) cooked potatoes
3 tablespoons double cream
2 oz (50 g) grated Cheddar
    cheese

Peel and chop the onion. Melt the butter in a saucepan. Add the onion and cook over a low heat until the onion is soft and transparent. Add the flour and mix well. Gradually add the milk, stirring continually over a medium high heat until the sauce comes to the boil and is thick and smooth. Add the cockles and parsley and season with pepper. Put in a shallow baking dish.

Mash the potatoes with the cream until smooth. Season with salt and pepper and spread over the cockle mixture. Sprinkle over the cheese and bake in a moderately hot oven (400°F. 200°C. Reg. 6) for about 15 minutes until the dish is hot through and the top is golden brown.

Gratin of Potatoes, Onion and Fish

I suppose you could call this a rather sophisticated version of a fish pie—whatever its name it is very good indeed, with the flavour of the fish impregnating the potatoes and the end result being an aromatic and warming main course. The fish you use should be of the firm, white-fleshed variety; choose coley, cod, huss, pollock or any other firm-fleshed fish.
Serves 4

1 lb (450 g) firm-fleshed white
    fish
1 large onion
1 lb (450 g) potatoes
8 anchovy fillets
1 oz (25 g) butter
3 eggs

½ pint (300 ml) single cream
salt and freshly ground black
    pepper
1½ oz (40 g) grated Gruyère
    cheese
1 tablespoon of oil from the
    anchovies

Fillet the fish, if necessary, and cut it into thin slices. Peel and finely chop the onion. Peel and thinly slice the potatoes. Cut each anchovy in half lengthwise. Heat the butter in a frying pan, add the onion and cook over a low heat, stirring to prevent sticking, until the onion is soft and transparent. Drop the slices of potato into fast-boiling, salted water and cook for 6 minutes. Drain well.

Butter a baking dish. Spread half the potato slices in the bottom of the dish and cover with half the onions. Top with the slices of fish and the anchovy fillets and then finish with the remaining onions and potato slices.

Beat the eggs with the cream until smooth and season with salt and pepper. Pour the custard over the casserole and shake the casserole so that the liquid seeps through the dish. Sprinkle over the cheese and dribble over the anchovy oil.

Bake the dish for 30 minutes in a moderately hot oven (375°F. 190°C. Reg. 5).

Serve the dish with a green vegetable and a tomato salad or grilled tomatoes.

Onion and Caper Sauce

Serve this with roast or boiled lamb, with roast chicken or with plainly cooked fish. The sauce has a delicious flavour and makes a good addition to a rather plain main course.
Serves 4

1 *large onion*	1½ *tablespoons flour*
1½ *tablespoons capers*	¼ *pint (150 ml) chicken stock*
2 oz (50 g) butter	¼ *pint (150 ml) double cream*
¼ *pint (150 ml) dry white wine*	*salt and white pepper*

Peel and finely chop the onion. Finely chop the capers. Melt the butter in a small saucepan. Add the onion and cook over a low heat, stirring every now and then, for 10 minutes. Add the wine, cover tightly and continue to cook for a further 10 minutes until the onion is almost softened to a purée. Add the flour and mix well. Gradually blend in the stock, stirring continually until the sauce comes to the boil and is thick and smooth. Add the capers, season with salt and pepper and mix in the cream. Do not boil the sauce once the cream has been added.

Temptation

This recipe is based on a Swedish dish of potatoes, onions and anchovies that goes under the name of Johnnson's Temptation. All I have done is to add some ham and hard-boiled eggs, making this delicious concoction into a substantial main course. Although the ingredients, and the dish itself, are simple, I think it is worthy of more than just supper fare and I often produce it at a Saturday night dinner party at home.

If the potatoes are new they should be parboiled to prevent them going brown.

Serves 5–6

8 oz (225 g) lean ham

3 hard-boiled eggs

5 large potatoes

2 large onions

1 tin anchovy fillets

oil from the tin of anchovies

2 oz (50 g) butter

½ pint (300 ml) single cream

freshly ground black pepper

Peel the potatoes and cut them into slices and then into thin matchstick strips. Peel and finely chop the onions. Cut the anchovies into half lengthwise. Cut the ham into thin slices and then into thin matchstick strips. Chop the hard-boiled eggs reserving one of the egg yolks.

Place half the potatoes in a lightly buttered, shallow baking dish and cover with half the onions. Top with the ham, sprinkle with the chopped hard-boiled eggs and then with the anchovies placed in a criss-cross pattern over the ham. Season with a little pepper and finish off with the remaining onions and then the potatoes. Pour over half the cream and the oil from the anchovies and dot with small pieces of butter. Bake the dish in a hot oven (425°F. 220°C. Reg. 7) for about 20 minutes or until the top of the potatoes is a golden brown. Pour over the remaining cream and continue to cook for a further 20 minutes or until the potatoes are tender throughout and crisp on the top.

Rub the reserved egg yolk through a coarse sieve and sprinkle the yolk over the dish just before serving.

Serve with a green vegetable.

Chicken and Ham with Shallots in a Golden Sauce

This is a delicious way of making a chicken stretch really well for a special party dish. The chicken is boiled and left to cool before being cut up and the rich stock it was cooked in is used to make the sauce. The dish does require advance preparation but the effort is well worth while.

Serves 8

1 *roasting or boiling chicken*	2 *egg yolks*
2 *oz (50 g) cooked ham*	3 *tablespoons single cream*
1 *lemon*	1 *tin lychees*
2 *onions*	24 *small shallots*
1 *carrot*	2 *oz (50 g) butter*
1 *large sprig parsley*	2 *tablespoons flour*
1½ *chicken stock cubes*	1 *teaspoon finely chopped tarragon*
1 *sprig tarragon*	2 *tablespoons dry sherry*
4 *bay leaves*	
salt and freshly ground black	
pepper	

Squeeze out and reserve the lemon juice. Quarter the onions. Clean and roughly chop the carrot. Place the chicken with the giblets in a saucepan. Add the lemon halves, onions, carrot, parsley, stock cubes, tarragon and bay leaves. Cover with cold water, season with pepper, bring to the boil, cover, and simmer slowly for about 1½ hours or until the chicken is almost but not quite tender. Remove from the heat and leave the chicken in the stock for 15 minutes. Remove the chicken and leave it to cool. Return the stock to the stove and boil to reduce it for 20 minutes. Strain the stock and leave it until cool and then chill in the refrigerator until the fat has formed a skin over the surface and can easily be removed.

Remove the meat from the chicken and cut it into strips about ½ inch (1½ cm) thick. Cut the ham into thin matchstick strips. Beat together the egg yolks and cream. Drain off the syrup from the lychees. Peel the shallots.

Heat the butter in a heavy saucepan, add the shallots and cook over a low heat, stirring every now and then to prevent burning, until the shallots are soft. Add the flour and mix well. Gradually blend in ¾ pint (450 ml) of the chicken stock and stir over a medium heat until the sauce is thick and smooth. Add the teaspoon of chopped tarragon, 1 tablespoon of the reserved lemon juice and the sherry, season with salt and pepper and simmer for 3 minutes. Lower the heat, beat in the cream and egg yolks and stir until the sauce has thickened slightly and is satiny. Add the chicken, ham and lychees and heat over a low flame until the meat is hot through.

Serve the chicken in a ring of fluffy boiled rice.

Duck with Onions, Red Peppers and Dubonnet

Another recipe which gives one the advantage of using the meat in a most economical way as well as providing the duck carcass for one of the best stocks of all.
Serves 6–8

1 *small duck*	$\frac{1}{2}$ *pint (300 ml) good chicken or*
2 *onions*	*duck stock*
2 *large red peppers*	1 *tablespoon cornflour*
2 *large sticks of celery*	$\frac{1}{4}$ *pint (150 ml) Dubonnet*
2 *cloves of garlic*	1 *tablespoon soy sauce*
1 *inch (2$\frac{1}{2}$ cm) fresh ginger root*	*salt and freshly ground black*
3 *tablespoons oil*	*pepper*

Peel the onions, cut them into thin slices and divide into rings. Remove the core and seeds of the peppers and cut the flesh into thin strips. Remove any tough strings from the celery and cut the stalks into very thin slices. Peel the garlic and crush the flesh. Peel the ginger root and cut the flesh into very thin strips.

Remove the skin from the duck (this can be cut into thin strips and fried in a little very hot oil over a high heat until it is crisp and golden, drained well on kitchen paper and then used as a garnish for the dish or served as a cocktail titbit). Cut the flesh of the duck into thin strips.

Heat the oil, add the onion, peppers and garlic and cook over a low heat for about 5 minutes until the onions are soft and transparent. Raise the heat, add the duck, and cook over a high heat, stirring now and then, until the duck is browned on all sides.

Add a little of the stock to the cornflour and mix to a smooth paste. Add the remaining stock, Dubonnet and soy sauce and mix well.

Pour the sauce over the duck and vegetables, season with salt and pepper and mix well, stirring over a medium heat until the sauce thickens and is glossy, and cooking for about 5 minutes until the duck is just tender.

Serve the duck in a ring of fluffy boiled rice.

Steak with Lots of Onions, an Orange Flavouring and White Cinzano

Serves 6

2 *lb (900 g) entrecôte or rump steak in one piece*
4 *large onions*
2½ *tablespoons olive or sunflower oil*
½ *oz (15 g) butter*
1 *tablespoon French Dijon mustard*

3 *tablespoons finely chopped parsley*
grated rind of 2 large oranges
8 *tablespoons white Cinzano*
salt and freshly ground black pepper

Cut the steak into 12 thin slices. Peel the onions, cut them into thin slices and divide them into rings. Heat a thin film of oil in a heavy frying pan, add the steaks two or three at a time, and brown them quickly on both sides over a high heat. Remove the steaks to a plate.

Add the remaining oil and butter to the juices in the pan, put in the onions and cook them over a low heat, stirring gently to prevent sticking, until they are soft and golden. Stir in the mustard, 2 tablespoons of the parsley, half the orange rind and all of the Cinzano, scraping the bottom of the pan with a wooden spoon to remove all the traces of meat. Bring the sauce to the boil, season with salt and pepper and mix well.

Remove half the onions with a slotted spoon and arrange them in a shallow baking dish, cover with the steaks and arrange the rest of the onions on top. Pour over the sauce, cover tightly with foil and bake in a moderate oven (375°F. 190°C. Reg. 5) for about 20 minutes until the meat is tender. Check seasoning, transfer carefully to a clean, heated serving dish and sprinkle over the remaining parsley and orange peel.

Serve with a green vegetable and rice or potatoes.

A Curry of Meat and Onions with Apricots and Almonds

The sweet and savoury combinations of the East are very evocative. In this dish inexpensive stewing steak is combined with plenty of onions and with dried apricots to give this special flavour and gently fried slivers of almonds give it an extra crunchy texture to finish.
Serves 4

1 lb (450 g) stewing steak
2 teaspoons saffron strands
3 large onions
2 cloves garlic
4 tablespoons vegetable oil
1 tablespoon hot curry paste (I use Elsenham's)

4 oz (100 g) dried apricots
$\frac{3}{4}$ pint (450 ml) yoghurt
$\frac{1}{4}$ pint (150 ml) good stock
salt
2 tablespoons slivered almonds
1 tablespoon finely chopped fresh mint

Cut the meat into cubes about 1 inch (2½ cm) square. Infuse the saffron in 2 tablespoons of warm water for 15 minutes. Peel and chop the onions. Peel and crush the garlic through a garlic press. Heat 3 tablespoons of oil in a large heavy frying pan. Add the onions and garlic and cook over a low heat, stirring every now and then, until the onions are soft and transparent. Add the curry paste, mix well and cook over a medium heat for 5 minutes. Raise the heat, mix in the meat and brown quickly on all sides. Add the apricots, yoghurt and stock, strain the saffron and add the liquid, cover and cook over a low heat for about 1¼ hours until the meat is really tender.

Heat 1 tablespoon oil in a saucepan. Add the almonds and cook them over a medium heat until they are crisp and golden.

Mix the mint into the curry, transfer to a serving dish and sprinkle over the almonds just before serving.

Serve with rice and curry accompaniments.

Pork and Onion Pies with Apple and Spring Onions

Good picnic food that makes a change from the inevitable quiches so often served at moveable feasts.

Makes 6 pies

12 oz (350 g) quiche pastry (see page 4)
10 oz (275 g) cold pork or cooked gammon
3 crisp eating apples
8 spring onions
2 hard-boiled eggs

1½ oz (40 g) butter
1 teaspoon finely chopped sage
salt and freshly ground black pepper
pinch of ground nutmeg
1 beaten egg

Roll out the pastry thinly, line 6 patty tins with the pastry and cut 6 smaller circles for lids. Chop the hard-boiled eggs. Very finely chop the pork or gammon. Trim and finely chop the spring onions. Peel and finely chop the apples. Combine the pork, eggs, apples and spring onions, add the sage, season with salt, pepper and nutmeg and mix well. Fill the cases with this mixture, dot with butter, damp the edges, put on the lids and press them firmly together. Make a slit in the centre and brush with beaten egg. Bake in a hot oven (400°F. 200°C. Reg. 6) for 30 minutes. Remove from the tins and leave to cool.

Peas of all kinds

I am a great believer in the 'do it yourself' attitude towards life, especially when it comes to growing your own vegetables. One thing that does fill me with amazement, however, is the trouble and time people will take to raise peas in vast quantities for the deep freeze. Why do so many spend so much of the summer podding, blanching, packing and freezing when, if you look at it cold-bloodedly, commercially frozen peas, picked and shelled by machines, are just as good as any you freeze yourself? Commercial peas, since they are harvested in such bulk, are very reasonable in price and, since they are frozen with a speed and at a temperature the domestic freezer cannot imitate, have a much longer shelf life than those that are home frozen.

Obviously if you happen to have a glut of peas on your hands, then there is a good argument for freezing the excess produce, but who actually wants to eat peas all the year round with every meal? The great joy about this late spring and early summer vegetable is the fresh taste and sunshine flavour; peas go with spring lamb and summer food and that is really where they belong.

The great joy of growing your own peas is, of course, that you can harvest them when they are really young, tender and sweet-fleshed and you can also enjoy a variety of flavours by growing different species of the pea family. All of them are relatively easy to grow providing they have a good loamy soil which has been well manured in the autumn or early winter.

Garden Peas

These were brought to England in the first place by the Romans but they were nearly always dried in those days and presented a rather dreary fare for the British peasant. Then the notion of eating fresh peas spread to this country from Europe and became so popular that, by the seventeenth century, they were a must at almost every upper-class meal during the summer months.

There are two basic varieties of the garden pea, with the round-seeded varieties being the hardier plant that is easier to bring on early and the wrinkled or marrowfat pea which has more flavour coming later in the season.

The secret of harvesting peas is to do the job regularly, every day if possible, and to pick them from the bottom of the plant upwards. Once all the peas have been picked, the vines are hoed back into the ground providing valuable nitrogen material for the soil. You don't, by the way, need to go to the trouble of gathering pea sticks from the hedgerows, the vines will grow perfectly well without support although they will be a little more arduous to pick.

Asparagus Peas

It is a pity that these peas are seldom grown for the commercial market but, if you do have your own garden, it is well worth having a row to provide a really interesting and unusual vegetable. They are extremely pest-resistant and will grow well if they are planted in fairly light soil in a sunny position. The asparagus pea (although not a member of the pea family, as its name suggests) has a very similar flavour to asparagus and the mature pods are eaten in rather the same way, with the seeds and the soft flesh of the pods being sucked through the teeth. The pods are angular seeds which two hundred years ago were grown as a garden ornament rather than as a vegetable. Mature asparagus peas are delicious served with melted butter—I provide each guest with a small pot of melted butter and serve the peas as a first course.

The younger and more tender peas, picked before they are 1 inch (2½ cm) in length, make an excellent vegetable and can be eaten whole. The peas are cooked in boiling, salted water and care should be taken that they are not overcooked.

Petit Pois

This is the pea that is most popular on the Continent. The seeds are small and their flavour is remarkably sweet. They were a passion of Louis XIV of France, who showed himself to be almost grotesquely greedy when they appeared on his table. Nowadays in France they are excellent tinned (in fact they are one of the only vegetables, I feel, that does tin well).

A point that must be made, I think, when talking about petit pois is that they are *not*, as many people believe, merely peas picked when they are very small. Petit pois are a small variety of pea in their own right (amongst which is an excellent variety called 'Gullivert') and if left too long on the stalk they will remain small but be just as tough as larger peas. Cook petit pois in boiling salted water with a small shallot or a few spring onion bulbs.

Mange Tout or Snow Peas

Unlike asparagus peas, this variety of the pea family is gaining in popularity in this country. It has always been a much-favoured vegetable in the Far East and growing it makes great sense since the pod as well as the pea is eaten, making it a vegetable with a minimum of wastage, and I am delighted to see it appearing in many shops and in the food sections of Marks and Spencer's. Once again the golden rule for harvesting the snow pea is not to leave it to reach full maturity when it will become tough and stringy, and the golden rule for cooking the vegetable is to ensure that it is served while still retaining a certain amount of crunchiness.

Again this is an easy vegetable to grow with the pods being ready to harvest about two months after they have been sown, so it is well worth staggering your planting so that you have at least two, if not three, crops.

The taste of the mange tout or snow pea has a delicious freshness and their texture is very special indeed. They are ideal for quick cooking and for dishes with Chinese overtones.

Green Pea and Chervil Soup

A lovely soup to make when the first of the summer's peas come in and also equally good to make with frozen peas. The flavour of the chervil is fairly pronounced and the two tastes complement each other greatly. I use green peppercorns in this soup, excellent flavouring ingredients which can now be bought from good delicatessen shops.

Serves 6–8

1 lb (450 g) shelled peas
1 bunch chervil
1 medium onion
2 cloves garlic
2 tablespoons olive or vegetable oil

2½ pints (1500 ml) good chicken stock
1 tablespoon green peppercorns
1 teaspoon lemon juice
salt

Reserve some of the chervil leaves for garnish and cut off any tough stalks. Peel and finely chop the onion and garlic. Heat the oil in a heavy-bottomed saucepan. Add the onion and garlic and cook over a low heat until the onion is soft and transparent. Add the chervil and peas and cook over a low heat, stirring until all the oil has been absorbed. Add the stock, peppercorns and lemon juice, season with salt, bring to the boil and simmer for about 20 minutes or until the peas are really tender. Purée the soup through a food mill, in an electric blender or food processor. Return it to a clean pan, check seasoning and garnish with some finely chopped chervil leaves.

Note: You can add a little fresh or soured cream to the soup before serving.

Soup of Young Pea Tops

As the tops of broad beans can be used to make a delicious vegetable soup, so too do the tops of young pea plants make a delicious soup which tastes of tender young peas.

Serves 4

½ lb (225 g) 2 inch (5 cm) tops of pea plants
½ lb (225 g) spinach
½ oz (15 g) butter

1 tablespoon flour
2 pints (1200 ml) stock
salt and freshly ground black pepper

Boil the pea tops with the spinach until tender. Drain really well and purée through a sieve, in a food mill or liquidizer.

Melt the butter in a saucepan, add the flour and mix well. Gradually add the stock, stirring continually until the soup is thickened and smooth and simmer for 10 minutes. Add the vegetable purée, season with salt and pepper, bring to the boil and simmer for a further 10 minutes.

Note: A little cream and a pinch of ground nutmeg can be added before serving.

Soup of Young Pea Pods

Make this when the peas are just beginning to mature and are not much bigger than very small beads. The flavour is truly spring-like and, since you can use the pea pods, there is no wastage. You really need a good mill in order to purée and sieve the pods but this is a gadget well worth having in the kitchen anyway; they are not expensive and there is no electric machine on the market which will perform the service of puréeing and sieving, at the same time, with quite the same efficiency.
Serves 4

1 *lb (450 g) small peas in their*
  pods
3 *new potatoes*
1 *medium onion*
½ *oz (15 g) butter*
1 *tablespoon olive or vegetable oil*
2 *celery stalks*

2½ *pints (1500 ml) good*
  chicken stock
small bunch parsley
2 *sprigs mint*
salt and freshly ground black
  pepper
1 *tablespoon finely chopped mint*

Shell the pods reserving the miniature peas. Peel and roughly chop the potatoes. Roughly chop the celery stalks and leaves. Peel and chop the onion.

Heat the butter and oil together in a large heavy saucepan. Add the onion and cook over a low heat, stirring until the onion is soft and transparent. Add the potatoes, celery, pea pods, parsley and mint sprigs, pour over the stock, season with salt and pepper, bring to the boil, cover and cook over a medium high heat for about 45 minutes until the pea pods are really tender. Purée the soup through a food mill and return it to a clean saucepan. Bring the soup back to the boil, add the shelled peas and cook for 5 minutes (the peas should still be slightly crunchy when the soup is served). Add the chopped mint just before serving.

Pea Soup with a Tomato Aioli

Serves 6

1 *lb (450 g) peas (fresh or frozen)*
2 *onions*
4 *sticks celery*
2 *tablespoons olive oil*
¼ *teaspoon oregano*
4 *oz (100 g) mashed potatoes*

salt and freshly ground black pepper
2½ *pints (1500 ml) stock*
1 *shallot*
2 *cloves garlic*
2 *tablespoons tomato ketchup*
3 *tablespoons mayonnaise*

Peel and chop the onions. Chop the celery stalks including the leaves. Heat the oil in a large, heavy saucepan. Add the onions and celery and cook over a medium heat, stirring to prevent sticking, until the onions are soft and transparent. Add the peas and oregano, season with salt and pepper, cover tightly and simmer for about 20 minutes or until the vegetables are all completely soft. Add the mashed potato and purée the vegetables through a fine food mill, in an electric blender or food processor. Put the purée into a clean saucepan, add the stock and bring to the boil stirring well.

Very finely chop or mince the shallot. Peel and crush the garlic. Add the shallot and garlic to the mayonnaise with the tomato ketchup, season if necessary and mix well.

Pour the soup into serving bowls and float a spoonful of the tomato aioli on top of each serving.

Very Special Pancakes with a Purée of Peas and Sole Cooked in Champagne

This is undoubtedly one of the most successful recipes I have ever produced. It takes time but the effort is unconditionally rewarded by the pleasure expressed by those who have tasted the dish. It is at the same time amazingly light and deliciously succulent.

Serves 6

6 *large or* 12 *small pancakes (see page 230)*

3 *fillets of lemon sole or John Dory*

13 *oz (400 g) fresh or frozen peas*

6 *spring onions*

12 *leaves sorrel*

3 *oz (80 g) butter*

salt and freshly ground black pepper

pinch of ground nutmeg

4 *tablespoons double cream*

¾ *pint (450 ml) champagne*

2 *oz (50 g) firm button mushrooms*

4 *oz (100 g) peeled, cooked prawns*

½ *oz (15 g) butter*

1 *tablespoon flour*

1 *egg yolk*

2 *oz (50 g) grated Gruyère cheese*

Trim the spring onions and roughly chop them. Wash and trim the sorrel. Melt 2 oz (50 g) butter in a saucepan, add the peas, spring onions and sorrel and cook over a medium heat, shaking the pan every now and then to prevent sticking, until the peas are tender. Season with salt and pepper and a pinch of nutmeg, and purée the vegetables through a fine sieve, a food mill or in an electric blender or food processor. Add 2 tablespoons double cream and mix well.

Place the fish fillets in a shallow pan. Cover with the champagne and cook over a low heat until the fillets are just tender. Lift the fillets out with a perforated fish slice, remove any skin and divide each fillet in half. Continue to boil the liquid until it is reduced to about ¼ pint (150 ml).

Thinly slice the mushrooms and sauté them over a high heat in ½ oz (15 g) butter for 3 minutes.

Divide the purée between the pancakes, spreading it along the centre, and place half a fish fillet (or a quarter if the pancakes are small) on top of the purée and then top with a few slices of mushroom and some prawns.

Melt ½ oz (15 g) butter in a small saucepan. Add 1 tablespoon flour and mix well. Gradually blend in the cooking liquid from the fish, stirring continually over a medium high heat until the sauce comes to the boil and is thick and smooth. Season with salt and pepper and stir in 2 tablespoons double cream and the egg yolk. Continue stirring, without boiling, until the sauce is smooth and satiny.

Pour the sauce over the pancake fillings. Turn in the sides of the pancakes, roll them up neatly and place in a shallow fireproof serving dish. Sprinkle over the Gruyère cheese and put under a hot grill until the cheese has melted and the pancakes are hot through.

Omelette with Sorrel, Ham and Peas

A truly amazing combination which makes a quick and satisfying meal at any time when sorrel is available. The secret of a good omelette is to stir the eggs to break them up rather than to beat them and then to serve the finished masterpiece the moment it is ready—omelettes, like soufflés, wait for no man.
Serves 2

2 oz (50 g) ham	1 bunch sorrel
6 oz (175 g) cooked peas	1½ oz (40 g) butter
5 eggs	salt and white pepper

Wash and finely chop the sorrel leaves, having removed the stalks. Melt just under a third of the butter, add the sorrel leaves and cook them over a low heat, stirring, for 4 minutes. Cut the ham into very thin strips, melt ½ oz (15 g) of butter, add the ham and peas and cook them over a low heat for just long enough to heat the ingredients.

Break up the eggs with a fork until they are smooth but not foaming, add the cooked sorrel and season the mixture with salt and pepper. Melt the remaining butter (there should be slightly more than ½ oz, 15 g) in an omelette pan. As soon as the butter begins to foam add the eggs, tipping the pan from one side to another so that egg runs all over the surface. Score the omelette through with a knife in four or five places and tip the pan again so that any runny egg falls into the slits. As soon as the eggs are

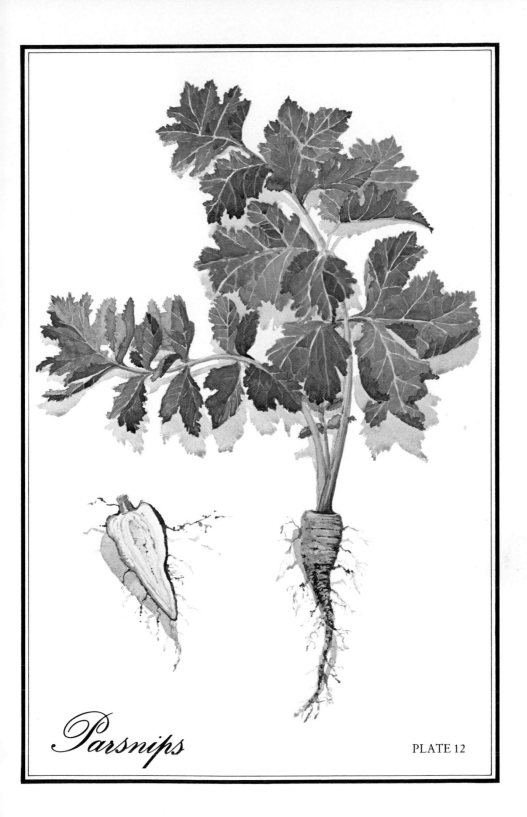

Parsnips

PLATE 12

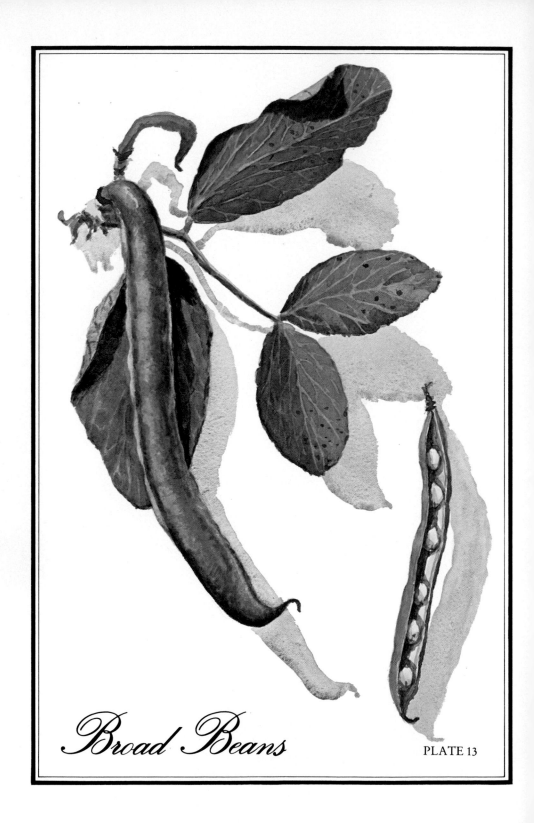

Broad Beans

PLATE 13

just set (they should still be slightly runny on top) place the ham
and peas in the centre and slide the omelette on to a serving plate,
folding it in two as you do so.

Crab Omelette with Peas

Serves 4–6

8 oz (225 g) white crab meat	1 tablespoon very finely chopped
12 oz (350 g) shelled peas	fresh ginger root
4 oz (100 g) firm button	salt
mushrooms	1 tablespoon vegetable oil
3 eggs	2 teaspoons soy sauce

Cook the peas in a little boiling salted water until just tender
and drain well. Finely chop the mushrooms. Beat the eggs lightly
and add the crab, peas, mushrooms and ginger and season with a
little salt.

Heat the oil in an omelette pan, add the egg mixture and cook
over a moderately high heat cutting through the omelette with
a knife so that the runny egg from the top slides on to the
surface of the pan. When the omelette is just set and golden
brown on the bottom, carefully turn it over and quickly brown
the other side. Slide the omelette on to a heated serving dish,
brush with the soy sauce and serve at once cut into wedge-shaped
slices.

You can serve the omelette as a light main course with new
potatoes and a salad or green vegetable or you can serve it as a
first course by itself.

Risotto with Peas, Beans and Chicken

Rice and peas crop up as a traditional native dish in many parts
of the world. You find it, for instance, as part of the regular fare
of people living in the West Indies, in Italy and in parts of the
Far East. In this recipe I have drawn inspiration from a combination of those traditional dishes, making a delicately spiced
risotto to serve as a main course.

Serves 4

G

8 oz (225 g) cooked chicken
6 oz (175 g) shelled peas
1 large onion
¾ inch (2 cm) fresh ginger root
2 cloves garlic
1 small red or green chilli pepper
3 tablespoons olive or vegetable
   oil

6 oz (175 g) long-grain, Patna
   or Basmati rice
1 pint (600 ml) chicken stock
salt and freshly ground black
   pepper
6 oz (175 g) thin French beans
1½ oz (40 g) soft butter

Peel and finely chop the onion. Remove the skin from the ginger root and grate the flesh, discarding any tough fibres. Peel and very finely chop the garlic. Finely chop the chilli, removing the seeds. Chop the chicken into small dice.

Heat the oil in a heavy, flameproof casserole. Add the onions, ginger, garlic and chilli and cook over a low heat, stirring, until the onion is soft and transparent. Add the rice and stir until it becomes transparent. Add the stock, season with salt and pepper, and continue to stir until the ingredients come to the boil. Cover tightly and cook over a low heat for 14 minutes. Add the peas, beans and chicken, mix well, cover tightly and continue to cook over a low heat for a further 6 minutes or until the vegetables and rice are just tender.

Add the butter, stir and serve at once with grated Parmesan cheese on the side.

Smoked Haddock Pie with Garden Peas

Fresh, young tender peas are delicious in a fish pie. In this recipe the ingredients are served in a large, rectangular *vol au vent* case. Serves 6

1 lb (450 g) frozen puff pastry
1 small egg, beaten
1 lb (450 g) smoked haddock
¼ pint (150 ml) milk
½ pint (300 ml) dry cider
4 oz (100 g) peeled, cooked
   prawns
3 hard-boiled eggs

8 oz (225 g) cooked peas
2 oz (50 g) butter
3 tablespoons flour
2 tablespoons double cream
salt and white pepper
pinch each cayenne pepper and
   ground nutmeg

Roll out the pastry to a rectangle about 12 × 8 inches (30 × 20 cm). Cut three-quarters of the way through the pastry 1 inch

(2½ cm) from the edge to make the lid. Brush the pastry with beaten egg, being careful not to let the egg dribble down the sides, and bake in a hot oven (425°F. 220°C. Reg. 7) for 20 minutes until well risen and golden brown.

Place the haddock in a shallow pan. Pour over the milk and cider and simmer very gently until the haddock is tender. Strain off the liquid, remove the skin and any bones and flake the flesh.

Roughly chop the hard-boiled eggs.

Melt the butter in a saucepan, add the flour and mix well. Gradually add the liquid in which the fish was cooked, stirring continually over a medium high heat until the sauce is thick and smooth. Add the cream and mix in the haddock, prawns, peas and hard-boiled eggs. Season with salt, pepper, nutmeg and a little cayenne.

Carefully remove the lid from the pastry case and pull out any soft pastry from the inside. Pour the haddock mixture into the case, replace the lid and re-heat in a moderately hot oven (375°F. 190°C. Reg. 5) for 15 minutes.

Summer Chef's Salad

I always love the idea of the chef's salads they serve in America; lots of bulk and not too fattening; but when they come they are all too often disappointing. The salad ingredients must be fresh and, what is even more important, the main protein ingredients must be of the top quality and not that awful plastic processed cheese, ham and any other cold meat that is added. Prepared well these salads make really first-class summer buffet party or lunch party main courses and they can look very attractive.

In this recipe I have really gone to town using fresh summer ingredients with the brightness of young peas predominating. Serves 4–6

12 oz (350 g) fresh young peas	4 oz (100 g) ham
12 baby carrots	3 tomatoes
4 sticks celery	¼ teaspoon dry English mustard
1 small bunch young radishes	6 tablespoons olive or vegetable oil
1 green pepper	2 tablespoons white wine vinegar
3 spring onions	2 tablespoons tomato juice
4 cooked new potatoes	small pinch sugar
2 small cooked beetroots	salt and freshly ground black
4 oz (100 g) cooked green beans	pepper
4 oz (100 g) tongue	pinch of paprika

Shell the peas and cook them in boiling salted water until tender. Scrape the carrots and place them in a saucepan. Add enough water to cover the bottom of the saucepan to the depth of ¼ inch (¾ cm), bring to the boil, cover tightly and simmer for 7 minutes. Drain off any excess liquid (this should be added to a stock pot) and leave the carrots to cool.

Trim the celery and thinly slice the stems. Thinly slice the radishes. Remove the core and seeds of the pepper and chop the flesh into small dice. Trim and thinly slice the spring onions. Cut the potatoes and beetroots into small dice. Cut the cooked beans into ¾ inch (2 cm) lengths. Cut the tongue and ham into thin matchstick strips. Cover the tomatoes with boiling water for 2 minutes, drain and then slide off the skins and slice the tomatoes.

Combine the mustard, oil, vinegar, tomato juice and sugar in a large bowl and season with salt, pepper and a little paprika. Mix well, add the vegetables and salad ingredients (except the lettuce and tomatoes) and toss lightly. Arrange the lettuce leaves around a large flat platter and arrange the tomato slices around the edge of the platter on top of the lettuce leaves. Pile the vegetables, meat and the dressing in the centre and chill before serving.

Peas with Kidneys and a Mustard Cream Sauce

Kidneys are not expensive and, if properly cooked, can be very good indeed. Soaking them in water to which a little vinegar has been added helps to take away their slightly sweet flavour. Small, young, fresh or frozen peas should be used for this dish; the mini petit pois are ideal.

Serves 4

4 *lambs' kidneys*
12 *oz (350 g) fresh or frozen*
  peas
1 *teaspoon white wine vinegar*

2 *shallots*
2 *oz (50 g) butter*
1 *tablespoon olive or vegetable oil*
1 *teaspoon flour*

½ pint (300 ml) double cream   salt and freshly ground black
1 tablespoon made English   pepper
   mustard

Slide the skin off the kidneys, cut them in half and snip out the
core with a pair of kitchen scissors. Cover the kidneys with cold
water, add the vinegar and leave for 15 minutes. Drain well, pat
dry and cut into ¾ inch (2 cm) thick slices.

Peel and finely chop the shallots. Heat the butter and oil in a
heavy frying pan. Add the shallots and cook over a medium heat
until they are soft and golden. Add the kidneys and peas, season
with salt and pepper, cover and cook over a low heat for about
8 minutes or until the peas are just tender. Sprinkle over the
flour, stir to blend and then stir in the cream and mustard.
Continue to stir gently until the sauce comes to the boil and has
thickened.

Transfer to a serving dish and garnish with triangles of crisply
fried bread.

Quickly Cooked Strips of Lamb with Carrots, Mange Tout Peas and a Cream Sauce

Here again we get a mixture of Chinese and French cuisine with
an economical use of meat, a dish that is very quickly cooked
and has the addition of a rich, glossy sauce.
Serves 4

1 lb (450 g) lamb cut from the   2 cloves garlic
   top of the leg in very thin   5 tablespoons vegetable oil
   slices   ¼ pint (150 ml) double cream
2 tablespoons cornflour   2 tablespoons finely chopped
3 tablespoons dry sherry   parsley
1 tablespoon soy sauce   ¼ pint (150 ml) chicken stock
3 medium-sized carrots   1 tablespoon brown sugar
1 lb (450 g) mange tout (snow   few drops Worcestershire or
   peas)   Harvey's sauce and a few drops
1 onion   Tabasco sauce

Cut the lamb into very thin matchstick strips about 1½ inches (4 cm) long. Place the lamb in a bowl, sprinkle over the cornflour and mix well. Pour over the sherry and soy sauce, mix well and leave to stand for 30 minutes. Drain and reserve excess marinade.

Peel the carrots, cut them into very thin lengthwise slices and then into matchsticks about 1½ inches (4 cm) in length. Peel and chop the onion. Peel and finely chop the garlic. Top and tail the peas and remove any tough strings from the sides. Blanch the peas in fast-boiling, salted water for 6 minutes and drain well.

Heat 4 tablespoons of the oil in a large, heavy frying pan or a Chinese *wok*. When the oil is smoking, throw in the onion, garlic and carrots, stirring over a high heat for 5 minutes until the carrot is tender but still crisp.

In a separate frying pan heat the remaining oil over a high heat. Add the meat and toss over a high heat for a few minutes until the meat is browned on all sides. Add the meat and peas to the carrots and onion and mix in the sugar, marinating liquid and the stock, stirring over a medium heat until the sauce is thick and smooth and the meat is just tender (about 5 minutes). Flavour with a little Worcestershire or Harvey's sauce and Tabasco, stir in the cream and boil, stirring, for 2 minutes to thicken the sauce.

Sprinkle over the parsley and serve with rice.

Quick-fried Chicken with Mange Tout Peas

Dishes like these are excellent when you want a meal in a hurry since they take very little time to cook. In this dish extra flavouring is provided by a little dry sherry.
Serves 4

12 oz (350 g) raw or cooked
   chicken
8 oz (225 g) mange tout (snow
   peas)
2 cloves garlic
1 onion
3 sticks celery
4 oz (100 g) mushrooms

4 tablespoons vegetable oil
1 tablespoon cornflour
½ pint (300 ml) chicken stock
1 tablespoon tomato purée
3 tablespoons dry sherry
salt and freshly ground black
   pepper

Peel the garlic and cut the cloves into very thin slivers. Peel the onion and finely chop the flesh. Top and tail the pea pods and remove any tough strings from the sides. Remove any tough strings from the sides of the celery stalks and thinly slice the stalks. Thinly slice the mushrooms. Cut the chicken and chicken skin into very thin strips. Combine the cornflour with the stock and tomato purée, beat until smooth and mix in the sherry.

Heat the oil in a large frying pan or a *wok*. Add the onion, garlic and celery and cook over a moderately high heat, stirring all the time, until the onion is soft and transparent. Add the peas and stir for a further 3 minutes. Add the mushrooms and chicken and toss over a high heat for 2 minutes. Add the sauce, season with salt and pepper and stir over a high heat for about 4 minutes until the chicken is just tender.

Serve with rice or with pasta shells.

Braised Beef with Onions and Peas

The long slow cooking in this dish transforms the peas and onions into a rich savoury purée that makes an excellent accompaniment to the meat.
Serves 4–6

A 2lb (900 g) topside of beef   salt and freshly ground black
1 lb (450 g) shelled peas   pepper
4 oz (100 g) butter   pinch allspice
2 large onions   wine glass white wine
3 juniper berries

Peel and very thinly slice the onions. Crush the juniper berries. Heat the butter in a large frying pan. Put in the meat and brown it quickly on all sides to seal in the juices. Remove the meat and take the pan off the heat. Season the meat with salt, pepper, allspice and the crushed juniper berries.

Pour the white wine into a casserole just large enough to take the meat and the vegetables and arrange the onions in the bottom of the dish. Place the meat on the onions and put the peas around and on top of the meat. Pour over the juices from the pan in which the beef was sealed, cover the casserole with a double thickness of foil and then with its lid and cook in a slow oven (275°F. 140°C. Reg. 1) for 2½ hours.

Take out the meat and cut it into thin slices. Arrange the slices on a heated serving dish. Beat the peas and onions with a wooden spoon into a coarse purée and spread the mixture over the slices of meat.

Peppers

First of all let me clear up a point that I know confuses many people when they buy peppers in the shops. Yes, green and red peppers (or capsicums to give them their correct name) are the same thing. The red, sweeter, pepper is merely a ripe green pepper and the only reason they are much more expensive to buy is that they take some considerable time longer to ripen than the green peppers and they have a shorter shelf life. I grow my own peppers and, as I use so many of them to give more colour and flavour to dishes, I always find I am hard put to leave them on the plant until they ripen to that glorious rich red which indicates that the peppery sharpness of their flesh has matured to a still crisp, but deliciously sweet, redness.

There are many advantages in growing your own peppers. First of all they are easily grown in pots (they need to be in a greenhouse or on a sunny windowsill), they look attractive and the difference between the crispness of a pepper you pick from your own plant and one that you buy in a shop is very marked.

Capsicum annunum, the pepper most usually found in Britain and certainly the most easy to grow in that climate, is a relative of both the potato and the tomato and it is a fruit/vegetable that is very high in vitamin C. There are reckoned to be over 200 varieties of this family and, on the whole, the strength of their peppery flavour tends to depend on the size of the pepper. None of the family is a true pepper but the seeds of all the fruit have that which, in some of the smaller varieties, adds the bite to chilli and Tabasco sauce and to paprika pepper.

The seeds of the pepper, and their cores, should always be

removed before the pepper is prepared (I sometimes add these to stock to give additional flavouring). Store your green or red peppers in the salad compartment of a refrigerator and, if you buy them, make sure they are shining and free of all blemishes or flabbiness.

If you grow your own capsicums watch out for greenfly, which find these particular plants very attractive. You can start picking the fruit when they are the size of a tennis ball but the longer you leave them the more mild and the sweeter will be their flesh. Small peppers, however, growing next to other fruits, should be culled fairly early on to give the stronger fruits a chance to develop.

Peppers add flavour and colour to almost any casserole, stew or braised dish and they are an invaluable crisply textured ingredient for salads and cold dishes. I very seldom skin the peppers I use, as by doing so you destroy much of the valuable properties of the fruit. If you wish to cut the peppers into rings, cut out the stalks and remove the core and seeds through the opening, leaving the fruit whole.

Bread Loaf Filled with a Savoury Omelette

Serves 4

1 *Vienna loaf or a fat French loaf*	1 *tablespoon finely chopped onion*
2½ oz (65 g) butter	2 oz (50 g) firm button
2 tablespoons olive or vegetable oil	mushrooms
12 oz (350 g) cooked new	1 green pepper
potatoes	5 eggs
4 oz (100 g) streaky bacon	salt and freshly ground black
4 oz (100 g) cooked chicken or	pepper
ham	

Cut a slice off the top of the loaf and pull out the soft bread inside leaving a case. Melt 1 oz (25 g) of butter and brush the inside of the bread case with melted butter and 1 tablespoon oil. Wrap the loaf in foil and bake it in a low oven (300°F. 150°C. Reg. 2) while making the omelette.

Thinly slice the potatoes. Remove the rinds from the bacon and chop the rashers. Finely chop the chicken or ham. Thinly slice the mushrooms. Remove the core and seeds from the pepper and chop the flesh. Lightly beat the eggs.

Melt the remaining butter with the remaining oil in a large omelette pan. Add the onion, bacon and pepper and cook over a low heat until the onion is soft and transparent. Add the potatoes and cook over a medium heat for 3 minutes. Add the mushrooms and continue to cook for another 2 minutes. Season with salt and pepper and pour over the eggs. Raise the heat and draw back the edges of the omelette as it cooks, so that the runny egg can flow underneath coming in contact with the pan. Remove the pan from the heat as soon as the omelette is just set – it should not be allowed to overcook.

Remove the bread case from its foil covering, slide the omelette into the case, put on the loaf top and serve as soon as possible with a green or mixed salad.

Spaghetti with a Meat Sauce Flavoured with Peppers and Aubergines

The sauce in this spaghetti dish is much more robust than the normal *Bolognese*. I find this a marvellous dish when you want to produce something relatively inexpensive for a large number of people. If you are in a hurry don't worry about peeling the peppers – this is a refinement that is worth doing if you can afford the time but which doesn't make all that much difference in the long run.
Serves 6

8 oz (225 g) minced lean raw
  beef or lamb
4 red peppers
1 lb (450 g) aubergines
1 onion
1 stick celery
1 carrot
2 oz (50 g) fat bacon rashers
4 tablespoons olive or vegetable oil
1 medium tin (14 oz, 392 g)
  tomatoes

1 tablespoon tomato purée
salt and freshly ground black
  pepper
4 tablespoons red wine
pinch oregano
1 tablespoon finely chopped parsley
1½ lb (675 g) spaghetti
1 oz (25 g) butter
1 oz (25 g) Parmesan cheese

Spear the peppers on a fork and hold them over an open flame, turning the peppers all the time, until the skin becomes burnt and blackened. Cool the peppers and rub off the skin with a damp cloth. Remove the core and seeds and cut the peppers into thin matchstick strips. Cut the aubergines into small dice. Peel and finely chop the onion. Finely chop the celery. Peel and finely chop the carrot. Cut the bacon into small dice.

Heat the oil in a large heavy pan. Add the onion, meat, bacon, peppers, aubergines, celery and carrot and cook over a medium heat until the meat is browned on all sides (stir during the cooking process).

Drain the juice from the tomatoes and chop up the tomato flesh (I do this in a bowl with kitchen scissors). Add the tomatoes, tomato purée, wine, oregano and parsley to the meat and vegetables, season with salt and pepper, mix well, cover and simmer for 1 hour – remove the lid for the last 15 minutes of cooking time to evaporate the liquid in the sauce which should be fairly dry.

Cook the spaghetti in boiling, salted water (stir it well to ensure the strands are separated), for about 20 minutes or until it is just tender but still holds its shape well. Drain the spaghetti, place it in a large, heated serving dish, dot with the butter and sprinkle over the Parmesan cheese. Toss the spaghetti with two forks to spread the butter and cheese and pour over the sauce.

Serve with a salad.

Chicken and Pepper Sauce for Spaghetti

If you travel through the countryside of Italy you can find literally thousands of different sauces to serve with pasta. Taking a leaf from the Italians' book I have been experimenting with some variations on their traditional sauces and come up with some really inexpensive and, I feel, most delicious variations on the spaghetti theme. Spaghetti and other pasta make such a good basis for a meal that it is a pity to confine their potential to merely sauce *Bolognese* and *Napolitano*. This is a typical example of a quick, easy and inexpensive sauce which makes spaghetti an interesting and satisfying main course.

Serves 4

8 oz (225 g) cooked chicken
1½ green peppers
3 large stalks celery
1 large onion
2 cloves garlic
4 oz (100 g) mushrooms
2 oz (50 g) butter
1 tablespoon vegetable oil

1 tablespoon finely chopped
  parsley
salt and freshly ground black
  pepper
¼ pint (150 ml) single or double
  cream
12 oz (350 g) spaghetti

Remove any tough strings from the celery and cut the stalks into very thin slices. Peel and chop the onion. Peel and finely chop the garlic. Thinly slice the mushrooms. Remove the core and seeds from the green peppers and chop the flesh. Cut the chicken into small dice.

Heat the butter with the oil in a saucepan. Add the celery, onion and garlic and cook over a low heat until the onion is soft and transparent. Add the peppers and continue to cook for a further 5 minutes, stirring to prevent sticking. Add the chicken, mushrooms and parsley, season with salt and pepper, mix in the cream and remove from the heat.

Cook the spaghetti in boiling salted water for about 20 minutes until tender and drain well. Return the spaghetti to the pan, add the sauce and toss over a medium heat until the sauce and spaghetti are hot through.

Serve with grated Parmesan cheese on the side.

Chicken Gizzards with Onions and Peppers in a Savoury Choux Pastry

I love the rich meaty flavour and the firm texture of chicken giblets and, when you can get them, they also make some of the most delicious and economical of meals. Chicken gizzards can be bought from large stores like Harrods and Selfridge's, from country market stalls and from some shops specializing in poultry.

Serves 4–6

choux pastry (see page 4)
1 *lb (450 g) chicken gizzards*
2 *onions*
2 *large green or red peppers*
3 *tablespoons vegetable oil*
1 *tablespoon flour*

stock
bouquet garni
salt and freshly ground black
 pepper
3 *tablespoons medium dry sherry*

Cut off any yellow stains on the gizzards and cut the gizzards in quarters. Peel and chop the onions. Remove the seeds and core from the peppers and chop the flesh.

Heat the oil in a heavy saucepan, add the onion and cook over a low heat until the onion is soft and transparent. Add the peppers and continue to cook for 2 minutes. Raise the heat, add the gizzards and stir over a high heat until the gizzards are nicely browned on all sides. Add the flour and continue to stir until the flour is browned. Mix in enough stock to cover the ingredients, add a bouquet garni, season with salt and pepper and bring to the boil and simmer for about 1¼ hours, until the gizzards are tender. Remove the bouquet garni and strain off the stock into a small saucepan. Add the sherry and boil the gravy until it is reduced by about a third and is glossy and syrupy. Add a little of the gravy to the gizzards, onions and peppers and check the seasoning.

Fill the choux puffs with the mixture, arrange them on a serving dish and heat through for about 20 minutes in a moderate oven (350°F. 180°C. Reg. 4). Pour over the remaining gravy just before serving.

Note: The gizzards can be cooked in a pressure cooker to save time.

Escalopes of Chicken with Peppers and Onions

Chicken breast cut into thin slices and lightly beaten can be cooked in the same way as now prohibitively expensive escalopes of veal. You can top the escalopes with rings of anchovy fillet filled with some capers and then merely pour over the juices from the pan to which you have added a little butter, some finely chopped parsley and a little lemon juice or you can serve them with a lemon-and-cream sauce flavoured with a little mustard.

Serves 4

2 *large chicken breasts*

2 *onions*

2 *green or red peppers*

1 *egg, beaten*

dried breadcrumbs

salt and freshly ground black pepper

3 *tablespoons vegetable oil*

2½ *oz (65 g) butter*

4 *anchovy fillets*

2 *teaspoons capers*

2 *teaspoons lemon juice*

1 *teaspoon French Dijon mustard*

Peel and very thinly slice the onions and divide them into rings. Cut out the stalks of the peppers and remove the core and seeds leaving the peppers whole. Cut the peppers into very thin rings. Slice the chicken breasts horizontally in two and place the slices on greaseproof paper. Cover with a second sheet of paper and gently beat the slices to double their size using the flat side of a meat mallet or a rolling pin. Season the slices with salt and pepper, dip them in beaten egg and then coat them with breadcrumbs.

Heat the oil in a heavy frying pan. Add the onions and peppers and cook over a medium heat, stirring to prevent sticking, for about 10 minutes or until the onions and peppers are soft and tender. Remove the onions and peppers with a slotted spoon, spread them over a shallow serving dish and keep them warm.

Add 1½ oz (40 g) butter to the pan (you may also have to add a little more oil – the pan should have about ⅛ inch (½ cm) depth of oil and butter mixed) and heat through until very hot. Add the escalopes of chicken and cook them over a high heat until they are golden brown on both sides. Remove the chicken from the pan with a slotted spoon and place them on top of the onions and peppers. Garnish each escalope with an anchovy in a ring filled with capers.

Add the remaining 1 oz (25 g) butter to the juices in the pan with the lemon juice and mustard. Heat through, scraping the pan, and strain the sauce through a fine sieve over the escalopes. Serve at once.

A Dish of Finely Minced Chicken with Whole Oats and Green Peppers

The origins of this dish lie in Arabia and it really is most delicious although it does help to have a food processor for the preparation of the chicken which should be as smooth as possible. You can buy whole oats from health food stores. Serves 4

1 *lb (450 g) raw chicken off the bone (the carcass can be used for stock)*
4 *oz (100 g) whole oats*
2 *oz (50 g) pine kernels or pistachio nuts*
1 *large onion*

3 *green peppers*
$\frac{1}{4}$ *teaspoon cumin seeds*
$\frac{1}{4}$ *teaspoon ground coriander*
salt and freshly ground black pepper
3 *tablespoons olive or vegetable oil*

Mince the chicken twice through the fine blades of a mincing machine. Crush the whole oats in a pestle and mince or very finely chop the nuts (these processes can all be done in an electric food processor). Peel and finely chop the onion. Remove the core and seeds from the peppers and thinly slice the flesh. Blanch the onion and pepper in boiling, salted water for 5 minutes and drain them well.

Season the chicken with salt and pepper and mix in the cumin and coriander. Oil a shallow baking dish and spread half the chicken over the bottom of the dish. Cover with crushed oats and nuts mixed together and then with the peppers and onions. Spread over the rest of the chicken pressing it down firmly with the back of a wooden spoon and then dribble over the oil.

Bake in a moderately hot oven (400°F. 200°C. Reg. 6) for 30 minutes, by which time the ingredients will have shrunk a little from the sides of the dish and the top should be crusty and golden.

Prawns Pil Pil

This is a dish for those who enjoy 'hot food'. The term *pil pil* is used in Portugal for a sauce that is made with a strong chilli flavour, served with or used to baste chicken and other ingredients. Personally I love, now and then, to have a good strong

taste of chilli in my food and I find this dish an admirable starter in the winter when it gives a good warming beginning to a meal and makes a good foil for a rather bland and perhaps rich main course. If you grow your own chilli peppers (and they are easy to grow in the greenhouse or in a pot on a windowsill) you can dry them by tying the chillies by their stalks in a long line and then hanging them in a cool, dry, dark place until they are shrivelled and crisp—be warned, however, that the taste of the chillies is even stronger when the fruit is dried and they can be very fiery indeed.
Serves 4

8 oz (225 g) peeled, cooked prawns
2 green peppers
3 carrots
1 small onion
2 cloves garlic
1 dried red chilli pepper

5 tablespoons olive or vegetable oil
3 tablespoons tomato purée
1 tablespoon sherry
1 tablespoon tomato ketchup
few drops Tabasco sauce
1 French loaf

Peel the carrots and cut them into very, very small dice. Remove the core and seeds of the pepper and very finely chop the flesh. Peel and very finely chop the onion. Peel and very finely chop the garlic cloves. Remove the seeds of the chilli pepper and finely chop the flesh (wash your hands after handling the pepper as those seeds are very fiery and if you put your hands near your face you can be in trouble).

Heat the oil in a saucepan with a heavy bottom. Add the onion, pepper, garlic, carrots and chilli and cook over a low heat, stirring every now and then, until the carrot is soft. Add the tomato purée, sherry, ketchup and Tabasco and mix well. Cover and simmer for 5 minutes. Add the prawns and stir over a moderate heat until they are hot through (they should not need cooking and in fact cooking will toughen them).

Cut the French loaf into long diagonal slices. Toast the slices or bake them in the oven until crisp. Serve the prawns pil pil on top of the toast.

Monkfish (Angel Fish) with Green Peppers

The texture of monkfish is very similar to that of shrimps. In this recipe small strips of monkfish are cooked with peppers producing a well-flavoured dish that makes an excellent starter. Monkfish tends to be a bit on the expensive side but there is little waste and you do not need a large quantity to make a good four servings.

If you serve the dish with rice it can make a good main course for lunch.

Serves 4

1 *lb (450 g) monkfish off the*
   bone
3 *large green peppers*
3 *large ripe tomatoes*
1 *clove garlic*
4 *spring onions*

5 *tablespoons sunflower oil*
salt and freshly ground black
   pepper
½ *teaspoon ground ginger*
¼ *pint (150 ml) boiling water*
2 *tablespoons soy sauce*

Cut the fish into strips about ¼ inch (¾ cm) thick and 1½ inches (4 cm) long. Remove the seeds and core of the peppers and cut them into strips the same width and length as the fish. Cover the tomatoes with boiling water for 2 minutes, drain and slide off the skins. Quarter the tomatoes. Peel and chop the garlic. Trim the spring onions and cut them in half lengthwise.

Heat the oil in a *wok* or deep frying pan, add the fish and cook, stirring, for 2 minutes. Add the peppers, garlic and ginger, season with pepper and cook for 1 minute, stirring to prevent sticking. Add the boiling water and soy sauce, bring to the boil, cover and cook for 3 minutes. Mix in the tomatoes, cook for a further 3 minutes and then stir in the onions and cook for a final minute. Serve as soon as possible.

Runner Beans

Strangely enough, the runner bean (still the most popular of the bean family in Britain, which was introduced there from Mexico in the seventeenth century) was originally valued for its flowers, small and bright scarlet, rather than for the pods which were completely ignored. Now the plant as a decorative flower has disappeared entirely but there are few vegetable gardens in England where runner beans are not grown as a summer crop. It is paradoxical that, while the runner bean actually came to Europe from America, the scarlet runner bean has never been very popular there; green, snap or fresh lima beans are very much popular leaders in the bean field.

If your garden area is small you can still combine the attractive appearance of runner beans with their food potential by growing them against the side of the house or along a fence. In a town garden they can be grown in tubs or even along a balcony. The advantage of the runner bean over the French bean is its cropping potential which is much higher and more prolific than the shorter and less hardy French bean but, like all other vegetables, they must be picked when they are still tender and supple and not allowed to grow on to their final length, which may be 15 inches or even more.

Once established, runner beans are little trouble to grow although the climbing varieties do have to have the support of bamboos or hazel sticks. They are on the tender side to start with though and will not germinate unless they are given fairly warm conditions, either being planted in a greenhouse or under glass or left to be put out into open ground until the weather has become reasonably warm in May.

The secret of getting a good crop of beans is constant picking when the season is under way. Pick the beans at least every other day, always removing any that are misshapen or show any signs of disease.

The younger the beans the more easy they are to deal with. Picked when they are still only about 6 inches long, they will just need to be topped and tailed and can be cooked whole like French beans and then used in the same way. The more mature beans, which will have a slightly rough skin, should have the strings from the sides of the beans removed, along with the tops and tails, and the beans should then be cut into thin diagonal or lengthwise strips.

When you buy beans in a shop always check that they look bright green and fresh. If you do find they become wilted and slightly soft before you can cook them, they can be refreshed by being put in a sealed plastic bag in the salad compartment of the refrigerator for a day or two.

French beans are really too tender for long cooking but runner beans, on the other hand, especially the larger ones, respond very well indeed to casseroling with meat, fish and poultry; the meat flavours the beans and the beans tenderize the meat, making an extremely good combination.

A Clear Soup of Runner Beans and Chicken with Other Vegetables

This soup is based on the Chinese 'stir and fry' principle with vegetables and meat being carefully prepared, quickly fried and then simmered for a short while in a good clear stock. If a good stock is not available you can use tinned consommé instead.
Serves 6

8 oz (225 g) runner beans
6 oz (175 g) raw chicken breast
1 small onion
1 clove garlic
1 red or green chilli pepper

½ inch (1½ cm) piece of fresh
  ginger root
1 carrot
1 small head lettuce
2 oz (50 g) firm button
  mushrooms

2 *sticks celery*
3 *tablespoons olive or vegetable oil*
2½ *pints (1500 ml) good clear*
  stock

2 *tablespoons soy sauce*
2 *tablespoons dry sherry*
salt and freshly ground black
  pepper

Peel and finely chop the onion. Peel and very finely chop the garlic. Remove the core and seeds from the chilli pepper and very finely chop the flesh. Peel the ginger and very finely chop the flesh. Top and tail the beans and cut them into very thin slices. Remove the leaves from the celery stalks and chop them finely. Cut the celery stalks into very thin matchstick strips. Cut the chicken breast into very thin matchstick strips. Coarsely shred the lettuce. Very thinly slice the mushrooms. Peel the carrot and cut it into very thin matchstick strips.

Heat the oil in a *wok* or heavy, deep frying pan until the oil is just smoking. Add the onion, garlic, pepper and ginger and stir over a high heat until the onion is soft and transparent but not browned. Add the carrot and celery and continue to stir until the vegetables have softened. Add the chicken and stir until the flesh has turned white. Add the lettuce, beans and mushrooms, stir for 1 minute and then add the stock. Bring to the boil, stir in the soy sauce, simmer for 5 minutes, season with salt and pepper, mix in the sherry and serve at once.

Grilled Fish with Runner Beans and an Almond Sauce

A delicate almond sauce makes this an attractive dish with the contrast of green and white giving a fresh, summery effect. I find that whiting fillets are the best fish to use for a recipe of this kind.
Serves 6

6 *large whiting fillets, skinned*
3 *tablespoons lemon juice*
1 *lb (450 g) runner beans*
salt and white pepper
flour

3½ *oz (90 g) butter*
1 *onion*
2 *oz (50 g) flaked almonds*
½ *pint (300 ml) single cream*

Place the fish in a shallow dish, pour over the lemon juice and leave to stand for 2 hours. Strain off the juice, pat dry with kitchen paper and coat the fish lightly with seasoned flour.

Peel and very finely chop the onion. Top and tail the beans and cut them into thin diagonal slices. Cook the beans in a little boiling, salted water until they are just tender and drain well. Arrange the beans in the bottom of a lightly greased heated serving dish and keep warm while cooking the fish and sauce.

Heat the butter in a frying pan. Add the fish and cook over a medium heat, turning once, for about 5 minutes or until the fish is golden and cooked through. Remove the fish with a fish slice and place the fillets on the beans.

Add the onion to the juices in the pan and cook over a low heat, stirring, until the onion is soft and transparent. Add the almonds and continue to stir until the almonds are golden and crisp. Add the cream and reserved lemon juice to the juices in the pan, heat through without boiling and pour the sauce over the fish.

A Summer Salad of Garlic Sausage and Runner Beans

The important thing in this dish is not to overcook the beans which should retain a definite crispness. The beans are cooked in stock to give them extra flavour and the stock should be reserved for making a soup.

Serves 4

6 oz (175 g) garlic sausage
12 oz (350 g) runner beans
¾ pint (450 ml) chicken or
  vegetable stock
4 ripe tomatoes
1 hard-boiled egg
4 tablespoons olive or vegetable oil

1 tablespoon white wine vinegar
1 teaspoon English or French
  Dijon mustard
salt and freshly ground black
  pepper
1 tablespoon finely chopped chives
  or spring onion tops

Top and tail the beans, remove any strings from the sides and cut the beans into diagonal slices about ½ inch (1½ cm) thick.

Bring the stock to the boil, add the beans and cook them for 4 minutes only. Drain the beans and leave them to cool.

Cover the tomatoes with boiling water for 2 minutes, drain them and then slide off their skins. Cut the tomatoes into thin slices and then arrange the slices around the edge of a shallow serving dish.

Cut the garlic sausage into thin strips. Finely chop the white of the hard-boiled egg. Combine the beans, garlic sausage and egg white in a bowl. Mix together the oil, vinegar, mustard and chives and season the vinaigrette with salt and pepper. Pour the dressing over the beans and toss the ingredients lightly together. Pile the salad in the centre of the dish and garnish with the hard-boiled egg yolk rubbed through a coarse sieve.

Spaghetti or Tagliatelle Verdi with Smoked Salmon and Runner Beans

I am a great advocate of pasta dishes and I also have an ever-lasting love affair with Italian food of all kinds since it seems to me to combine both economy and speed with the most rewarding results. This dish is a wonderful mixture of luxury and restraint; it is based on the famous Carbonara sauce and makes good use of the untidy off-cuts of smoked salmon which can be bought from any shop which cuts its own smoked salmon. You can serve it as a first course but I would personally serve it as the main dish of the meal with a good green or mixed salad.

If you have a pasta-making machine (these can be bought at Divertimenti in Marylebone Lane, London W.1) it is well worth making your own tagliatelle verdi with a spinach base, but if you live in London, home-made pasta, made fresh daily, can be bought from Camisa & Son in Old Compton Street, Soho, and is absolutely delicious. The green ribbon noodles made by Butoni can also be bought from most good delicatessen shops and are a useful standby to have in the larder.

Serves 6–8

1 *lb (450 g) spaghetti or
    tagliatelle verdi*
6 *oz (175 g) smoked salmon
    pieces*
1 *lb (450 g) runner beans*
3 *oz (75 g) butter*

¼ *pint (150 ml) single cream*
freshly ground black pepper
1 *tablespoon finely chopped
    parsley*
2 *oz (50 g) finely grated
    Parmesan cheese*

Top and tail the runner beans and cut them into very thin diagonal slices and then into 1 inch (2½ cm) lengths. Cook the beans in a little boiling, salted water until they are just tender but still crisp. Drain them well. Finely chop the smoked salmon.

Cook the spaghetti or tagliatelle in plenty of boiling salted water for about 12–15 minutes until it is just tender and drain it well.

In a large clean pan, melt the butter, add the beans and smoked salmon to the butter and season with plenty of pepper. Add the cream, mix well and then add the spaghetti or tagliatelle and toss lightly until the pasta is warmed through. Turn on to a heated serving dish, sprinkle with finely chopped parsley and serve at once with the grated Parmesan in a bowl on the side.

Casserole of Runner Beans

Serves 4

1 *lb (450 g) runner beans*
2 *rashers streaky bacon*
1 *onion*
1 *oz (25 g) butter*
1 *sprig savory*

½ *pint (300 ml) vegetable or chicken stock*
salt and freshly ground black pepper

String and slice the beans and blanch them in boiling salted water for 5 minutes. Remove the rinds of the bacon and finely chop the rashers. Peel and very thinly slice the onion and divide it into rings.

Melt the butter in a flameproof casserole. Add the bacon and onion and cook over a low heat, stirring to prevent sticking, until the onion is soft and transparent. Add the beans, savory and enough stock just to cover the ingredients, season with salt and pepper, cover tightly and cook over a low heat for 30 minutes. Remove the savory before serving.

Runner Beans with Cream and Savory

Serves 4

1 *lb (450 g) runner beans*
¼ *pint (150 ml) single cream*
1 *teaspoon finely chopped savory*

salt and freshly ground black
pepper

String and slice the beans and cook them in fast-boiling salted water until just tender. Drain well.

Combine the cream and finely chopped savory in a saucepan, season with salt and pepper, bring to the boil and simmer for 5 minutes.

Add the beans, toss lightly and heat through.

Ham with Runner Beans and Cream

Ham is always a good ingredient for a quick meal. I cook my own gammon, in one piece, and then use it for countless dishes like this. The ham keeps well providing it is lightly covered with polythene film and stored in the refrigerator.

Serves 4

4 *slices cooked ham ½ inch*
  (1½ cm) thick
1 *lb (450 g) runner beans*
1 *oz (25 g) butter*
2 *teaspoons olive or vegetable oil*
2 *shallots or 1 small onion*
1 *tablespoon flour*

¼ *pint (150 ml) chicken stock*
4 *tablespoons medium dry sherry*
1 *teaspoon tomato purée*
freshly ground black pepper
pinch ground nutmeg
¼ *pint (150 ml) double cream*

Peel and very finely chop the shallots or onion. Heat the oil and butter in a large frying pan, add the ham slices and cook over a medium heat until the slices are lightly browned. Remove the ham with a slotted spoon. Add the shallots or onion to the juices in the pan and stir over a low heat until they are soft and transparent. Add the flour and mix well. Add the stock, stirring continually until the sauce is thick and smooth. Add the sherry and the tomato purée and season with pepper and nutmeg. Stir in the cream and remove from the heat.

Top and tail the beans and cut them into thin, diagonal slices. Cook the beans in boiling salted water until tender and drain them really well. Arrange the beans in a lightly buttered shallow baking dish, cover with the slices of ham and pour over the sauce. Cover really tightly and bake in a moderate oven (350°F 180°C. Reg. 4) for 20 minutes.

Dark Chicken Meat with Runner Beans and a Devil Sauce

Many of the dishes in this book use only part of the chicken. This recipe uses only the legs and the joy of these dishes is that you can, from a fairly sizeable chicken, get up to four meals of four servings and be left with the raw carcass which can then be used to make a delicious stock to use as a soup base. This is an excellent and spicy dish with a good robust flavour.
Serves 4

2 *large chicken legs*
12 *oz (350 g) runner beans*
1 *large onion*
3 *tablespoons vegetable oil*
2 *tablespoons Worcestershire sauce*

1 *tablespoon French Dijon mustard*
¼ *pint (150 ml) chicken stock*
salt and freshly ground black pepper

Peel and very finely slice the onion and divide into rings. Remove the skin from the chicken, cut the flesh off the legs and then cut it into very thin strips. Top and tail the runner beans, remove any strings from the sides and cut the beans into very thin, diagonal strips.

Heat the oil in a heavy frying pan. Add the onion and stir over a high heat until the onion is brown and crisp. Remove the onion with a slotted spoon and drain on some kitchen paper.

Add the runner beans to the oil in the pan and cook them for 3 minutes, stirring to prevent browning. Add the chicken and continue to stir over a medium high heat for 3 minutes. Add the Worcestershire sauce and mustard and mix well. Add the stock, bring to the boil, cover and cook over a low heat for about 15 minutes or until the chicken and beans are tender. Season the dish with a little salt and pepper and garnish it with crisply fried onion rings.

Serve with rice, and a good cabbage dish would go well as an accompanying vegetable.

Runner Beans with Chicken

This is a dish with both Chinese and Hungarian overtones and one that I have found very popular at home. I serve it with rice and a salad and although it is very economical indeed it is certainly sophisticated enough to serve at a dinner party.
Serves 4

8 oz (225 g) raw or cooked
   chicken
12 oz (350 g) runner beans
2 cloves garlic
1 onion
4 oz (100 g) mushrooms
1 tablespoon flaked almonds
4 tablespoons olive or vegetable oil

1 tablespoon apple purée
1 tablespoon tomato ketchup
¼ pint (150 ml) chicken stock
salt and freshly ground black
   pepper
finely chopped celery leaves
   (optional)

Top and tail the beans, remove any tough strings and cut the beans into very thin, lengthwise strips or thin slices. Peel the garlic and cut it into thin slivers. Peel and finely chop the onions. Very thinly slice the mushrooms. Cut the chicken into very thin matchstick strips.

Cook the beans in a little boiling salted water for about 5 minutes or until they are *just* tender and still crisp.

Heat the oil in a heavy frying pan. Add the onion, garlic and almonds and cook over a medium high heat until the onion is golden brown and the garlic and almonds are crisp and brown. Add the mushrooms and chicken and toss over a medium high heat for about 5 minutes (less if the chicken is already cooked) until the chicken is tender.

Mix together the apple purée, tomato ketchup and stock and stir the sauce into the bean and chicken mixture. Season with salt and pepper, heat through and serve in the centre of a rice ring or on top of a bed of fluffy boiled rice. Sprinkle some finely chopped celery leaves over the top just before serving.

Pork Casserole with Runner Beans

Good, country-style food that smells as good on the stove as it is to eat. Serve it with baked, jacket potatoes, a hot potato salad or with slices of potatoes, layered with onions, cream, a little butter and plenty of seasoning, tightly covered and baked in the oven.
Serves 6

1½ lb (675 g) lean hand of pork
   or boned shoulder of pork
12 oz (350 g) runner beans
2 shallots
1 medium onion
1 clove garlic
1½ tablespoons vegetable oil
1 sprig thyme
3 bay leaves

2 teaspoons paprika
pinch mixed spice
salt and freshly ground black
   pepper
1 heaped tablespoon flour
an inexpensive dry white wine
3 oz (75 g) stuffed green olives
1 green pepper

Cut the pork into 1 inch (2½ cm) cubes. Peel and chop the shallots and onion. Peel and finely chop the garlic. Heat the oil in a heavy, flameproof casserole and when it is really hot, add the pork and brown the cubes on all sides over a high heat. Add the shallots, onion, garlic, thyme and bay leaves, season with salt, pepper, paprika and mixed spice and stir over a low heat for 3 minutes. Add the flour and stir until the flour is lightly browned. Stir in enough wine to cover the ingredients and continue to stir until the sauce comes to the boil. Cover tightly and simmer over a very low heat (the liquid should only just move in the dish) for 1 hour.

Top and tail the beans and cut them into thin diagonal slices. Slice the stuffed olives. Remove the core and seeds from the green pepper and cut the flesh into thin slices.

Remove any fat that has risen to the surface of the casserole (the easiest way to do this is with a sauce ladle), add the beans, olives and pepper to the meat and continue to simmer, tightly covered, for a further 30 minutes. Check seasoning before serving.

Fillet of Pork with Runner Beans

Serves 4

1 *fillet pork, approximately* 1 *lb*
  (450 g) in weight
1 *lb (450 g) runner beans*
1½ *tablespoons cornflour*
¼ *teaspoon paprika*
1 *tablespoon soy sauce*

1 *onion*
2 *cloves garlic*
4 *tablespoons vegetable oil*
½ *pint (300 ml) chicken stock*
1 *tablespoon tomato purée*

Cut the pork fillet into ¼ inch (¾ cm) slices. Place the slices between two sheets of greaseproof paper and beat them with a wooden mallet or rolling pin until they are flattened to about double their size.

Combine the cornflour, paprika and soy sauce and mix well. Add the slices of fillet and mix until the slices are well coated with the mixture. Leave to stand for 30 minutes.

Top and tail the beans and cut them into very thin diagonal slices. Peel and finely chop the onion and garlic. Heat 1 tablespoon of oil in a frying pan. Add the onion and garlic and cook over a low heat until the onion is soft and transparent. Add the beans and cook over a low heat, stirring, for 3 minutes. Add the stock, mix in the tomato purée, cover, and cook over a moderate heat for about 6 minutes or until the beans are just tender.

In a second frying pan, heat the remaining oil. Add the slices of meat and cook them over a high heat for only about 2 minutes on each side until the meat is browned and tender. Remove the slices of meat and keep them warm. Strain off the liquid from the beans and add it to the juices in the pan in which the meat was cooked. Stir over a high heat for 2 minutes.

Arrange the beans on a heated serving dish, top with the meat and strain over the liquid.

Pork Fillet with Beans, Cooked in Milk and Served in a Rice Ring

Cooking pork in milk is an old-fashioned idea but one that can well be brought back into fashion. The disadvantage is that you always get some sediment in the sauce but the great advantage is that the flavour of the pork is exquisite and the texture so tender that it really does 'melt in the mouth'. I use pork fillet in this dish but you could use a less expensive cut of pork and, if necessary, cook it for a little longer. The secret of the dish lies in the slow cooking.

This is a useful dish to make with beans when they are not quite as tender as they might be.
Serves 6

1½ lb (675 g) pork fillet
1 lb (450 g) runner beans
1 onion
1 clove garlic
3½ oz (90 g) butter
milk
bouquet garni (sprig thyme,
    2 bay leaves, parsley and sage)
salt and freshly ground black
    pepper
¼ teaspoon paprika

12 oz (350 g) long-grain rice
8 oz (225 g) courgettes
1½ oz (40 g) grated Parmesan
    cheese
1 tablespoon flour
4 tablespoons double cream or sour
    cream
1½ tablespoons finely chopped
    parsley
1 red pepper or tinned pimento

Cut the meat into slices ¼ inch (¾ cm) thick. Top and tail the beans and cut them into thin diagonal slices. Peel and chop the onion and garlic.

Heat 1 oz (25 g) butter in a heavy frying pan. Add the slices of meat and brown them on both sides over a high heat. Put the beans, onion and garlic into a heavy saucepan. Arrange the slices of meat on top of the vegetables and add the bouquet garni. Season with salt, pepper and paprika and add enough milk just to cover the ingredients. Bring gently to the boil and then cook, uncovered, over a very low heat so that the liquid is only just moving, for 1½ hours. Remove the bouquet garni and strain off the remaining liquid from the ingredients.

While the pork is cooking, put the rice into a saucepan with a little salt. Add double the quantity of water, bring to the boil, stir once and then cover tightly and cook over a very low heat for 20 minutes. Remove the cover, stir the rice vigorously to get rid of the steam, cover again and leave to stand for 10 minutes.

Coarsely grate the courgettes and mix them into the rice with 1½ oz (40 g) butter and the Parmesan cheese and season the mixture with salt and pepper. Pack the rice mixture into an oiled ring mould pressing it down firmly, cover with foil and bake the ring in a moderate oven (350°F. 180°C. Reg. 4) for 20 minutes.

Melt 1 oz (25 g) butter in a saucepan, add the flour and mix well. Gradually add the liquid in which the pork cooked, stirring continually over a medium high heat until the sauce comes to the boil and is thick and smooth. Add the meat and vegetables and mix lightly. Check the seasoning and stir in the cream and parsley.

Remove the core and seeds of the red pepper and chop finely.

Turn the mould on to a circular serving dish and spoon the pork mixture into the centre of the ring. Sprinkle over the pepper or pimento and serve at once with a green or mixed salad.

Julienne de Boeuf Sauté

This dish is, in a way, similar to a *boeuf stroganoff* but it has the addition of runner beans and green pepper instead of just onions and mushrooms. The secret of the dish is not to overcook the beans which should still retain a slight crispness – the flavour is, I think, delicious and like so many of the dishes in this book it is extremely quick to make.

Serves 4–6

1 *lb (450 g) rump steak*	4 *tablespoons chicken stock*
8 *oz (225 g) young runner beans*	*salt and freshly ground black*
2 *onions*	*pepper*
1 *green pepper*	¼ *pint (150 ml) sour cream*
2 *oz (50 g) mushrooms*	½ *tablespoon paprika*
2 *tablespoons olive or vegetable oil*	1 *tablespoon tomato purée*
2 *oz (50 g) butter*	1 *tablespoon finely chopped parsley*

Top and tail the beans, remove any strings and cut the beans lengthwise into very thin slices. Peel and thinly slice the onions and divide them into rings. Remove the core and seeds of the green pepper and cut the pepper into thin rings. Thinly slice the mushrooms. Cut the rump steak into very thin slices against the grain and then into thin strips about $\frac{1}{8}$ inch ($\frac{1}{2}$ cm) wide.

Heat $1\frac{1}{2}$ tablespoons of oil with 1 oz (25 g) butter in a heavy frying pan. Add the onion and pepper and cook over a low heat until the onion is soft and transparent. Add the beans and mix well. Mix in the stock, cover tightly and cook over a low heat for 10 minutes.

Mix the sour cream with the tomato purée and paprika.

Heat the remaining oil and butter in a second frying pan. Add the meat and cook over a very high heat, tossing the pan, until the meat is browned on all sides.

Add the meat and the mushrooms to the vegetables and pour over the sour cream mixture. Season with salt and pepper and cook over a moderate heat, stirring every now and then for about 10 minutes or until the meat is just tender.

Transfer to a serving dish and sprinkle with finely chopped parsley.

Serve the meat in a ring of fluffy boiled rice or mashed potatoes and accompany with a green or mixed salad.

Lettuces

PLATE 14

Turnips

PLATE 15

Salsify and Scorzonera

These may both be ugly-looking vegetables but their flavour makes them a real winter delicacy. The two vegetables come from the same family but whereas salsify is basically white overall, the scorzonera (which many maintain has the better flavour) has a tough black skin. Both roots bleed when they are cut so they should be scrubbed and boiled in water, to which a little lemon juice and salt has been added, until they are tender. The roots are then peeled, cut into bite-sized pieces and tossed in butter or served in a cream sauce.

Salsify and scorzonera are, quite rightly, often called the 'oysters of the earth' because their smooth texture when cooked is not unlike that of oysters and the almost silvery-white colour is also similar to the flesh of cooked oysters. Scorzonera is also supposed to have some magical properties – in Spain it is thought to have originated from the plant called *escarzo* (or 'serpent') and is believed to be an antidote for snake bites.

Salsify and scorzonera both grow easily and well in a moderate soil and they can be left in the ground until they are required, being lifted from September onwards; the roots can also be lifted and stored in sand in the same way as carrots or other root vegetables.

The exciting and peculiar thing about both of these vegetables is their almost chameleon ability to take on the flavours of other ingredients, which makes them so very valuable to the home cook. Cooked, sliced salsify or scorzonera for instance, combined with scallops, doubles the quantity of a dish while still retaining the gentle flavour of the scallops. The roots also go well with

H

chicken and any other light meat and combine excellently with almost any fish.

Cooked, peeled and cooled scorzonera and salsify are also delicious in cold dishes and salads. Combined with other ingredients in a mayonnaise they make good first courses and they are invaluable to combine with chicken or shellfish in main-course salad dishes.

In the eighteenth century there was a time when salsify was a popular and much-used vegetable, then it fell from favour (perhaps because of the ugly appearance of the vegetable) and about ten years ago it was difficult to buy salsify seeds at all. Now, however, salsify is making a come-back and scorzonera is also gaining in popularity. They may be slightly tedious vegetables to prepare but the rewards are well worth the effort and I cannot recommend both vegetables too highly as crops that are invaluable to grow in your garden.

Pastry Cases Filled with Sweetbreads and Salsify in a White Sauce

I usually serve this dish as a starter for a dinner party but it could just as well be produced for a main course. The flavours of tarragon and lemon go well with the slight blandness of the salsify and sweetbreads and the texture of the dish is very special indeed. Tarragon is a very strongly flavoured herb and should be used with care to prevent the taste becoming too dominating.
Serves 4

12 oz (350 g) quiche pastry (see page 4)
6 oz (175 g) sweetbreads
1 lb (450 g) salsify
3 teaspoons lemon juice
1 onion
1 carrot
bouquet garni
salt and freshly ground black pepper
1 teaspoon dried tarragon
2 oz (50 g) butter
2 tablespoons flour
½ pint (300 ml) chicken stock
1 egg yolk
¼ pint (150 ml) single cream

Cover the sweetbreads with cold water and leave them to stand for 2 hours. Drain off the water, place the sweetbreads in a saucepan with the onion and carrot, peeled and roughly chopped, and the bouquet garni. Cover with cold water, bring gently to the boil and then simmer gently for 25 minutes. Drain off the liquid, place the sweetbreads on a plate, cover with another plate and weigh down with a heavy weight. Leave in a cool place for 4 hours. Remove any fatty membrane from the sweetbreads and cut them into thin slices.

Wash the salsify and boil them in water, to which 1 teaspoon of lemon juice has been added, for about 30 minutes or until they are just tender. Leave to cool and then remove the skin and cut the roots into thin slices.

Roll out the pastry very thinly and line 8 small tartlet cases with the pastry. Prick the pastry, line the cases with foil and fill them with dried beans and freeze the cases until they are solid. Put the frozen cases in a hot oven (400°F. 200°C. Reg. 6) and bake them for about 8 minutes. Remove the beans and foil and return the cases to the oven for a further 5 minutes or until they are crisp and golden.

Soak the tarragon in 2 teaspoons of lemon juice for 5 minutes. Melt the butter in a saucepan. Add the flour and mix well. Gradually blend in the stock, stirring continually over a medium high heat until the sauce is thick and smooth. Beat the cream with the egg yolk until smooth. Add the tarragon and lemon juice to the sauce and heat in the cream, stirring all the time over a low heat (do not allow to boil) until the sauce is shining and satiny. Add the sweetbreads and salsify to the sauce and season with salt and pepper.

Fill the cases with the sweetbread filling and heat them through in a moderate oven (350°F. 180°C. Reg. 4) for 15 minutes before serving.

Note: The filling and cases can be made and filled in advance and then re-heated when they are required.

Scallops and Salsify in a Cream Sauce

The texture of cooked salsify is very similar to that of scallops; if they are cooked together the scallops flavour the salsify, making this a surprisingly inexpensive dish.
Serves 4

4 *large scallops*
12 *oz (350 g) salsify*
2 *tablespoons olive or vegetable oil*
3 *teaspoons lemon juice*
1 *shallot or small onion*
2 *oz (50 g) button mushrooms*
flour
salt

freshly ground black pepper
pinch cayenne pepper
2 *oz (50 g) butter*
1 *small glass white wine*
¼ *pint (150 ml) single cream*
1 *oz (25 g) grated Parmesan*
cheese

Remove the black vein from around the scallops, cut off the coral and the white parts of the scallops and cut into very thin slices. Combine the oil and 2 teaspoons of lemon juice, add the scallops and leave them to marinate for 1 hour.

Scrub the salsify roots and cook them in salted water with 1 teaspoon of lemon juice until just tender. Drain well, leave to cool, remove their skins and then thinly slice the salsify. Peel and finely chop the shallot. Thinly slice the mushrooms.

Drain the scallops and toss them in flour that has been seasoned with salt, pepper and a little cayenne.

Melt the butter in a heavy frying pan. Add the scallops and cook gently over a low heat for 5 minutes. Remove the scallops with a slotted spoon and place them in four scallop shells or shallow dishes. Add the salsify to the juices in the pan with the shallot and mushrooms and cook over a low heat, stirring, until the shallot is soft and transparent. Add the wine to the vegetables, raise the heat and cook until the wine has been reduced by half. Add the cream, season with salt and pepper and cook over a very low heat, stirring, for 2 minutes. Pour the vegetables over the scallops, sprinkle over the Parmesan cheese and brown quickly under a hot grill.

Scallops with Bacon and Salsify or Scorzonera

Scallops need only the very shortest of cooking times. In this dish they are combined with bacon and salsify or scorzonera, making a quick and delicious first course or light lunch dish.
Serves 4

8 *scallops (large or medium size)*   *flour*
4 *salsify or scorzonera roots*   *salt and white pepper*
4 *oz (100 g) streaky bacon*   ¼ *pint (150 ml) dry white wine*
1 *teaspoon lemon juice*   2 *oz (50 g) white breadcrumbs*
2 *shallots*   1 *oz (25 g) butter*
1½ *oz (40 g) butter*   1 *tablespoon very finely chopped*
1 *tablespoon olive or vegetable oil*   *parsley*

Separate the white part from the coral of the scallops and remove any black veins. Thinly slice the white part of the scallops and halve the corals. Lightly coat the scallops in seasoned flour. Remove the rinds from the bacon and cut the rashers into thin strips. Wash the salsify or scorzonera and boil them in boiling salted water, to which the lemon juice has been added, until the roots are tender. Drain and peel when cool enough to handle. Cut the salsify or scorzonera into thin slices. Peel and finely chop the shallots.

Heat 1½ oz (40 g) butter in a frying pan with the oil. Add the shallots and bacon and cook over a low heat until the shallots are soft and transparent. Add the scallops and continue to cook over a low heat for 5 minutes. Add the salsify or scorzonera and heat through. Remove the scallops and vegetables with a slotted spoon and put them into a shallow baking dish. Turn up the heat under the juices in the pan, add the wine and mix well. Boil until the sauce is reduced by one-third, pour it over the scallops and sprinkle the breadcrumbs on top. Dot with 1 oz (25 g) butter and put under a hot grill for a few minutes until the topping is crisp and golden. Sprinkle with the parsley.

Mussels with Salsify and Spinach

In this dish salsify is combined with mussels in a rich yellow saffron sauce. The bright green of the spinach adds an extra attraction to the dish.

Serve the mussels this way as a first course or as a main course with rice and a salad.

Serves 6 as a first course, 4 as a main course.

2 quarts (2400 ml) mussels,
   cleaned
6 salsify
1 small onion or shallot
2 bay leaves
bunch parsley
¼ pint (150 ml) water
½ teaspoon saffron strands
1 teaspoon lemon juice

8 oz (225 g) spinach
2 oz (50 g) butter
1½ tablespoons flour
scant ¼ pint (150 ml) milk
salt and freshly ground black
   pepper
1 egg
2 oz (50 g) fresh white
   breadcrumbs

Peel and finely chop the onion. Place the onion in the bottom of a large, heavy saucepan with the water, parsley and bay leaves. Add the mussels, cover tightly and cook over a high heat for about 5 minutes until the mussels have opened. Remove the mussels and strain the liquid from the pan. Measure ½ pint (300 ml) of the liquid from the pan and pour ¼ pint (150 ml) of the hot liquid over the saffron. Leave to infuse for 20 minutes. Discard the shells of the mussels.

Scrub the salsify and cook it in boiling salted water with a teaspoon of lemon juice and boil for 20 minutes or until the salsify is tender. Drain and leave to cool. When you can handle the salsify, peel off the skins and cut the roots into slices about ½ inch (1½ cm) thick.

Cook the spinach in a little boiling, salted water for only about 3 minutes. Drain, squeeze out excess liquid and roughly chop the leaves. Toss the leaves in 1 oz (25 g) melted butter and season with salt and pepper. Melt 1 oz (25 g) butter in a saucepan, add the flour and mix well. Gradually add the milk, stirring continually over a medium high heat until the sauce is thick and smooth. Add the strained saffron liquid and the other ¼ pint (150 ml) cooking liquid from the mussels, mix well, bring to the boil and simmer for 3 minutes. Season the sauce with salt and pepper.

Beat the egg until smooth and blend it into the sauce. Place the spinach in the bottom of a serving dish, cover with the mussels and salsify, and pour over the sauce. Sprinkle the breadcrumbs on top, put under a hot grill and heat through until the dish is piping hot and the top is a golden brown.

Chicken Salad with Salsify in a Yoghurt Dressing Served in Cucumber

If you like the Eastern dish of cucumber in yoghurt which is often served with curries you will undoubtedly find this dish a great success. The recipe is light, excellent for slimmers and the perfect dish for lunch on a hot summer's day. The combination of salsify and chicken is very good indeed.
Serves 4

8 oz (225 g) cooked chicken
4 salsify roots
2 stubby cucumbers
1 teaspoon lemon juice
1 small tin (7 oz, 200 g) tuna
1 carton (5 fl. oz, 150 ml) yoghurt

1 teaspoon French Dijon mustard
1 clove garlic
salt and white pepper
1 tablespoon finely chopped chives

Peel the cucumbers, cut each one in half horizontally and scoop out the seeds. Sprinkle the cucumbers with salt and leave them to 'sweat' for 20 minutes. Scrub the salsify, cook the roots in boiling salted water with 1 teaspoon of lemon juice until tender. Drain, leave to cool and then peel off the skins.

Cut the chicken into very small dice, and flake the tuna. Dice the salsify. Add the mustard to the yoghurt with the garlic squeezed through a garlic press, season with salt and pepper and mix well. Add the chicken, tuna and salsify.

Pat off excess liquid from the cucumbers with kitchen paper and cut a thin slice from the bottom of each half so that they will stand upright. Spoon the chicken salad into the cucumber halves and sprinkle over the chives.

Note: Instead of cutting cucumbers in half you can peel them, cut them into 2 inch (5 cm) lengths, remove the seeds and fill the cucumber with the salad.

Chicken Breasts with Salsify

Chicken breasts prepared like escalopes of veal are crisply fried and served with salsify, chopped and sautéd in butter, making a delicious combination of flavours.
Serves 4

2 *large chicken breasts*
1 *lb (450 g) salsify*
1 *teaspoon lemon juice*
1 *egg, beaten*
dried breadcrumbs
2 *oz (50 g) butter*

1 *tablespoon finely chopped parsley*
salt and freshly ground black
  pepper
vegetable oil for frying
4 *anchovy fillets*
1 *tablespoon capers*

Wash the salsify and cook the roots in boiling salted water with 1 teaspoon of lemon juice until just tender. Drain, cool, remove the skins and cut the roots into ½ inch (1½ cm) lengths.

Slice each chicken breast in two, horizontally. Place the slices between two sheets of greaseproof paper and beat gently with a wooden mallet or rolling pin to tenderize and stretch the slices. Dip the chicken slices in beaten egg and then coat in breadcrumbs.

Melt the butter in a saucepan, add the salsify and toss over a medium heat until the butter has been absorbed. Add the parsley, season with salt and pepper, turn the salsify on to a heated serving dish and keep warm.

Heat the oil in a frying pan, add the chicken breasts and cook over a medium high heat for about 3 minutes on each side until crisp, golden and tender. Drain the chicken breasts on kitchen paper, place them on top of the salsify and garnish each slice with a circle of anchovy fillet filled with capers.

Kidneys with Salsify in a White Wine Sauce

The texture of salsify is an experience I always enjoy and when I first tried this dish I discovered that not only do the salsify roots complement the kidneys but they also become impregnated with the flavour of the kidneys in a most satisfactory manner.

The dish is garnished in the traditional way with triangles of crisply fried bread and it can be served with rice and a salad. Serves 6

9 *lambs' kidneys*
1 *lb (450 g) salsify*
2 *teaspoons lemon juice*
4 *oz (100 g) butter*
salt and freshly ground black
  pepper
pinch ground nutmeg and mace

2 *teaspoons very finely chopped*
  parsley
1 *tablespoon flour*
¼ *pint (150 ml) dry white wine*
3 *tablespoons good stock*
4 *slices white bread*
oil for frying

Wash the salsify and cook the roots in boiling salted water, to which 1 teaspoon of lemon juice has been added, until they are just tender (they must not be overcooked). Drain, cool and skin the roots and cut them into slices about ¼ inch (¾ cm) thick.

Trim off the skin and core of the kidneys and cut them into thin slices.

Melt ½ oz (15 g) butter in a small saucepan. Add the sliced salsify, toss over a medium heat until the butter is absorbed and set them to one side.

Melt half the remaining butter in a heavy frying pan, add the slices of kidney and cook over a high heat until the slices are browned on both sides. Season them with salt, pepper, nutmeg and mace and mix in the parsley. Sprinkle over the flour and stir in the wine, stock and salsify. Cook over a slow heat for 5 minutes, mix in the remaining lemon juice and butter and check the seasoning.

Remove the crusts from the bread and cut each slice into four triangles. Fry the bread in hot oil until crisp and golden and drain the slices on kitchen paper.

Transfer the kidneys to a heated serving dish and tuck the triangles around the edge. Serve at once.

Spinach

The Victorians stuffed their children so full of spinach, usually overcooked and swimming in water, because it 'would do them good', that it is little wonder their children left the nursery vowing they would never eat spinach again. In fact the vegetable became so unpopular that during the 1920s it was seldom served in Britain and Good King Henry, a cultivated weed similar to spinach and once a feature of almost every cottage garden, went completely out of fashion. Then came Popeye the Sailor Man. Remember him and his weedy girlfriend, Olive Oil, and the amazing effect a little spinach had on his muscles and sex life? All he had to do in a crisis was to consume one tin of spinach, and Olive Oil and everything else fell into his lap.

By the 1940s Popeye and spinach were synonymous and as a child I remember being taken in by my nanny's assurance that if I ate enough of the stuff I would grow big and strong like a sailor (something I have been trying to avoid ever since). Surprisingly my fondness for spinach, in all its many forms, remained and I now grow six varieties in my kitchen garden, harvesting the leaves almost all the year round, shredding them, cooking them *en branche*, puréeing them, using them as a colouring ingredient and as a salad ingredient in the place of lettuce.

Spinach, by the way, really is good for you – providing the vegetable is not overcooked, the leaves contain a high level of iron and potassium. If you happen to be lacking in these vital elements a good drink can be made by saving the water the spinach has been cooked in, cooling and then combining it with vodka, pepper, celery salt and Worcestershire sauce and shaking it up with some cracked ice. Like most good things, however, spinach also has its dangers – too much of the vegetable (and I do mean really large quantities) can be a contributory cause of kidney stones, due to its oxalic acid content. In fact our hero Popeye was banned from New Zealand because the oxalic content was supposed to be on the high side in the tinned produce.

Spinach can be difficult to establish, with the summer variety ('Long Standing Round') disliking hot, dry weather, and the winter variety turning up its toes if subjected to too much wet or cold. Far more hardy is spinach beet, often known as perpetual spinach, which grows all the year round, thrives on being cut for the kitchen and has crisp, green leaves.

New Zealand spinach (perhaps their answer to Popeye) is not in fact a true spinach but it is useful to grow because it can stand both poor soil and drought. The leaves are small and rather mild in flavour but they are extremely good in salads.

Seakale beet (Swiss chard) also comes into the spinach category as its leaves are used in the same way, but here the advantage is that you can use the thick white stems as well as the green leaves. Trim off the green leaves from the ribs (I do this with kitchen scissors) and use them in place of spinach. The stalks can be tied into bundles, cooked in the same way as asparagus and served with melted butter or an hollandaise sauce. Ruby chard is also a variety of the seakale beet but although it looks very attractive in the garden its flavour is not so good as the silver beet.

The secret of cooking spinach is *never*, ever, to overcook it. The leaves need only a few minutes and they should retain their shape and texture when they are served unless, of course, the spinach is to be creamed or puréed. Cook the leaves in only about 1 inch ($2\frac{1}{2}$ cm) of boiling, salted water over a high heat for about 4 minutes.

The spinach will usually have to be well washed before being cooked to remove any grit or dirt from the leaves. It should be dried on a kitchen towel before being cooked and should be very well drained after cooking. The liquid in which the spinach was cooked can be used in vegetable stocks.

Spinach Soup with Chicken Dumplings

The dumplings in this rich green soup are based on a Chinese recipe for steamed pork dumplings. The addition of an egg white makes them light and their texture is superb. The addition of the dumplings makes this into a hearty and nourishing soup which, for a simple meal, need only be followed by fruit and cheese. If you serve it as a first course it should be followed by something light.

Instead of using spinach for the soup you can make it from young nettles (using the tops only), young turnip tops, beetroot tops or seakale beet.

Serves 6

2 lb (900 g) fresh spinach
1 onion
2 oz (50 g) butter
1½ oz (40 g) flour
2 pints (1200 ml) stock
salt and freshly ground black
  pepper
pinch each cayenne pepper and
  grated nutmeg

2 oz (50 g) white bread with
  the crust removed
4 tablespoons chicken stock
12 oz (350 g) raw chicken
½ inch (1½ cm) piece fresh
  ginger root
1 egg, separated
¼ pint (150 ml) single cream

Pick over and wash the spinach leaves. Peel and finely chop the onion. Heat the butter in a large saucepan. Add the onion and cook over a low heat until it is soft and transparent. Add the flour and mix well. Add the spinach and stir over a medium heat for 2 minutes. Gradually blend in the 2 pints (1200 ml) of stock, bring to the boil and simmer until the spinach is tender. Purée the soup through a fine sieve, a fine food mill or in an electric liquidizer or food processor.

Soak the bread in the 4 tablespoons of stock. Put the chicken twice through the fine blades of a mincing machine (this can be done in an electric food processor). Peel and finely grate the ginger.

Combine the chicken, bread and ginger and mix well. Season with salt and pepper and beat the egg yolk into the mixture which should be smooth and almost like a thick pasta. Lightly beat the egg white and gently mix it into the other ingredients.

Using well-floured hands form the mixture into small walnut-sized balls — a messy business but well worth the effort.

Put the spinach purée into a clean pan, season it with salt, pepper, cayenne and nutmeg and bring it to the boil. Drop the chicken dumplings into the soup and cook over a high heat for about 7 minutes, by which time the dumplings should have risen to the surface of the soup and be cooked through. Lower the heat, add the cream, check the seasoning and serve at once.

Poached Eggs with Mayonnaise on a Bed of Seakale Beet

This makes a really good and unusual starter. The eggs should be poached in boiling water and the whites should be trimmed with scissors to give them a uniform shape.
Serves 4

1 *lb (450 g) seakale beet*
4 *eggs*
2 *tablespoons olive or sunflower oil*
½ *teaspoon French Dijon mustard*
1 *tablespoon white wine vinegar*

salt and freshly ground black pepper
6 *tablespoons mayonnaise*
1 *tinned pimento*

Wash and dry the seakale beet, having cut out any tough stalks. Cook the seakale beet in a little boiling salted water until just tender and drain well pressing out any excess water. Roughly cut up the seakale beet with kitchen scissors. Combine the oil, vinegar and mustard, season with salt and pepper and mix well. Toss the seakale beet in the dressing and arrange it in four small dishes. Chill in the refrigerator.

Poach the eggs in boiling salted water until just set. As soon as they are ready, remove them from the water and plunge them into cold water. Drain and trim the eggs neatly with kitchen scissors. Place the eggs on the seakale beet, spoon over the mayonnaise and garnish with very thin strips of pimento.

Terrine of Pork and Swiss Chard with a Piquant Mayonnaise

Serves 6

1 lb (450 g) pork (this should
    have about a third as much fat
    as lean meat)
1 lb (450 g) Swiss chard
1 small onion
2 cloves garlic
1 oz (25 g) butter
salt and freshly ground black
    pepper
pinch each ground allspice,
    nutmeg and mace

1 crisp lettuce
2 tinned red pimentos
1 tablespoon finely chopped capers
1 tablespoon finely chopped
    dill-pickled cucumber
½ pint (300 ml) home-made
    mayonnaise
few drops chilli or Tabasco sauce
few drops Worcestershire sauce

Pick over the chard and cook it in a very little boiling salted water until it is just tender. Drain well and press out all the excess water by wrapping the chard in a cloth or squeezing it with your fingers. Finely chop the chard.

Mince the pork through the fine blades of a mincing machine. Peel and finely chop the onion and very finely chop the garlic.

Melt the butter in a small frying pan. Add the onion and garlic and cook over a low heat, stirring to prevent sticking, until the onion is soft and transparent.

Combine the spinach, pork, onion and garlic and the juices from the pan, season with salt, pepper, allspice, mace and nutmeg and mix well. Press the mixture firmly into a lightly buttered terrine. Cover with a double thickness of well-buttered grease-proof paper and then with a lid or with foil. Stand the terrine in a baking tin half filled with hot water and cook in a very moderate oven (325°F. 170°C. Reg. 3) for 1 hour. Leave to cool and then chill.

Turn out the terrine on to a bed of lettuce leaves. Very finely chop or mince the pimentos. Add the pimentos, capers and dill-pickled cucumber to the mayonnaise and flavour with a little chilli, Tabasco and Worcestershire sauce.

Serve the mayonnaise on the side, cut the terrine into thin slices and accompany with hot toast or French bread.

The terrine can be served as a first course or as a main course for a summer lunch with new potatoes and a mixed salad.

Ham and Spinach Soufflé in Tomato Cases

A really excellent luncheon dish or starter to a meal. The tomatoes provide attractive and pleasantly tasting vehicles for the soufflés and the combination of flavours is one that is hard to beat. Whenever possible use those large Mediterranean tomatoes which can be grown out of doors in Britain in a good summer.
Serves 8

4 oz (100 g) lean ham	6 eggs, separated
12 oz (350 g) spinach	1½ oz (40 g) grated Parmesan
8 very large tomatoes	cheese
3 oz (75 g) butter	salt and freshly ground black
2 tablespoons flour	pepper
½ pint (300 ml) milk	pinch ground nutmeg

Cut a slice from the top of each tomato and carefully scoop out the core, seeds and most of the flesh without piercing the skin. Turn the tomatoes upside down and leave them to drain.

Pick over and wash the spinach and cook it without extra water over a medium heat for about 4 minutes or until it is just tender. Drain well and squeeze out all excess moisture. Finely chop the spinach and toss it in 1 oz (25 g) of melted butter until the butter has been absorbed. Mince or very finely chop the ham.

Melt the remaining 2 oz (50 g) butter in a clean saucepan. Add the flour and mix well. Gradually add the milk, stirring continually over a medium high heat until the sauce comes to the boil and is thick and smooth. Remove from the heat and beat in the egg yolks one by one, making sure the mixture is smooth after each addition. Add the Parmesan cheese, ham and spinach, season with salt, pepper and a little ground nutmeg. Beat the egg whites until stiff and lightly fold them into the mixture.

Fill the tomatoes three-quarters of the way up with the soufflé mixture and bake for about 25 minutes in a hot oven (400°F. 200°C. Reg. 6) and serve at once.

Risotto Dauphine

I find this one of the most satisfactory of dishes for both its looks
and its taste. It is quick and simple to make, utilizes small leftover amounts of cooked chicken and has an exquisite flavour.
You can double the quantities to serve four people.
Serves 2

24 *large spinach leaves*
4 *oz (100 g) cooked chicken*
6 *oz (175 g) spring onions*
6 *oz (175 g) long-grain rice*
1½ *tablespoons vegetable or olive*
   oil
¼ *pint (150 ml) tomato juice*

¼ *pint (150 ml) chicken stock*
salt and freshly ground black
   pepper
1 *oz (25 g) freshly grated*
   Parmesan cheese
1 *oz (25 g) butter*

Trim off the stalks of the spinach leaves. Trim the spring
onions and thinly slice the stalks and bulbs.

Heat the oil in a heavy saucepan. Add the spring onions and
cook over a low heat until they are soft and transparent. Add the
rice and stir over a low heat until the rice is transparent. Add the
tomato juice and stock, stir well, season with salt and pepper,
bring to the boil, cover tightly and cook over a very low heat
for 15–20 minutes until the rice is just tender.

Steam the spinach leaves over boiling water for 5 minutes.
Butter a bowl large enough to take the risotto and line it with
the spinach leaves, overlapping the leaves and leaving their tops
hanging out over the sides.

Very finely chop the chicken. Mix the chicken and Parmesan
cheese into the cooked rice mixture with the butter. Check the
seasoning and pack the rice mixture into the lined bowl, pressing
it in firmly. Fold over the ends of the spinach leaves and bake the
dish in a moderate oven (350°F. 180°C. Reg. 4) for 15 minutes.
Turn out on to a heated serving dish and serve with salad and,
if you like, a tomato sauce.

Savoury Pancakes Filled with Spinach, Chicken and Cream Sauce

Serves 6

The pancakes:
4 oz (100 g) plain white flour
2 eggs
2 egg yolks
2 tablespoons olive or vegetable oil
4 tablespoons milk
4 tablespoons cold water

2 oz (50 g) butter
2 tablespoons flour
½ pint (300 ml) milk
salt and freshly ground black
   pepper
pinch ground nutmeg
3 oz (75 g) grated Gruyère
   cheese
1 oz (25 g) finely grated
   Parmesan cheese

The filling:
1 lb (450 g) spinach
6 oz (175 g) cooked chicken

Combine the 4 oz (100 g) plain flour with the eggs, egg yolks, oil, milk and water and whisk with a wire, rotary or electric whisk until the mixture is smooth. Leave to stand for 1 hour.

Wipe an omelette pan with a film of oil and heat until smoking, add a large tablespoon of the batter, swirling it around the pan so that it forms an even coating (these pancakes are thicker than usual and resemble the texture required for making Russian *blini*). Cook for 1 minute, shaking the pan to prevent the pancake sticking, then turn over and cook for a further minute on the other side. Remove the pancake to a warmed plate. Continue in the same way until all the batter is used up. Pile the pancakes, one on top of another, on a plate, to keep warm while making the filling.

Pick over and wash the spinach and cook it without extra water for about 4 minutes or until it is just tender. Drain the spinach well and press out any excess moisture. Finely chop the spinach. Chop the chicken.

Melt the 2 oz (50 g) butter in a saucepan, add the 2 tablespoons flour and mix well. Gradually add the milk, stirring continually over a medium high heat until the sauce comes to the boil and is thick and smooth. Season with salt, pepper and a pinch of nutmeg, add the Gruyère cheese and stir over a low heat for 3 minutes. Add the spinach and the chicken to the sauce, mix lightly and check the seasoning.

Place some of the filling on each of the pancakes, spreading it down the middle of the pancake, roll up neatly and place the pancakes on a lightly buttered serving dish. Sprinkle over the Parmesan cheese and put under a hot grill for a few minutes until the Parmesan has melted and the pancakes are hot through.

Pancakes with Spinach and Mussels in a Saffron-flavoured Sauce

Serves 6

The pancakes:
4 oz (100 g) plain white flour
pinch salt
1 egg
½ pint (300 ml) milk
olive oil

The filling:
24 cooked mussels
6 oz (175 g) cooked spinach
1 teaspoon strand saffron
2 tablespoons boiling water

2 oz (50 g) butter
2 tablespoons flour
¼ pint (150 ml) milk
scant ¼ pint (150 ml) white wine
2 tablespoons double cream
salt and freshly ground black
    pepper
2 oz (50 g) grated Cheddar
cheese
½ oz (15 g) grated Parmesan
cheese

Combine the 4 oz (100 g) flour with a pinch of salt, the egg and milk and beat with a wire, rotary or electric whisk until the batter is smooth. Leave to stand for 30 minutes. Heat a little olive oil in an omelette pan, swirling the oil around until the pan is coated with a thin film and the oil begins to smoke. Add about 1 tablespoon of pancake batter, swirling that round too until it sets in a thin film. Cook over a high heat for 3 minutes until the bottom of the pancake is lightly browned, turn over and continue to cook until the other side is a nice golden brown. Slide the pancake on to a plate and continue in the same way with the rest of the batter, stacking the pancakes, one on top of the other, until all the batter has been used.

Put the saffron into a small bowl and pour over 2 tablespoons of boiling water. Leave to stand for 5 minutes and then strain off the liquid.

Melt the butter in a saucepan. Add the flour and mix well.

Gradually blend in the milk, stirring continually over a high heat until the sauce comes to the boil and is thick and smooth. Add the wine, saffron water, cream and mussels, season with salt and pepper and simmer for 3 minutes.

Spread a little of the cooked spinach on each pancake, cover with the sauce and roll up neatly. Place the pancakes on a lightly buttered baking dish and sprinkle over the combined Cheddar and Parmesan cheese. Bake in a hot oven (400°F. 200°C. Reg. 6) for about 10 minutes until the pancakes are hot through and the cheese is golden brown.

Eggs with Spinach and Anchovies

A delicious summer dish. Use only young leaves that have not become too bitter. If you grow your own sorrel this makes a very good alternative to the young spinach leaves.
Serves 4

4 eggs
8 oz (225 g) young spinach
   leaves
2 oz (50 g) butter
3 tablespoons double cream
salt

freshly ground black pepper
pinch ground nutmeg
four 3 inch (8 cm) circles of
   bread
olive oil
8 anchovy fillets

Cook the eggs in boiling water for 5 minutes. Plunge them immediately into cold water and peel them as soon as they are cold enough to handle. Take care, as the eggs are only semi hard-boiled.

Remove the stems of the spinach leaves. Melt the butter, add the spinach and cook over a low heat, stirring frequently, until the spinach is soft. Purée the spinach through a food mill, a sieve or in an electric liquidizer and return to a clean pan. Add the cream and season with salt, pepper and a little nutmeg. Heat through.

Fry the bread in olive oil until crisp and golden brown, drain on kitchen paper, put each egg on a slice of fried bread and spoon over the spinach. Top with an anchovy fillet.

Old-fashioned Devilled Chicken or Turkey with Spinach

Devilling was a popular process in British food of the eighteenth and nineteenth centuries. If you like things on the hot and spicy side then this is a delicious method of cooking a great many cuts of meat or poultry and also dealing with leftovers. In this recipe devilled chicken or turkey (it is a useful way of using those joints of turkey you can now buy all the year round) is combined with lightly cooked spinach to give a delicious flavour and an interesting texture. The dish is served with rice and a good accompaniment would be tomatoes halved, rubbed with a little garlic, seasoned with salt and freshly ground black pepper, brushed with oil, then grilled or baked.
Serves 4

1 *lb (450 g) uncooked chicken or turkey off the bone*	1 *tablespoon lemon juice*
	few drops chilli sauce
8 *oz (225 g) spinach or seakale beet*	1 *tablespoon dark brown sugar*
	1 *tablespoon oil*
1 *onion*	3 *oz (75 g) butter*
1 *tablespoon mushroom ketchup*	*little cayenne pepper and plenty of*
2 *teaspoons Harvey's sauce*	*freshly ground black pepper*
1½ *teaspoons dry English mustard*	2 *tablespoons flaked almonds*

Peel and chop the onion. Cut the chicken or turkey into very thin strips. Thinly shred the spinach. Combine the mushroom ketchup, Harvey's sauce, mustard, lemon juice, chilli sauce and sugar and mix well until smooth.

Heat the oil with the butter in a heavy frying pan. When the butter has melted, add the onion and cook over a medium heat until the onion is golden brown. Add the chicken and stir over a high heat for about 3 minutes until the chicken has lost its opaque look. Stir in the sauce and continue to stir over a medium heat for about a further 3 minutes until the sauce has thickened and the chicken is just tender. Add the spinach and stir over a medium heat for yet another 3 minutes until the spinach has become soft but has not lost its fresh green colour and still has a slightly crisp texture. Season with cayenne pepper and black pepper.

Spread the almonds on an oiled baking sheet and roast them

in a hot oven (400°F. 200°C. Reg. 6) for 2 minutes until they are
golden brown.

Transfer the chicken mixture to a serving dish, surround it
with fluffy boiled rice and scatter the almonds over the top.

Chicken and Bacon Pies with Spinach

An old-fashioned hot-water crust, crisp and succulent, encases a
well-spiced mixture of chicken, bacon and pork fat combined
with finely shredded spinach or seakale. The pies are good hot
but perhaps even better cold and they make really excellent
picnic eating. This kind of pastry is used for making pork and
raised pies; it is easy to make and should be used warm rather
than being chilled like most pastry.

It is important that the stock used for topping up the pies
once they have been cooked should be really well jellied and if
necessary some gelatine should be added to the stock, although a
better result is achieved by cooking one or two pig's trotters
with the stock in the first place.

Serves 4–6

The pastry:
1 *lb (450 g) flour*
4 *oz (100 g) lard*
½ *pint (300 ml) water*
1 *teaspoon salt*
1 *beaten egg*

The filling:
10 *oz (275 g) raw chicken*
4 *oz (100 g) streaky bacon with*
    the rinds removed

4 *oz (100 g) pork fat*
8 *oz (225 g) spinach or seakale*
    beet
salt and freshly ground black
    pepper
pinch each ground mace and
    ground nutmeg
jellied chicken stock

Mince the chicken, bacon and pork fat through the coarse
blades of a mincing machine. Very finely chop the spinach or
seakale beet. Combine the chicken, bacon, pork fat and spinach
and season well with salt, pepper, mace and nutmeg.

Combine the water and salt and lard in a saucepan, heat until
the lard has melted, then bring to the boil and add the flour all
at once. Remove the pan from the heat and stir with a wooden
spoon until the mixture forms a ball. Turn on to a floured board

and knead lightly until the dough is smooth.

Roll out the pastry to about ⅛ inch (½ cm) thickness on a well-floured board. Set aside one-third of the pastry to use as lids and use the remainder to line eight patty tins. Three-quarters fill the patties with the chicken mixture, cut circles for the lids, damp the edges of the pastry, place on the lids and press the edges firmly together. Cut an air vent in the centre of each lid and bake the pies in a hot oven (425°F. 220°C. Reg. 7) for 10 minutes and then lower the heat to moderate (350°F. 180°C. Reg. 4) and continue to cook for a further 10 minutes. Brush with beaten egg and return to the oven for another 10 minutes, by which time the pastry should be crisp and golden brown and the filling tender. Leave the pies to stand for 10 minutes and then remove them from their tins.

Using a small funnel, pour stock into the pies until they are full to the brim. Leave the pies to cool before eating.

Note: More stock may have to be added after the pies have been left to cool for an hour or so. The more stock that is added the more moist and delicious the pies will be.

Lamb or Mutton and Spinach Pies

These are delectable, fragrant and extraordinarily light individual pies made with raised pie pastry (hot-water crust) and with a filling of finely chopped lamb or mutton and chopped spinach. They should really be eaten straight from the oven but are almost as good cold as they are hot, so that they make excellent hot weather and picnic eating.
Serves 4–6

The pastry:
4 oz (100 g) good dripping or lard
½ pint (300 ml) boiling water
1 teaspoon salt
1 lb (450 g) plain white flour

The filling:
12 oz (350 g) lean mutton or lamb
1 lb (450 g) spinach
1 onion
1 tablespoon oil

salt and freshly ground black   2 *teaspoons brown sugar*
  pepper   1 *tablespoon mushroom ketchup*
½ *teaspoon ground nutmeg*   *a little milk*
grated peel of 1 *lemon*   *gravy*

Add the lard or dripping to the boiling water and boil until
the lard or dripping has dissolved. Add the salt and pour in the
flour all at once. Remove the pan from the heat and beat with a
wooden spoon until the mixture has formed a dough and comes
away from the sides of the pan. Leave until cool enough to
handle and then knead on a floured board until smooth. Remove
a third of the dough and roll out the rest to about ¼ inch (¾ cm)
thickness. Line 6 patty tins with the dough.

Finely chop the onion. Very finely chop (or grind in a food
processor) the lamb or mutton. Heat the oil, add the onion and
cook over a low heat until the onion is soft and transparent.
Cook the spinach in a little boiling salted water until it is just
tender, drain well and chop the spinach very finely (this can also
be done in a food processor).

Combine the onion, lamb or mutton and the spinach in a
bowl, season with salt and pepper and nutmeg, mix in the lemon
peel and brown sugar and moisten with the mushroom ketchup.

Fill the patty cases with the meat mixture. Roll out the remaining pastry cut into lids, damp the edges and press the lids on to
the bases. Brush with milk, cut an air vent in the centre of each
pie and bake in a moderate oven (350°F. 180°C. Reg. 4) for
40 minutes. Fill up the pies through the air vents, using a small
funnel, with a little extra gravy before serving.

A Savoury Concoction of Duck Wrapped in Seakale Beet Leaves

The mixture of duck, vegetables, herbs and spices turns out
rather like a really well-flavoured sausage. The seakale beet
leaves provide the packaging materials for the dish and both
tenderize the meat and give it additional flavour.
Serves 8

1 *small duck or duckling*
8 *large seakale beet leaves*
8 *oz (225 g) parsnips*
1 *onion*
2 *cloves garlic*
4 *rashers streaky bacon*
1 *oz (25 g) butter*
2 *oz (50 g) fresh white
   breadcrumbs*
1 *egg*
*pinch each ground mace, nutmeg
   and cayenne pepper*

*salt and freshly ground black
   pepper*
1 *tablespoon finely chopped
   parsley*
*small pinch each finely chopped
   thyme and sage*
1 *tin consommé (or ¾ pint,
   450 ml, good stock)*
1 *teaspoon tomato purée*

Cut out the thick white stalk from the seakale beet leaves. Cut the white stalks into 2 inch (5 cm) lengths and then into thin matchstick strips. Blanch the leaves in boiling salted water for 3 minutes and drain well. Blanch the stalks in boiling salted water for 5 minutes and drain well.

Peel the parsnips and cook them in boiling salted water until just tender, drain well and mash with a potato masher or fork. Peel and very finely chop the onion and garlic.

Remove the skin from the duck and mince the flesh (the skin can be cut into thin strips and fried, in a little oil, over a very high heat until it is crisp and golden brown and used as a garnish for the dish or served as a cocktail titbit). Remove the rinds from the bacon and mince the rashers.

Melt the butter in a small pan. Add the onion and garlic and cook over a low heat until the onion is soft and transparent. Combine the duck, bacon, onion, garlic and breadcrumbs and mix well. Beat the egg, add it to the duck mixture, season with salt, pepper, mace, nutmeg and cayenne, add the herbs and mix really well.

Spread the seakale beet leaves out flat, divide the duck stuffing between the leaves, shape the filling into a sausage and neatly wrap the leaves around the filling. Place the stuffed leaves in a buttered baking dish and cover with the blanched stalks.

Combine the consommé or stock with the tomato purée and mix well. Pour the liquid over the stuffed leaves, cover tightly with foil and bake in a moderate oven (350°F. 180°C. Reg. 4) for 1¼ hours.

Serve with rice and a salad.

Liver and Onions with Crisply Fried Spinach

Liver is cut into very thin slices (ask for the liver in one piece because I have never found a butcher in this country who will cut the liver as thin as thinly sliced bacon which is the important thing in this dish) and then very quickly fried with onions. The liver and onions are surrounded by very crisply fried spinach (a delicious taste sensation) and topped with a piquant sauce. Spinach very finely shredded and deep fried tastes remarkably like that delicious Japanese crisply fried seaweed.
Serves 4

1 *lb (450 g) calf's liver*
12 *oz (350 g) spinach or seakale beet*
2 *large onions*
3 *oz (75 g) butter*
1 *tablespoon oil*
salt and freshly ground black pepper

2 *tablespoons tomato ketchup*
¼ *pint (150 ml) good stock*
3 *tablespoons white wine*
few drops Worcestershire sauce
2 *tablespoons finely chopped parsley*
deep oil for frying

Buy the liver in one piece, and using a very sharp knife, cut it into wafer-thin slices (the thinner they are the better the dish will taste). Peel the onions, cut them into very thin slices and divide them into rings. Pick over the spinach (wash it if necessary, but make sure it is dried really well) and very finely shred the leaves.

Heat the butter and oil in a heavy pan. Add the onions and cook over a low heat until the onions are really soft and transparent. Raise the heat and add the liver, a slice at a time, stirring for about 3 minutes with the onions until the slices are nicely browned and tender but still just pink in the middle. Using a slotted spoon transfer the onions and liver to a warm serving dish, piling them in the centre of the dish, and keep warm.

Add the tomato ketchup, stock, wine and Worcestershire sauce to the juices in the pan and season with salt and pepper. Stir well to amalgamate all the flavours in the pan, bring to the boil and simmer for 4 minutes. Mix in the parsley and pour the sauce over the liver. Keep warm again.

Heat the oil until just smoking. Add a handful of shredded spinach and cook over a high heat until the spinach has become crisp and is just turning brown. Remove the spinach with a slotted spoon, draining off all excess oil, and put it on to kitchen paper to drain. Fry the rest of the spinach in the same way.

Surround the liver with the fried spinach and serve at once.

Tomatoes

I remember once reading a tirade by a well-known cookery writer about the over-use of tomatoes and tomato purée in cooking. Personally I don't believe one can really have too much of a good thing and the culinary use of tomatoes is something I would hate to be without. For one thing their colour can do a lot for an insipid or dreary-looking dish and, for another, their flavour has the ability to enhance a great many other ingredients. Certainly one does not want to overdo the tomato flavouring and the rich red, concentrated tomato purée should be used with care but, on the whole, if you want to give more flavour or colour to a dish there are few better ways of doing it than by adding tomatoes in one form or another.

You will notice that in most of my recipes using tomatoes I suggest that they should be skinned. Providing you cover the tomatoes with boiling water for a minute or two this is an easy process to do as the skins will slide off easily once the tomatoes have been drained. I do this because not only do the skins tend to be a little on the tough side but they are also invaluable for adding to stock in order both to colour and flavour the liquid. In most cooked dishes I also remove the seeds and any tough central core.

The flavour of tomatoes increases the longer you cook them and when you are using fresh (or for that matter tinned) tomatoes for a sauce or purée they will need to be cooked over a high heat without a cover so that the liquid evaporates and their taste is intensified.

Tomatoes feature greatly in my garden. We grow the red and

also the lovely mild and sweet golden varieties in the greenhouse for harvesting from May onwards. Later on we have the ugly Mediterranean variety, which has a marvellous flavour and which can be grown out of doors, and the outdoor cocktail tomato (Suttons 'Mixed Ornamental'), a miniature variety which is delicious in salads and hors d'oeuvres.

One of the joys of tomatoes is that you can grow them even in the most confined of spaces provided there is plenty of sunlight, that they are kept well moistened and that you give them a feed every now and then to help their growth and development. Across from my tiny mews house in London a neighbour has them overflowing every summer from a small window-box where they drip brilliantly coloured fruit over a dusty London back street. Other friends grow tomatoes successfully in patio tubs and although they do need a certain amount of looking after there is no doubt at all that the effort is worth while for, however cheap the tomatoes in the greengrocer's shop are, they are always picked green or 'pink' and ripened artificially, and nothing compares with the marvellous sweet/ sharp flavouring of the fruit you pick from your own plants which are left to ripen on the plant.

Tomatoes made a surprisingly late entry on to the European culinary scene. They seem to have made their first appearance as a weed in the maize fields of the Andes but for some time they were thought to be poisonous and that the pips caused appendicitis. They were actually introduced into Europe about four centuries ago and since they were called 'golden apples' it seems as if these early varieties were the golden-coloured fruit which is now slowly making a come-back. Over the years their name, in Britain at any rate, was changed to 'love apple' as the fruit was thought not to be poisonous at all but, instead, a powerful aphrodisiac and gradually they gained in popularity, becoming an integral feature of the 'mixed salad'. In Europe the tomato, now red, became an important feature of everyday diet and in many places it is still one of the major ingredients of a peasant diet, adding colour and flavour for a minimal cost to even the most simple of food. In Italy, for instance, a tomato sauce served with pasta still acts as a substantial main course, in Malta a spicy tomato sauce spiked with wild capers is eaten on bread as a midday meal and many of the classic dishes of Spain are based on the flavour of sun-ripened tomatoes.

The tomatoes grown in Britain do not have the strength of those ripened by the Mediterranean sun and it is for that reason that I frequently recommend the addition of a little tomato purée to increase their strength when you are cooking them. If tomatoes are out of season or expensive to buy, the tinned varieties, especially those which come from Italy, are very good value and hard to tell from the fresh fruit when cooked.

A Soup of Tomatoes, Beetroot and Parsnips

This is an excellent aromatic and colourful soup. I make it with yellow tomatoes and golden beetroot when I have them but it is just as delicious made with the more conventional red tomatoes and beetroot. Home-made duck stock makes an excellent base for the soup.

A last-minute garnish of sour cream and dill-pickled cucumber gives the soup a sophisticated touch.
Serves 6–8

1 *lb (450 g) tomatoes*
2 *medium beetroots*
2 *parsnips*
1 *onion*
1 *clove garlic*
2 *pints (1200 ml) stock*
1 *tablespoon oil*
½ *inch (1½ cm) fresh ginger root*

2 *bay leaves*
salt and freshly ground black
    pepper
¼ *pint (150 ml) single cream*
1 *dill-pickled cucumber*
1 *carton (5 fl. oz, 150 ml) sour*
    cream

Roughly chop the tomatoes. Peel and finely chop the onion and garlic. Peel the ginger root and cut the flesh into very small strips. Peel and roughly chop the beetroots and parsnips.

Place the parsnips and beetroots in a saucepan, cover with the stock, bring to the boil and simmer for 45 minutes until the vegetables are tender.

Heat the oil in a frying pan, add the onions, garlic and ginger and cook over a low heat until the onion is soft and transparent. Add the tomatoes and bay leaves, season with salt and pepper and cook over a low heat, stirring every now and then for 20 minutes. Strain off the liquid from the beetroot, parsnip and tomato mixture and rub the vegetables, discarding the bay leaves, through a fine food mill or a sieve. Return the vegetables to a clean pan, add the cooking liquids, check the seasoning and bring to the boil. Lower the heat and stir in the cream. Do not boil once the cream has been added.

Finely chop the dill-pickled cucumber, mix it with the sour cream and put a spoonful of the mixture into each serving of soup.

Tomatoes with a Seafood Topping

This makes an excellent starter to a meal and it looks very attractive too. The tomatoes are not actually stuffed but they are peeled and halved and their seeds should be removed.
Serves 4

4 *medium to large tomatoes*
4 *oz (100 g) peeled, cooked*
  prawns
4 *oz (100 g) white crab meat*
6 *fl. oz (175 ml) mayonnaise*
1 *teaspoon lemon juice*

few drops Worcestershire and
  Tabasco sauce
2 *tablespoons double cream*
salt and white pepper
a little finely chopped chives

Cover the tomatoes with boiling water and leave them to stand for 2 minutes. Drain them and slide off their skins. Halve the tomatoes and scoop out the seeds and any coarse central stem with a small teaspoon.

Finely chop the prawns. Combine the mayonnaise with the lemon juice, add a few drops of Worcestershire and Tabasco sauce, season if necessary and mix in the cream. Add the crab meat and the prawns to the mayonnaise and mix lightly.

Arrange two halves of tomato cut side up on four small individual serving dishes. Spoon the mayonnaise mixture over the tomatoes, sprinkle over the chives, and chill before serving with thin slices of buttered brown bread.

A Savoury Dish of Tomatoes Stuffed with Peppers and Ham

A versatile dish that can be served as a first course, as a vegetable accompaniment or as a lunch or supper main-course dish. The best tomatoes to use are the large and sometimes misshapen Mediterranean variety, which can easily be grown at home, out of doors, provided there is anything like a reasonable amount of sun during the summer months.
Serves 4

4 *large ripe tomatoes (or use*
   8 *smaller tomatoes)*
1 *small onion or shallot*
2 *cloves garlic*
1 *large green pepper*
4 *oz (100 g) ham*
3 *tablespoons olive or vegetable oil*

6 *oz (175 g) cooked rice*
a little stock
salt and freshly ground black
   pepper
¼ *teaspoon oregano*
4 *anchovy fillets*

Cut a slice off the top of the tomatoes and reserve the tops. Scoop out and discard the core and seeds (a grapefruit spoon is the best instrument for this), and then scoop out the flesh leaving a layer of about ⅛ inch (¼ cm) thickness, reserving any juice. Finely chop the flesh. Peel and finely chop the onion or shallot and the garlic. Remove the core and seeds and very finely chop the flesh of the pepper. Very finely chop the ham.

Heat 2 tablespoons of the oil in a saucepan, add the pepper, onion and garlic and cook over a low heat until the onion or shallot is soft and transparent. Add the ham and cook for a further 2 minutes. Add the rice and tomato juice and flesh and mix well, moistening with a little stock to make a thick pulp. Season with salt and pepper and mix in the oregano. Simmer for 3 minutes, stirring, and then fill the tomato cases with the mixture.

Cut the anchovies in half lengthwise and place them on top of the tomatoes. Put on the lids, brush with the remaining oil and bake in a moderate oven (350°F. 180°C. Reg. 4) for 45 minutes.

Tomato and Salmon Quiche

If you have golden tomatoes in your garden or can buy them in the summer, make this quiche with those more delicately flavoured fruit rather than with the more mundane red tomatoes. A good-quality frozen imported salmon does well for this dish. You can serve it hot, warm or cold and it is a perfect ingredient for a summer picnic.
Serves 6

1 *partially baked* 10 *inch (25 cm) quiche case (see page 4)*
1½ *lb (675 g) ripe tomatoes*
½ *lb (225 g) cooked salmon*
1 *large onion*
1 *oz (25 g) butter*
3 *eggs, beaten*
½ *pint (300 ml) single cream*
2 *oz (50 g) Cheddar cheese, grated*

1 *oz (25 g) Parmesan cheese, grated*
1 *tablespoon finely chopped chervil*
salt and freshly ground black pepper
1 *oz (25 g) Gruyère cheese, grated*

Peel and thinly slice the onion and divide it into rings. Cover the tomatoes with boiling water for 2 minutes, drain and then slide off the tomato skins. Thinly slice the tomatoes. Flake the fish removing any skin and bones.

Heat the butter in a frying pan, add the onion and cook over a low heat, stirring every now and then, until the onion is soft and transparent. Leave to cool.

Spread the onion over the bottom of the quiche case, cover with the flaked salmon and then with the slices of tomato.

Beat the eggs with the cream until smooth. Add the Parmesan, Cheddar cheese and chopped chervil, season with salt and pepper and mix well. Pour the mixture over the ingredients in the quiche case and sprinkle over the Gruyère.

Bake the quiche in a moderately hot oven (375°F. 190°C. Reg. 5) for about 25 minutes or until the quiche is puffed up and golden brown.

A Provençal Quiche with Ham

A delicious quiche this, full of aromatic flavour and rich in texture. Serve it with a salad and, in season, some minted new potatoes.
Serves 6

1 *partially baked* 10 *inch* (*25 cm*) *quiche shell* (*see page 4*)
1 *large onion*
1 *green or red pepper*
8 *oz* (*225 g*) *aubergines*
¾ *lb* (*350 g*) *tomatoes*
8 *oz* (*225 g*) *cooked ham*
3 *tablespoons olive or vegetable oil*
1 *tablespoon finely chopped parsley*
pinch finely chopped fresh or dried oregano

3 *eggs*
½ *pint* (*300 ml*) *single cream*
2 *oz* (*50 g*) *finely grated Cheddar cheese*
½ *oz* (*15 g*) *finely grated Parmesan cheese*
salt, freshly ground black pepper and a pinch of cayenne pepper
1 *oz* (*25 g*) *grated Gruyère cheese*

Peel and finely chop the onion. Remove the seeds and core of the pepper and chop the flesh. Cut the aubergines into very small dice. Cover the tomatoes with boiling water and leave to stand for 2 minutes. Drain well and slide the tomato skins off. Cut the tomatoes into thin slices. Cut the ham into thin matchstick strips.

Heat the oil in a heavy frying pan. Add the onion and cook over a low heat, stirring to prevent sticking, for about 4 minutes until the onion is soft and transparent. Add the peppers and aubergines and continue to cook over a low heat, stirring every now and then, for about 6 minutes until the vegetables are all soft. Add the parsley and the oregano, season with salt and pepper and cayenne and mix well. Leave to cool for about 10 minutes.

Beat the eggs with the cream until smooth. Add the Cheddar and Parmesan cheese and season with a little salt and pepper.

Arrange the onions, aubergines and pepper in the partially baked quiche shell, cover with the ham and then with the sliced tomatoes and pour over the egg, cream and cheese mixture. Top with the Gruyère cheese and bake in a moderately hot oven (375°F. 190°C. Reg. 5) for about 25 minutes or until the quiche is puffed up and golden brown.

Serve the quiche hot or cold with a salad or green vegetables.

I

Dabs or Small Sole Céleste

I use very small dabs or, if I can get them, miniature sole like they have in Italy, for this spectacular dish. Although the fish are normally much smaller than those one would normally serve for each portion, the addition of the vegetables and a robust mornay sauce make this a substantial meal. Dabs, when they are available, are extremely good value for money and I completely disagree with those that maintain they have a slightly muddy flavour; providing the dabs are small I feel they compare very favourably with the much more expensive sole and they are certainly infinitely preferable to plaice.

Serves 4

4 small dabs or sole, skinned	2 tablespoons flour
2 tablespoons olive or vegetable oil	$\frac{1}{2}$ pint (300 ml) milk
2 oz (50 g) butter	2 oz (50 g) grated Gruyère
1 medium aubergine	cheese
1 large onion	1 oz (25 g) grated Parmesan
3 large ripe tomatoes	cheese
salt and freshly ground black	$\frac{1}{4}$ pint (150 ml) single cream
pepper	1 egg

Heat the butter with $\frac{1}{2}$ tablespoon of the oil in a large frying pan. Add the fish and cook over a moderate heat for about 4 minutes on each side or until the fish are just cooked through (do not overcook the fish).

Cut the aubergine into very small dice. Peel and finely chop the onion. Cover the tomatoes with boiling water for 2 minutes, drain them well and slide off the skins. Remove the core of the tomatoes and chop the flesh. Heat $1\frac{1}{2}$ tablespoons of oil in a small saucepan. Add the onion and cook over a low heat until the onion is soft and transparent. Add the aubergine and continue to cook, stirring, for 3 minutes over a medium heat. Add the tomatoes, season with salt and pepper, mix well and simmer for 20 minutes without a lid, stirring every now and then to prevent sticking, until the aubergine is tender and the liquid has been absorbed – the mixture should be fairly dry.

Remove the fish from the pan, draining off any fat, arrange them on a serving dish and spread the aubergine mixture neatly over the fish.

Transfer the juices from the frying pan to a saucepan, add the flour and mix well. Gradually add the milk, stirring continually over a medium high heat until the sauce comes to the boil and is thick and smooth. Add the Gruyère and Parmesan cheese and stir over a low heat until the cheese has melted – the sauce should be of a thick coating consistency.

Beat the cream with the egg until smooth. Add the cream and egg mixture to the sauce and stir over a low heat (do not boil) until the sauce is smooth, thick and satiny. Spoon the sauce over the fish so that the vegetables are completely coated and grill under a hot flame until the top is a golden brown crust and the fish is hot through.

Serve as a first course or as a main course with new or mashed potatoes and a green vegetable.

Home-made Tomato Purée

Reducing peeled, seeded and cored tomatoes with a little onion and garlic results in a rich and sharp tomato purée which can be added to sour cream, whipped cream or mayonnaise to produce a delicious sauce for fish, cold chicken or meat or for a dish of hard-boiled eggs. This is well worth making when tomatoes are very cheap or when you have a glut of your own home-grown tomatoes. The mixture can be frozen and it also makes a delicious base for a tomato soup (add stock and cream) or a little can be used to flavour soups, sauces and gravies. As our home-grown tomatoes do not have the intense flavour of those grown on the Continent I have also added a tablespoon of concentrated tomato purée but this may not be necessary if the weather has been exceptionally good.
Serves 4

1½ *lb (675 g) ripe tomatoes*
1 *shallot or onion*
1 *large clove garlic*
salt and freshly ground black
   pepper

1 *teaspoon sugar*
1 *tablespoon tomato purée*

Cover the tomatoes with boiling water and leave them to stand for 2–3 minutes. Drain well, slide off the skins, remove the core and seeds and chop the flesh. Peel and finely chop the shallot and garlic. Blend the shallot, garlic and tomatoes in an electric blender or food processor until they are almost smooth. Put the ingredients into a saucepan with the sugar and tomato purée and season with salt and pepper. Bring to the boil and boil over a high heat for about 20 minutes without covering until the sauce is thick and reduced to about a third of its volume. Leave to cool before adding to sour cream, whipped cream or mayonnaise.

Tomato, Horseradish and Yoghurt Sauce

Pretty, pink and delicately flavoured, this makes a perfect summer sauce to serve with fish pâtés or terrines. It also makes a colourful topping for plainly cooked fish dishes or for green vegetables.
Serves 4

4 *large ripe tomatoes*
1 *onion*
2 *cloves garlic*
1 *tablespoon olive oil or sunflower oil*
1 *teaspoon finely chopped fresh oregano (or ½ teaspoon dried oregano)*
2 *teaspoons freshly grated horseradish root*

1 *tablespoon tomato purée*
2 *teaspoons white wine vinegar*
1 *teaspoon sugar*
salt and freshly ground black pepper
1 *carton (5 fl. oz, 150 ml) yoghurt*

Roughly chop the tomatoes. Peel and chop the onion. Peel and finely chop the garlic. Heat the oil in a small saucepan. Add the onion and garlic and cook over a low heat until the onion is soft and transparent. Add the tomatoes, oregano and horseradish, season with salt and pepper. Mix in the tomato purée, vinegar and sugar, bring to the boil, cover and simmer for 20 minutes, removing the lid for the last 5 minutes of cooking time so that the mixture becomes fairly thick.

Rub the purée through a food mill or fine sieve and leave to cool. Stir in the yoghurt, check the seasoning and serve warm or cold.

Turnips and Parsnips

Turnips and parsnips have both, in terms of popularity, seen better days. Once they featured almost daily at the main meal in the autumn and winter months but during the last fifty years and especially since the last war, they have become almost ignored—a sad state of affairs and one that should be rectified because both have an admirable flavour, contain a great deal of goodness and can be used as an inexpensive ingredient to give flavour and bulk to a great many really delicious dishes.

The original turnips came from Asia and are, in fact, yet another member of the brassica family. There are many varieties, varying from the small, tender and nutty white turnips which come in the early summer to the coarser and rather strongly flavoured root which is lifted in the winter. One of the great advantages that turnips, like other root vegetables, have is that they absorb other flavourings and do not disintegrate or lose their texture during cooking. This, of course, makes them ideal for cooking in casseroles and also for cooking with rather fatty dishes like pork or duck. Turnips have, in their time, been reported to have almost magical qualifications: in 1593 Sir Thomas Elyot said they 'augmenteth the sede of man; provoketh carnall lust'—a claim that might well make them more popular in the greengrocer's shop.

While the best turnips are undoubtedly those of the white variety (with a slight purplish bloom to their skin), which come in the early summer and should be lifted when not much larger than the size of a tennis ball, the yellow winter variety also contains plenty of nourishment and is very much an inexpensive form of food. All turnips need to be well peeled as the peel is often hard and stringy and, as well as being braised or stewed, they are delicious roasted around a joint.

Parsnips figured greatly in the diet of the first British Elizabethans when they were used not only as a vegetable but also as the basis of sweets, combined with honey and cream. I find the sweetness of their flesh to be part of their charm but it does have to be carefully counteracted or it can overpower a dish.

Seasoning helps to counteract this flavour, so does long, slow roasting and cooking with a rather sharp red wine. Like turnips, parsnips can be roasted alongside a joint, they can be mashed with butter and cream and well seasoned to make an excellent side vegetable and they do make the most delicious fritters.

Both turnips and parsnips are easy to grow and can be stored throughout the winter. The green leaves of the turnip are also good to eat and in Portugal they provide a commonplace everyday vegetable, cooked, drained and tossed in lemon juice, olive oil and seasoning.

Turnip and Carrot Soup with Fresh Herbs

An unusual clear soup made from good stock flavoured with turnips (they should be the summer white variety) and then strained. Thin julienne strips of carrot are added and the soup is finished with a dusting of finely chopped fresh parsley and savory leaves.
Serves 6

1 *lb (450 g) turnips*
8 *oz (225 g) carrots*
2 *oz (50 g) butter*
1 *teaspoon sugar*
3 *pints (1800 ml) good stock*
  (chicken, beef or veal—or use
  consommé)

2 *teaspoons lemon juice*
2 *tablespoons dry sherry*
1 *tablespoon finely chopped*
  parsley
1 *teaspoon finely chopped savory*

Peel the turnips and cut them into small dice. Melt the butter in a large heavy saucepan, add the turnips and cook over a low heat until the butter has been absorbed. Sprinkle over the sugar and mix well; cook over a moderate heat, stirring until the

turnips are golden brown. Add the stock and lemon juice, bring
to the boil and simmer for 20 minutes.

Peel the carrots and cut them into very thin matchstick strips.
Strain the stock and discard the turnips. Return the stock to a
clean pan, bring to the boil, add the carrots and cook for about
5 minutes until the carrots are just tender—they should still
have a crisp quality to them. Check the seasoning and stir in the
sherry. Serve the soup with a dusting of fresh herbs on each plate.

Risotto of Chicken and White Turnips

Although it may not sound anything much this dish has a
delicacy and subtlety which makes it memorable. You must use
the small, white, summer turnips and the result is a most wonderful combination of textures and flavours with an almost creamy
consistency. I use the meat from a chicken's breast but you could
also use the meat from the thighs or wings.
Serves 6

12 oz (350 g) raw chicken
12 oz (350 g) white turnips
1 onion
4 tablespoons vegetable oil
10 oz (275 g) long-grain or
    Patna rice

1 pint (600 ml) chicken stock
salt and freshly ground black
    pepper
2 oz (50 g) butter
1 tablespoon finely chopped
    parsley

Peel and chop the onion. Peel the turnips, cut them into thin
slices and then into very thin matchstick strips. Cut the chicken
into thin strips.

Heat the oil in a heavy flameproof casserole. Add the onion
and cook over a low heat, stirring to prevent sticking, until it is
soft and transparent. Add the turnip and continue to cook over a
medium heat, stirring, for a further 4 minutes. Add the chicken
and stir until the meat has lost its opaque quality. Add the rice
and stir for 1 minute and then pour in the stock. Season with salt
and pepper and bring to the boil slowly, cover very tightly and
cook over a low heat for 20 minutes by which time the rice and
other ingredients should be tender. Add the parsley and butter
cut into small pieces and toss the rice with two forks. Pile on to a
serving dish and serve with a salad and, if you like, some grated
Parmesan cheese.

Chicken with Turnips and Other Vegetables

A fragrant stew of chicken with the delicate flavour of young turnips adding both a texture and an interest to the dish. Use the subtle white turnips in the summer or make a more hearty dish in the winter by using the yellow turnips. Any leftovers from the dish can be made into an excellent soup by chopping the chicken and vegetables and adding some chicken stock and, if you like, some cream.
Serves 6

A 3 lb (1350 g) chicken
3 onions
2 cloves garlic
2 carrots
1½ lb (675 g) turnips
3 rashers streaky bacon
1 oz (25 g) butter
2 tablespoons vegetable oil
1 medium tin (14 oz, 392 g)
*   tomatoes*

3 bay leaves, 2 sprigs parsley,
*   1 sprig marjoram (tied in a*
*   bunch)*
salt and freshly ground black
*   pepper*
juice and coarsely grated rind of
*   1 orange*
2 tablespoons finely chopped
*   parsley*

Remove the legs from the chicken, separate the joints and chop each in half with a meat cleaver. Remove the wings and separate at the joints. Halve and then quarter the breast (on the bone) of the chicken.

Peel and roughly chop the onions. Peel and finely chop the garlic cloves. Peel the carrots and cut them into dice. Peel the turnips and cut them into dice. Remove the rinds from the bacon and cut the rashers into thin strips.

Melt the butter and oil in a large heavy frying pan. Add the bacon, onion and garlic and cook over a low heat until the onion is soft and transparent. Remove the onion, garlic and bacon to a casserole with a heavy spoon. Raise the heat, add the chicken pieces and brown quickly on all sides. Remove the chicken to the casserole, add the tomatoes and the juice to the cooking juice, mix well, bring to the boil and simmer for 5 minutes.

Surround the chicken with the turnips and carrots and pour over the tomato sauce. Add the herbs, season well with salt and pepper, cover the casserole with a tight-fitting lid or a double thickness of foil and cook in a low oven (300°F. 150°C. Reg. 2) for 1½ hours. Remove the herbs, spoon off any fat from the surface and mix in the orange juice.

Blanch the orange rind in boiling water for 2 minutes and drain well. Sprinkle the orange rind and parsley over the dish before serving.

Ragout of Lamb and Turnips

Ragouts seem to have faded from the cookery scene during the last hundred years and yet they make a delicious and light way to combine meat or poultry and vegetables. In this version of a ragout the lamb is combined with turnips, shallots and carrots, making a satisfying and well-flavoured dish.
Serves 4

1 lb (450 g) lean lamb
3 white turnips
4 carrots
14 small shallots
1 pint (600 ml) chicken or lamb
  stock
bouquet garni with 3 bay leaves

salt and freshly ground black
  pepper
1½ oz (40 g) butter
1½ tablespoons flour
1 tablespoon very finely chopped
  parsley
2 egg yolks

Peel the turnips and cut them into neat ¾ inch (2 cm) cubes. Peel the carrots and cut them into cubes the same size as the turnips. Cut the lamb into slightly larger cubes. Peel the shallots and leave them whole. Combine the vegetables in a heavy saucepan, add the lamb, cover with the stock, add the bouquet garni and season with salt and pepper. Bring slowly to the boil, skim off any scum from the surface, cover and simmer gently for about 1 hour or until the lamb is tender. Remove the bouquet garni and strain off the liquid from the pan.

Heat the butter in a clean saucepan. Add the flour and mix well. Gradually add the cooking liquid, stirring continually over a medium high heat until the sauce comes to the boil and is thick and smooth. Add the parsley and check the seasoning. Beat in the egg yolks, stirring over a low heat for 2 minutes. Mix the meat and vegetables into the sauce and heat through without boiling.

You can serve a ragout in a ring of rice or mashed potatoes and accompany with a green vegetable.

K

Lamb Curry with Turnip Tops and Yoghurt

Turnip tops make good eating and should not be thrown away. They have the texture of spinach or seakale beet but a rather stronger flavour which goes well in a curry dish. You can, of course, use spinach or seakale beet in the place of the turnip tops and I have also made the dish with those delicious red-veined beetroot tops.

Serves 4–6

1½ lb (675 g) lean lamb from a leg or shoulder
1½ lb (675 g) turnip tops
1 onion
3 tablespoons vegetable oil
1 teaspoon sugar
1 carton (5 fl. oz, 125 ml) yoghurt
½ teaspoon ground chilli
2 teaspoons ground coriander
1 teaspoon ground turmeric
¼ pint (150 ml) stock
1½ teaspoons garam masala
salt
1 tablespoon finely chopped celery, lovage or coriander leaves

Cut the meat into 1 inch (2½ cm) cubes. Wash the turnip tops and cook them in a heavy saucepan until the leaves are just tender (they will not need any water, the moisture left on the leaves from washing will be enough to prevent them burning). Reduce the leaves to a purée by passing them through a sieve or puréeing them in an electric blender or food processor. Peel and thinly slice the onion.

Heat the oil in a large heavy frying pan. Add the onion and cook it over a low heat until soft and transparent. Add the sugar and cook for 1 minute, stirring until the sugar has caramelized. Raise the heat, add the lamb and brown quickly on all sides. Add the yoghurt, chilli and coriander, season with salt and stir over a medium high heat until most of the liquid has disappeared. Add the turnip top purée and the stock, mix in the turmeric and simmer over a low heat, without covering and stirring from time to time, for about 30 minutes or until the lamb is very tender. Mix in the garam masala and cook over a low heat for a further 3 minutes, stirring gently.

Top with celery or coriander leaves and serve with rice and curry accompaniments.

Leg of Lamb with Turnips

A good dish to make with the slightly less tender legs of imported lamb. Use the small white turnips rather than the more strongly flavoured autumn and winter variety.
Serves 6

1 *small leg lamb*	½ *teaspoon oregano*
4 *small turnips*	*bouquet garni with a sprig of*
2 *carrots*	*parsley and thyme and 2 bay*
2 *onions*	*leaves*
2 *oz (50 g) butter*	2 *wine glasses white wine*
1 *tablespoon vegetable oil*	¼ *pint (150 ml) good chicken*
salt and freshly ground black	*stock*
pepper	

Peel and chop the onions. Peel the carrots and turnips and cut them into quite large dice.

Heat the butter with the oil in a large flameproof casserole. Add the leg of lamb and brown it on all sides over a high heat. Remove the lamb, add the vegetables to the juices in the pan and cook them over a medium heat, stirring, for 5 minutes until the onions are transparent and most of the fat has been absorbed. Place the lamb on top of the vegetables, add the oregano, season with salt and pepper and add the bouquet garni, wine and stock. Cover the pan tightly and simmer for about 1½ hours or until the leg is quite tender. Remove the bouquet garni, transfer the leg to a serving dish and surround it with the vegetables taken from the dish with a slotted spoon.

Serve the meat with the Onion and Caper Sauce on page 166.

Knuckle End of Leg of Lamb, Marinated and Braised with Five Vegetables

A lot of people actually dislike cold lamb so that by cooking a whole leg you often have to spend a considerable time converting the leftovers into made-up dishes. The leftovers can be avoided if you buy the knuckle end of a young lamb instead of the whole

leg and these can be found at good butchers and from the meat
departments of Marks and Spencer's stores where they are very
popular with Asian immigrants. The meat is well flavoured,
succulent and delicious and if it is braised in this manner with a
combination of vegetables it makes a most economical meal. To
add extra flavour the meat is marinated overnight in oil and wine
and the marinade is then used, together with a little cider, to
provide the cooking juice for the vegetables.
Serves 4–6

1½ lb (675 g) knuckle end of leg   1 large onion
    of young lamb   12 oz (350 g) turnips
¼ pint (150 ml) olive or   12 oz (350 g) potatoes
    vegetable oil   6 oz (175 g) cabbage
½ pint (300 ml) dry white wine   2 courgettes
1 teaspoon oregano   cider
4 bay leaves   salt and freshly ground black
1 clove garlic   pepper

Place the lamb in a bowl. Combine the oil with the white
wine, season it with salt and pepper and mix in the oregano and
the garlic clove, peeled and chopped. Add the bay leaves and
pour the marinade over the lamb. Marinate in the refrigerator
for at least 12 hours, turning the leg every now and then when
you think about it.

Drain off the marinade, spoon a little of the oil into a casserole
dish and brown the leg over a high heat on all sides to seal in the
juices.

Peel and roughly chop the onion. Peel the turnips and potatoes
and cut them into 1 inch (2½ cm) dice. Shred the cabbage.
Thickly slice the courgettes.

Surround the lamb with the vegetables, pour over the remains
of the marinade and add enough cider to come half-way up the
vegetables. Season with salt and pepper, cover tightly with two
layers of foil and cook in a moderate oven (350°F. 180°C. Reg. 4)
for 1¼ hours, removing the foil for the last 15 minutes of cooking
time so that the vegetables become golden brown on the top.

Remove the lamb and cut it into thickish slices. Remove the
vegetables with a slotted spoon on to a serving dish, cover with
the slices of lamb and pour over the cooking juices. Serve at once.

Belly of Pork with Turnips and Onions – Cooked in Cider

Pork and cider make excellent partners; in this dish they are cooked together with turnips and onions and the resulting juices are thickened to a rich sauce with cream and egg yolks flavoured with finely chopped parsley.

Serves 4

1½ lb (675 g) boned belly of pork
1 lb (450 g) turnips
2 onions
2 tablespoons vegetable oil
salt and freshly ground black pepper
pinch each finely chopped sage and thyme

¼ pint (150 ml) dry cider
¼ pint (150 ml) single cream
2 egg yolks
1 tablespoon finely chopped parsley
3 tablespoons double cream

Peel and thinly slice the turnips and onions. Roll the pork up tightly and tie it in four places. Cut through the string to make four thick slices.

Heat the oil in a frying pan. Add the onion and cook over a medium heat, stirring to prevent browning, until the onion is soft and transparent.

Arrange the onion in the bottom of the casserole dish, which should be just wide enough to take the slices of pork in one layer. Arrange the slices of turnip over the onions, seasoning the layers and sprinkling them with a little finely chopped sage and thyme. Place the slices of pork on top of the vegetables, season the pork slices and pour over the cider.

Bake the dish in a moderate oven (350°F. 180°C. Reg. 4) for 1½ hours, basting every now and then with the juices in the casserole, until the slices of pork are well browned and tender.

Carefully pour out the juices without disturbing the pork and vegetables. Beat the egg yolks with the single cream until smooth. Put the cooking liquid into a saucepan and beat in the egg yolks and cream, stirring continually over a low heat (without boiling) until the sauce thickens and is smooth and satiny. Add the parsley and double cream, check the seasoning, heat through without boiling and pour the sauce over the casserole.

Spiced Rolled Skirt of Beef with Turnips

Beef skirt is a marvellously lean and well-flavoured cut of meat and it is also very reasonably priced. Because of its leanness, however, skirt should be cooked slowly and therefore responds well to being braised with vegetables. This recipe can, of course, be cooked in a pressure cooker or slow-cook pot with good results.

Serves 6

2 *lb (900 g) beef skirt in one piece*
1 *lb (450 g) white turnips*
1 *clove garlic, crushed*
1 *tablespoon tomato purée*
1 *teaspoon French Dijon mustard*
salt and freshly ground black pepper
½ *teaspoon allspice*

2 *large onions*
3 *tablespoons vegetable oil*
1 *medium tin (14 oz, 392 g) tomatoes*
stock
3 *sprigs parsley*
1 *sprig marjoram*
8 *bay leaves*

Lay the meat out flat and spread one side with the crushed garlic, tomato purée and mustard. Season with salt, pepper and allspice, roll up tightly and tie in two places to make a firm parcel. Peel and roughly chop the onions and turnips.

Heat the oil in a large frying pan, add the meat and brown quickly on all sides. Transfer the meat to a casserole just large enough to take the meat and vegetables. Add the onions and turnips to the juices in the pan and cook over a medium heat, stirring, until the onions are transparent and the oil has been absorbed. Surround the meat with the vegetables and add the tinned tomatoes and enough stock just to cover the meat. Season with salt and pepper and place the parsley, marjoram and bay leaves on top of the ingredients. Cover tightly with two thicknesses of foil and cook in a very moderate oven (300°F. 150°C. Reg. 2) for 2½ hours. Remove the meat and vegetables to a serving dish and serve the gravy separately.

Turnip, Potato and Beef Pie

Serves 4

The pastry:
6 oz (175 g) plain flour
2 oz (50 g) lard
1 oz (25 g) butter
a little milk

The filling:
1 lb (450 g) chuck steak

1 lb (450 g) potatoes
1 large turnip
salt and freshly ground black
  pepper
¼ teaspoon finely chopped
  parsley, thyme and sage
¾ pint (450 ml) beef stock

Peel and thinly slice the potatoes. Peel the turnip and cut it into thin slices. Cut the beef into cubes about 1 inch (2½ cm) square.

Place a layer of potato in the bottom of a pie dish. Cover with half the turnip and with the beef. Season with salt and pepper and add the herbs. Cover the meat with the remaining turnip and with the rest of the potatoes. Pour over the stock and cook in a moderate oven (350°F. 180°C. Reg. 4) for 1½ hours.

Put the flour into a bowl with a pinch of salt. Add the fats, cut into small pieces, and rub into the flour with the fingertips. Add enough water to make a stiff dough and knead on a floured board until just smooth. Chill the pastry before rolling out.

Roll out the pastry to about ¼ inch (¾ cm) thickness. Damp the edges of the pie dish, place the pastry over the meat, and press the edges down firmly. Brush with a little milk and bake in a hot oven (400°F. 200°C. Reg. 6) for 5 minutes, then reduce the heat to moderate (350°F. 180°C. Reg. 4) and continue to cook for a further 15 minutes until the pastry is golden brown.

Kingsbridge Mixed Vegetables

In the winter there is a tendency these days to turn to frozen vegetables, eating peas, beans and other spring vegetables out of season. If you grow your own vegetables you should have enough to keep you going on fresh foodstuffs all the year round; if you buy your vegetables, don't scorn the mundane root varieties – they have plenty of nourishment and can be delicious if well cooked.

Serves 4

¾ *lb (350 g) carrots*
½ *lb (225 g) swede*
½ *lb (225 g) turnip*
1½ *oz (40 g) butter*
salt

freshly ground black pepper
1 *teaspoon sugar*
1 *tablespoon finely chopped*
    parsley or chives

Peel the vegetables and cut them into small dice. Cook separately in boiling salted water until just tender.

Melt the butter in a heavy-bottomed saucepan. Add the vegetables and season with the salt, pepper and sugar. Cook over a high heat until the vegetables are well coated with the butter and the sugar has melted and turned slightly brown. Add the parsley or chives, toss lightly and serve at once.

A Flat Cake of Meat, Potato and White Turnip with a Delicious Vegetable Sauce

This mixture of a potato pancake and a hamburger may seem like mundane fare but in fact it makes a dish that ends up as being highly sophisticated and very colourful. Work quickly with the ingredients for the flat cake so that the mixture does not become too liquid with the juices from the potatoes and turnip.
Serves 4

12 *oz (350 g) good quality raw*
    minced beef
12 *oz (350 g) potatoes*
8 *oz (225 g) turnip*
1 *large egg*
salt and freshly ground black
    pepper
pinch each ground nutmeg and
    cumin
2½ *tablespoons olive oil*
12 *very small shallots or large*
    spring onion bulbs
3 *medium carrots*

6 *very small, firm courgettes*
1½ *oz (40 g) butter*
¼ *pint (150 ml) dry white wine*
salt and freshly ground black
    pepper
½ *teaspoon ground fenugreek*
1 *tablespoon tomato ketchup*
1 *dessertspoon cornflour*
¼ *pint (150 ml) chicken stock*
1 *tablespoon finely chopped*
    parsley
1 *tablespoon finely chopped*
    borage (optional)

Wash and parboil the potatoes and turnips for 15 minutes. Cool them and remove the skins.

Grate the potato and peeled turnip through the coarse blades of a grater. Combine the potato, turnip and meat, add the egg, season with salt and pepper, add the nutmeg and cumin and mix well.

Heat 2 tablespoons of the oil in a large frying pan (a non-stick variety is best for this), press the meat mixture down firmly in the pan and cook over a high heat for 10 minutes. Brush the top of the cake with the remaining oil, put the pan under a hot grill and cook for about 8 minutes longer to brown and crisp the top. Slide the cake (or invert it) on to a heated serving dish and keep warm while making the sauce.

Peel the shallots or trim the spring onion bulbs. Peel and finely dice the carrots. Cut the courgettes into small dice (they should be a little larger than the carrots). Melt the butter in a saucepan, add the shallots and carrots and cook over a low heat, stirring every now and then, until the butter has been absorbed. Add the wine and continue to cook for 10 minutes. Season with salt and pepper, add the fenugreek, tomato ketchup and courgettes, mix lightly, cover and continue to simmer for a further 10 minutes.

Combine the cornflour with the stock, add the mixture to the vegetables and stir gently until the sauce has thickened and become glossy. Stir in the parsley (and borage) and pour the sauce over the meat cake.

Note: This vegetable sauce makes a good accompanying dish in its own right when courgettes are plentiful.

Mashed Potato with Swede

Swede always tends to be a little on the sweet side but it is good mixed with potatoes and with the addition of a little lemon juice and a good seasoning of salt and freshly ground black pepper. This was a dish we had often when the potato shortage was in full swing.

Serves 4

1 *medium swede*
1 *lb (450 g) potatoes*
salt and freshly ground black
  pepper

1 *teaspoon lemon juice*
1½ *oz (40 g) butter*
2 *tablespoons milk or cream*

Peel and chop the swede. Peel the potatoes. Cook potatoes and swede separately in salted water until tender. Drain well, combine swede and potato, add the lemon juice and mash until really smooth. Beat in the butter and milk or cream, season generously with salt and pepper, reheat and pile on to a serving dish.

Swede Tops

These used to be a popular vegetable dish, with a flavour not at all unlike that of seakale. Cut off the shoots from the swedes and trim away the green leaf from the stalks. Tie the stalks in bundles and cook in boiling salted water, to which a little lemon juice has been added, for about 30 minutes. Serve like asparagus with some melted butter and freshly ground black pepper, or smother them in a rich white sauce.

Parsnip Cakes

Parsnip cakes can be topped with a fried egg and served with crisp bacon as a quick supper dish, but they also make a delicious alternative to potatoes for a slap-up dinner party.
Serves 4

1½ *lb (675 g) parsnips*
juice ½ lemon
salt and freshly ground black
  pepper

brown breadcrumbs
lard or dripping for frying

Peel and roughly chop the parsnips and cover with cold water. Add the lemon juice, bring to the boil and simmer until the parsnips are soft. Drain off the water, season with salt and pepper and mash until smooth and creamy. Leave until cold and then shape into cakes about 3 inches (8 cm) across and ¼ inch (¾ cm) thick.

Press the cakes into the breadcrumbs and fry in hot lard or dripping until golden brown and crisp on each side.

Pork with Rice and Parsnips

An unusual combination which has Hungarian overtones. It is a substantial and economical dish and tastes very good on a cold winter's evening.
Serves 4

8 oz (225 g) lean pork
4 parsnips
1 onion
5 ripe tomatoes
5 oz (150 g) long-grain, Patna
　or Basmati rice

5 tablespoons sour cream
3 tablespoons milk
1 oz (25 g) dripping or lard
1 oz (25 g) butter
salt and freshly ground black
　pepper

Cut the meat into long thin matchstick strips about 1½ inches (4 cm) long. Season the meat with salt and pepper. Peel and chop the onion. Cover the tomatoes with boiling water for 2 minutes, drain and then slide off the tomato skins. Slice the flesh. Peel the parsnips and cut them into thin chips.

Heat the lard or dripping in a frying pan until very hot. Add the onion and meat and cook over a high heat until the meat is browned on all sides. Remove the meat and onion with a slotted spoon, add the parsnips and cook over a high heat, stirring, until the parsnips are just soft.

Throw the rice into boiling salted water and cook for 12 minutes. Drain the rice well.

Butter a casserole dish and place a layer of half the rice in the bottom. Cover with a layer of half the sliced tomatoes, season with a little salt and pepper and put in a layer of half the parsnips and meat. Continue with the remaining ingredients and pour over the sour cream beaten with the milk until smooth. Dot with butter, cover and cook in a hot oven (400°F. 200°C. Reg. 6) for 25 minutes.

Braised Loin of Pork with Vegetables

A small boned loin of pork is sealed and then surrounded by vegetables, flavoured with herbs and braised in some cider until the meat is tender. The bone from the pork helps flavour the juices. The vegetables are finished with some cream and finely chopped parsley and the dish emerges as a most aromatic and pleasing combination.
Serves 6–8

2½ lb (1125 g) loin of pork.
  Bone it, keep the bone and
  remove all the skin
4 tablespoons olive or vegetable oil
1 clove garlic
½ teaspoon dried oregano
2 tablespoons sesame seeds
1 large onion
6 oz (175 g) cabbage
8 oz (225 g) parsnips
12 oz (350 g) potatoes, peeled

salt and freshly ground black
  pepper
little finely chopped fresh sage
  and thyme
cider
2 tablespoons fresh orange juice
¼ pint (150 ml) single or double
  cream
1½ tablespoons finely chopped
  parsley

Place the pork in a casserole dish. Score the fat with a sharp knife and rub it with the peeled garlic clove. Season with salt and pepper and rub the seasoning and ground oregano into the skin. Sprinkle with the sesame seeds, pour over 2 tablespoons of oil and roast in a hot oven (425°F. 220°C. Reg. 7) for 20 minutes to seal in the juices.

Peel and chop the onion. Shred the cabbage. Peel the potatoes and parsnips and cut them into 1 inch (2½ cm) cubes.

Remove the pork from the oven and surround it with the vegetables. Place the bone from the loin on top of the vegetables, season with salt and pepper and sprinkle over the thyme and sage and pour in enough cider to come half-way up the vegetables. Add the orange juice and dribble over remaining oil. Cover with two layers of foil, then the casserole lid, and cook in a moderate oven (350°F. 180°C. Reg. 4) for 1¼ hours, removing the foil for the last 15 minutes of cooking time so that the vegetables and meat become golden on top.

Remove the meat and cut it into thin slices. Add the cream and parsley to the vegetables and mix lightly. Arrange the vegetables on a shallow serving dish and place the slices of pork on top.

Parsnip and Sweetbread Fritters

Parsnip fritters are excellent on their own but combined with blanched sweetbreads they make a first-rate first course— delicious and unusual. The sweetbreads are blanched and then have any membrane and skin removed; they are chopped and combined with a purée of parsnips to make a subtle combination that goes well with a rich, home-made, tomato sauce.
Serves 6

12 oz (350 g) sweetbreads
1 lb (450 g) parsnips
1 teaspoon lemon juice
salt and freshly ground black
  pepper

2 eggs
3 oz (75 g) butter
5 tablespoons flour
$\frac{1}{4}$ pint (150 ml) milk
deep oil for frying

Peel and roughly chop the parsnips. Cover them with cold water, bring to the boil and cook for about 25 minutes or until the parsnips are tender. Drain off the water and mash the parsnips to a purée.

Soak the sweetbreads in cold water for 2 hours, changing the water three or four times during the soaking period. Drain off the water. Place the sweetbreads in a saucepan, cover them with cold water, add a little salt and 1 teaspoon of lemon juice, bring slowly to the boil and simmer for 3 minutes. Drain off the water and plunge the sweetbreads immediately into a bowl of ice-cold water. When they are cold remove any tough membranes and bloody tissue. Finely chop the sweetbreads.

Beat the eggs until smooth. Melt the butter. Add the flour to the parsnips and mix until smooth. Add the eggs and butter to the parsnips, add the milk and mix well until the ingredients are smooth. Season with salt and pepper and mix in the sweetbreads.

Heat some oil in a deep pan until smoking, add spoonfuls of the parsnip and sweetbread mixture and cook over a high heat until the fritters are crisp and golden brown. Drain them on kitchen paper and keep warm while frying the remaining fritters, Serve at once with wedges of lemon and a tomato sauce.

Note: If, when you fry the fritters, they have a tendency to break up you may need to add a little more flour to bind them.

Fish and Mushroom Pie with a Potato and Parsnip Topping

This is a traditional fish pie but a combined potato and parsnip topping gives an unusual touch and a delicious extra dimension. Leftover vegetables can be added to the fish to stretch the quantities and provide extra interest. The fish can be poached in the milk to give extra flavour to the sauce.

Serves 4

12 oz (350 g) cooked white fish
or salmon
8 oz (225 g) parsnips
1 lb (450 g) potatoes
1 teaspoon lemon juice
3 oz (75 g) butter
2 tablespoons single cream
2 hard-boiled eggs
6 oz (175 g) mushrooms
2 tablespoons flour

¾ pint (450 ml) milk
2 oz (50 g) Cheddar cheese,
grated
2 oz (50 g) Gruyère cheese,
grated
salt and freshly ground black
pepper
pinch ground nutmeg and cayenne
pepper

Peel and roughly chop the parsnips and potatoes, and cook them together in boiling salted water with 1 teaspoon lemon juice until the vegetables are tender. Drain well and mash until smooth with ½ oz (15 g) butter and the cream. Season with salt and pepper.

Peel and roughly chop the eggs. Flake the fish. Thinly slice the mushrooms and cook them over a high heat in 1 oz (25 g) melted butter for 3 minutes, tossing the pan over the heat.

Melt 1½ oz (35 g) butter in a saucepan, add the flour and mix well. Gradually add the milk, stirring continually over a medium high heat until the sauce comes to the boil and is thick and smooth. Add half the Cheddar and Gruyère cheese, season with salt, pepper, nutmeg and a little cayenne pepper and mix well.

Fold the flaked fish, mushrooms and eggs into the sauce and turn it into a baking dish. Top with the mashed potatoes and parsnips and sprinkle over the remaining cheese.

Bake the dish in a moderate oven (350°F. 180°C. Reg. 4) for 30 minutes until the topping is golden brown and the dish is hot through.

Appendix

Some Other Vegetables: How to Prepare, Cook and Serve Them

JERUSALEM ARTICHOKES

Despite their name in English, Jerusalem artichokes have nothing whatsoever to do with the Holy Land and they do not belong to the artichoke family. An early explorer in America, finding them being grown by a tribe of Indians, described them as having the taste of globe artichokes; and 'Jerusalem' is a corruption of the French *girasol* or sunflower.

The roots are easily recognized by their gnarled shape, although they can sometimes be confused with roots of fresh green ginger. I have twice amazed greengrocers by buying either one Jerusalem artichoke or three pounds of fresh green ginger—the first being useless on its own and the second enough to last a family for about six months.

The taste of Jerusalem artichokes is a delicious and subtle one and their relative unpopularity lies in the difficulty of removing their skins. The roots abound in small nodules which make peeling an arduous job. Since they are quite inexpensive I feel it is worth cutting off the nodules and merely peeling the central body of the vegetable. An alternative method is to boil or steam the artichokes in their skins and rub off the skins when the roots are tender. The flesh is smooth and almost satiny in texture and, since they discolour easily, the roots should be dropped into cold water to which a little wine vinegar or lemon juice has been added if they are to be peeled before cooking.

Jerusalem artichokes can be boiled and served with butter and finely chopped parsley, roasted with a joint, cut into chips and fried, or puréed. They also make an excellent soup which is, understandably, called 'Palestine' soup. Jerusalem artichokes make a useful crop in the garden because they grow tall and quickly and can therefore form an excellent windbreak. They can be kept in sand through the winter although since they have such a distinctive taste most people do not like to eat too many of them.

GLOBE ARTICHOKES

Due to a concentrated drive to promote the Brittany globe artichoke crop, these round, plump, multi-leaved vegetables are appearing much more frequently in our greengrocer's and very good they are too. Globe artichokes are also easy to grow in your own garden and require little more than some good soil and a sunny position. If you grow your own try picking them when they are very young, as they do on the Continent, and especially in Italy where they appear at Christmas time; then cook and eat them whole, with some of the stalk and the leaves, and dress the hot vegetables with olive oil and vinegar. Choose globe artichokes that are firm, heavy for their size, unblemished and bright green in colour. Cut off the stalks, rub the bases of the artichokes with lemon juice and cook them in plenty of boiling salted water to which some lemon juice has been added, until a knife easily enters the base. Drain the artichokes upside down in a colander to get rid of the water and serve them hot with melted butter or cold with an aioli mayonnaise or a vinaigrette dressing.

The leaves of cooked, hot or cold, artichokes are pulled off one by one and the soft base of the leaves is sucked off by pulling them through your teeth as you hold the top end. When the 'choke', the hairy centre, is reached this is scraped off and discarded and the base (or *fond*) of the artichoke, the prize, is liberally dressed with butter, mayonnaise or vinaigrette and eaten with a knife and fork.

Globe artichokes can also be stuffed (sometimes the stuffing is pushed between the leaves and sometimes the centre is removed before cooking and its place filled with a mixture of finely chopped bacon, onions and mushrooms). Very young artichokes can be cut in half and deep fried.

Artichokes that are bought and need to be kept for a day or two should have their stalks put into water, like flowers, and be kept in a cool dark place until required, with the water being changed every day.

WHITE AUBERGINES

Aubergines were originally, like many other vegetables, grown mainly for their attractive flowers and decorative fruit, as a feature rather than a vegetable. Most varieties are deep red or purple but you may sometimes see the white variety (which gives the vegetable its alternative name of 'eggplant') on sale in areas that specialize in foreign produce—I have seen them on a number of occasions in Soho greengrocers' in recent years. The white aubergines taste exactly like the purple ones and are treated in the same way (see pages 25 and 26). When you buy them their skin should be shining (watch out for any worm holes) and the vegetables should feel heavy for their size.

BEAN SPROUTS OR MUNG SPROUTS

Bean sprouts and the similar Mung sprouts, which can be grown at home like mustard and cress, or soaked and then placed in a jar topped with muslin in only a few days, are on sale in many health-food shops and supermarkets these days and they make an excellent vegetable or addition to a vegetable soup. They can also be added to 'stir-fried' recipes or used raw in salads.

Bean sprouts and mung sprouts must be eaten fresh or they develop an unpleasant taste and smell. Use them the same day they are bought and rinse them well in plenty of cold water. Stir fry them in oil until they are tender or cook them in fast-boiling salted water. For use in salads they need only be rinsed in cold running water.

CHINESE CABBAGE

A number of similar pale-leaved forms of the brassica family come under the heading of Chinese cabbage. Since the Chinese forms of cabbage started to be grown in Israel they have gradually begun to be imported into Britain and are becoming more and more popular as a raw or cooked vegetable. Chinese cabbages look more like large, pale, cos lettuces than our usual cabbages, and one of their main advantages is that they can be used like a lettuce in salads or as a cooked vegetable equally successfully. They also have the extra advantage that if wrapped in a polythene bag and stored in the bottom of the refrigerator, they will keep fresh for weeks.

Chinese cabbages are more expensive than our own home-grown varieties but have virtually no wastage since they are trimmed before selling. Watch out for the price as you can be confused by the vegetable being sold by the pound rather than by each individual head; choose cabbages that look fresh and crisp and are free from blemishes. Thinly slice or shred the cabbages for salads or slice more thickly for using as a vegetable. They need very little cooking and should be eaten when still slightly crisp and firm.

CORIANDER LEAVES

Coriander is an easy herb to grow in the garden and both the leaves and the seeds, which are easy to dry, can be used to great advantage in a wide range of soups, casseroles, stews and other dishes. The seeds are crushed and the leaves finely chopped. Use the leaves in the same way as parsley.

Coriander leaves are often sold in markets and greengrocers' which specialize in vegetables and fruits for immigrants and they are well worth buying if you do not grow your own for their flavour is exciting and delicious. You can recognize the leaves by their smell, which is slightly of aniseed; they look like large-leaved parsley and should be fresh and bright green when you buy them. Stand the stalks in cold water and use the leaves as a garnish for soups, as an addition to salads, as a topping for curried eggs or fish dishes, or add them to stews, soups and sauces as a flavouring ingredient.

CUSTARD MARROW

The nicest thing about the custard marrow is its appearance but although this vegetable is now seen quite frequently during the summer in some of the better greengrocers' (they can also be grown in your garden in the same way as courgettes) the flesh is, I consider, very disappointing to eat and it is best used for decoration. Custard marrows look like thick flowers with curving edges that resemble petals; they can be almost white in colour, green and yellow in stripes or custard yellow. The marrows should be used when young and can be eaten raw in salads, sliced but not peeled, or in any recipe that calls for courgettes. Custard marrows, sometimes called squash, are very popular in America where they are often served stuffed or in soup.

OKRA

Okra are often known as lady's fingers, although I would call them witch's rather than lady's fingers and my son has a set of false, black, plastic nails that look exactly like the shape of okra pods.

In some markets and areas, especially where there are West Indian communities, okra are easily available, so if you see them buy some and give them a try. The flesh is curiously bitter-sweet and has a kind of jelly consistency that slips down very nicely indeed. Slicing, sprinkling with salt and leaving for half an hour or so draws some of this jelly out, if you don't like the slimy texture. Okra make an excellent partner for any of the Mediterranean vegetables (aubergines, tomatoes, sweet-fleshed onions and peppers). From India there is a fabulous but exacting recipe for stuffing the pods with a curried meat or vegetable mixture, or they can be added to stews or soups. Whatever use they are put to care should be taken, except in the cases of soup or ratatouille-type mixtures, not to overcook the okra so that they disintegrate. Okra can also be bought in tins and they seem to respond well to this treatment. They need only to be heated through and can then be added to stews, casseroles and vegetable mixtures at the last minute.

CHILLI PEPPERS

Green and red peppers, and even sometimes yellow peppers, are usually fairly easy to find and a great asset they have proved to be to our everyday diet in both hot dishes and cold food. Now you will also see miniature peppers, both green and red, in many greengrocers' throughout the summer months but *take care* because these in no way have the sweetness of the green or red capsicums which we are used to. The red chilli peppers are fiery, mouth-burningly hot (even hotter if you do not remove the core and seeds) and the green chillies are only a little less strong. When you prepare the chillies you should do so wearing gloves and take great care never to let your hands get near your eyes.

The chillies, with the core and seeds removed and the flesh very finely chopped, can be added in small quantities to soups, stews and casseroles to give flavour and are very much a part of Chinese 'stir-fried' dishes. One or two red chilli peppers added to a bottle of vodka and then frozen in a deep freeze for at least three days produces a most fantastic drink (mind-blowing might be an accurate description), to be served in small glasses and drunk in one draught, with caviar or, slightly lower down the scale, smoked salmon, mackerel or with a good bortsch soup. Chilli peppers can also be pickled to serve as an accompaniment to curries and cold meats. You can dry them by stringing them on a line and storing them in an airing cupboard or some other warm, dry place.

PUMPKIN

I haven't included recipes for pumpkin in this book for the simple reason that it is not a taste of which I am particularly fond and although I have grown magnificent specimens in my English garden I ended up by giving almost all of them away. The most successful way I have ever had this fruit/vegetable was when our New Zealand farm manager, Pancho, made us a traditional New Zealand 'hangi' for harvest thanksgiving. A whole lamb was roasted in a pit in which a fire had been burning and then raked out. It was smothered in vegetables, buried and steamed over the hot coals, then opened about eight hours later. Sliced pumpkins played a great part in that feast and, flavoured with the lamb and other vegetables, steamed in that pit, they were very delicious indeed.

Pumpkins are becoming quite popular in the British Isles and are quite easy to find now at the beginning of autumn. Their large, golden-orange shape (like giant cantaloupe melons) is easy to recognize and they are not expensive. They can be used to make soup, puréed as a vegetable, baked in sweet pies, fried in slices, and roasted with a joint. They can be stored for months in a cool, dry place, but should be eaten very quickly after having been opened. The pips can be cleaned off and roasted in the oven to serve with drinks.

KALE

Since we live on a farm where kale is grown for the cattle and I hate to throw anything away, we eat it quite often in spite of its strong flavour. Kale is a member of the cabbage family, with slightly frilled leaves. The main priority if you buy it (and do not do this unless it is very inexpensive indeed) is that it should be fresh, bright green, and crisp. Once bought, the kale leaves should be washed and picked over and any tough stems should be cut off. It should then be cooked in very little boiling salted water until just tender and served with plenty of butter and freshly ground black pepper. For the purposes of this book kale is too strongly flavoured to cook with meat, fish or poultry for it would swamp their flavour, but I have found it reasonably acceptable if it is dressed with oil and lemon juice, after it has been cooked and drained, and served as a vegetable accompaniment.

SWEETCORN

A cookery book like this one should, I believe, be personal and the reason why you will not find a chapter on sweetcorn which, after all, appears on the market frequently during the summer and can be easily grown in the garden, is because I feel they are best eaten from the cob with melted butter and not 'messed' around with in any way. When you buy corn on the cob they should look bright and firm and the grains should be even, plump and a good golden colour. Strip off the leaves and silken hair inside the leaves, trim the stalk and cook the corn in a pan of half water and half milk, brought to the boil and salted, for about 10 minutes until the kernels are just tender. Serve the cobs at once with melted butter and eat them in your hands with more salt and plenty of freshly ground black pepper.

If you grow your own corn and have a plentiful crop, try boiling the very young and immature cobs until they are tender and eating them whole.

SPAGHETTI MARROW (OR VEGETABLE MARROW)

This is an easy marrow to grow yourself (treat it in exactly the same way as courgettes) and it is fun to produce – providing you do not have too many of them, because although the texture is unusual and very pleasant the flavour is not really that special. You can find vegetable or spaghetti marrows on sale in local country markets during the summer; they are oval and a pale, golden yellow and should be picked when about 10 inches (25 cm) long. The marrows are boiled for about 20 minutes until the skin is just becoming soft to the touch. Drain the marrows, cut them in half, scoop out the seeds and serve half to each person with plenty of melted butter. The marrow is eaten with a spoon and the spaghetti-resembling flesh scooped out and seasoned with plenty of salt and freshly ground black pepper. I have also used the flesh in recipes which required pumpkin.

Index